# I'll Have What They're Having

## LEGENDARY LOCAL CUISINE

# I'll Have What They're Having

## LEGENDARY LOCAL CUISINE

Linda Stradley

Guilford, Connecticut
An imprint of The Globe Pequot Press

ThreeForks is a trademark of The Globe Pequot Press.

Page design by Casey Shain
Spot art images © 2002 www.arttoday.com

Library of Congress Cataloging-in-Publication Data
Stradley, Linda.
    I'll have what they're having : legendary local cuisine / Linda Stradley.—
        1st ed.
        p.  cm.
    Includes bibliographical references and index.
    ISBN 0-7627-1146-9
    1. Cookery, American.  I. Title.

TX715 .S895 2002
641.5973—dc21                                      2002069759

Manufactured in the United States of America
First Edition/First Printing

# Contents

# Acknowledgments

**When we no longer have good cooking in the world,
we will have no literature,
no high and sharp intelligence, nor friendly gatherings,
no social harmony.**

*—Marie (Antonin) Antoine Carême (1783–1833),
celebrated French cook and gastronomist*

This book belongs not only to me but to my wonderful husband, Don Stradley. He shared my goal and enthusiasm in writing it. Without his support and encouragement, I would not have been able to produce this regional cookbook in such a timely manner. He was always willing to taste test and give his comments on each new dish that I created.

I also want to thank my editor, Megan Hiller, whose enthusiasm, attention, and patience made it possible for me to pursue my love of culinary history. She encouraged me when the idea was just a spark in my mind.

I am filled with gratitude and want to give special thanks to my wonderful sister, Carol Arroyo, and my good friend Andra Cook. Carol and Andra both spent many hours reading, proofing copy, testing recipes, and suggesting ideas. I extend a heartfelt thanks for their testing, tasting, comments, and timely advice. I cannot tell them enough how much I appreciate their help and support.

I also want to thank my mother, Dorothy Hagerman, for her support and my friends Karen Calanchini and Roxanne Sienkiewicz and my daughter, Brenda Weller, for their enthusiastic help in testing recipes.

# Introduction

**We may live without poetry, music and art;**
**We may live without conscience and live without heart;**
**We may live without friends; we may live without books;**
**But civilized man can not live without cooks.**

**He may live without books,—what is knowledge but**
     **grieving?**
**He may live without hope,—what is hope but deceiving?**
**He may live without love,—what is passion but pining?**
**But where is the man that can live without dining?**

*—Owen Meredith, pseudonym of Edward Robert Bulwer-Lytton*
*(1831–1891), British poet*

This book is a celebration of one of the world's greatest cuisines—American. It tells the story of what Americans eat and why. Many people think that American food has become homogenized and nationalized, but this book shows that regional cuisine is very much alive. It has expanded to include new and exciting foods and dishes that we now call our own.

Most of us grow up taking local specialties for granted. It is when we move away that we realize our beloved dish is missing and just how much we enjoyed it. Even if we can find it in other parts of the country, though, it never tastes quite as good as when we had it in our hometown.

The United States first developed as distinct regions isolated from one another, much like individual countries. New immigrants tended to settle according to nationality, forming tight urban and rural communities with strong threads of languages and cuisines. In each region, the people brought with them their customs and adapted them to indigenous foods and ingredients.

Americans have taken Old World cuisines and combined them with regional ingredients and traditions to create foods uniquely American. Local restaurants have kept most regional cuisine alive. Throughout this country, local eateries revive and continue to redesign classic regional dishes.

It has been a challenge to search out the origins of the foods we eat and their culinary histories and traditions. Together, the recipes and stories in this cookbook tell a wonderful tale. Let us rediscover the flavors and traditions and renew our love of true American cuisine. Let us also discover cooking trends and culinary fads and fashions of today.

As you travel the fifty states be sure to sample local specialties. I offer the following recipes and histories so you will know what you are eating when you get there. With this book as a guide, you can look toward the locals and say with confidence, "I'll have what they're having." Or, if you can't get there, you can at least enjoy a region's specialty at home.

# Appetizers & Snacks

# Boiled Peanuts

**Sitting by the roadside on a summer day,**
**Chatting with my messmates, passing time away,**
**Lying in the shadow underneath the trees,**
**Goodness how delicious, eating goober peas!**

**Peas! Peas! Peas! Peas! Eating goober peas!**
**Goodness how delicious, eating goober peas!**

*—from the song "Goober Peas"*
*Written in 1866 with words by A. Pindar and music by P. Nutt.*

Boiled peanuts are a traditional snack in South Carolina, Georgia, northern Florida, Alabama, and Mississippi. They are an acquired taste, but according to southerners, they are totally addictive. From May through November, all over the South, you will see roadside stands—ranging from woodsheds to shiny trailers—offering fresh boiled peanuts. A traditional way that old-timers like to eat boiled peanuts is to drop the shelled peanuts into a bottle of cold RC Cola and gulp down the combo.

Boiled peanuts are green or raw nuts that are boiled in salty water for hours outdoors over a fire. A green peanut is not green in color, just freshly harvested. It takes ninety to a hundred days to grow peanuts for boiling, and they are available only during May through November throughout the southern states. One of the drawbacks of boiled peanuts is that they have a very short shelf life unless refrigerated or frozen.

No one knows just why southerners started boiling peanuts or who was the first to boil them. However, it is known that boiled peanuts have been a southern institution since at least the Civil War, when Union General William T. Sherman led his troops on their march through Georgia. When troops of the Confederacy were without food, peanuts were an important nutritional source. Soldiers roasted the peanuts over campfires and boiled them. They also adopted peanuts as a cheap coffee substitute. Some history books note that Confederate soldiers from Georgia were known as "goober grabbers."

It was during the slave-trading years of the seventeenth and eighteenth centuries that the peanut was first brought to the southeastern United States, and for a long time it was assumed that the peanut had originated in Africa. However, peanuts actually originated in Brazil and Peru.

## Boiled Peanuts

Judging from the many variations on recipes for boiled peanuts, there appears to be no wrong way to boil green peanuts. The important thing is the many tastings needed to determine when they are done. You must taste test the boiled peanuts for saltiness and firmness, as some people prefer soft nuts to firmer ones.

*4 to 5 pounds green (raw) peanuts in shell*

*4 to 6 quarts water*

*1 cup plain salt*

1. Wash unshelled peanuts thoroughly in cold water until water runs clear, then soak in cool, clean water for approximately 30 minutes before cooking. In a large pot, place soaked peanuts and cover completely with water. Add 1 cup of salt per gallon of water.

2. Cook, covered, on high heat for 4 to 7 hours. (Note: The cooking time for boiled peanuts varies according to the maturity of the peanuts used and the variety of peanuts. The cooking time for a "freshly pulled" or green peanut is shorter than for a peanut that has been stored for a time.) Boil the peanuts for about 4 hours, then taste. Taste again in 10 minutes, both for salt and texture. Keep cooking and tasting until the peanuts reach desired texture (when fully cooked, the texture of the peanut should be similar to that of a cooked dry pea or bean). Remove from heat and drain peanuts after cooking, or they will absorb salt and become oversalted.

3. Peanuts may be eaten hot or at room temperature, or chilled in the refrigerator and eaten cold, shelling as you eat them. For long-term storage, freeze in airtight containers.

*Boiled peanuts for sale at the state fair.* Bill Korlath photo.

**I'll Have What They're Having**

# Buffalo-Style Chicken Wings

The now-famous (and nationally beloved) Buffalo Chicken Wings were originally created at Frank & Teressa's Anchor Bar in Buffalo, New York, on October 30, 1964, by owner Teressa Bellissimo. They are deep-fried chicken wings served with a hot sauce, celery stalks, and blue cheese dressing.

The Anchor Bar's Buffalo Chicken Wings were an instant success and their impact on Buffalo was so great that former mayor Stanley M. Makowski proclaimed Friday, July 29, 1977, as "Chicken Wing Day." The city's proclamation noted that because of Mrs. Bellissimo's kitchen, "thousands of pounds of chicken wings are consumed by Buffalonians in restaurants and taverns throughout the city each week."

The Anchor Bar is a favorite stop for visiting celebrities and dignitaries from all over the world. The walls of the cafe are lined with awards, celebrity pictures, national comic strips, newspaper articles, and proclamations about the famous Anchor Bar Wings.

The following story on the origin of Buffalo Chicken Wings was written by Dom Bellissimo and sent to me by Ivano Toscani, executive chef/manager, of the Anchor Bar:

I would like my customers to know the real story behind our chicken wings. One Friday night back in 1964, I was working behind the bar. It was busy that night. My mother, Teressa, was in the kitchen cooking and dad, Frank, was in the restaurant greeting customers. It was one of those good Friday nights.

At about 11:30 P.M., a group of my friends came through the door, and they were starving! I told them to wait until midnight so they could have what they wanted. I served another round of drinks. By midnight, they were really hungry. I asked my mother to fix something for them. About ten minutes later, she brought out two plates and set them on the bar. They all asked, "What is this?" and to tell you the truth, I also was curious to know what those things were! They looked like chicken wings, but I was afraid to say so!

To make a long story short, yes, they were chicken wings. She was about to put them in the stock pot (for soup). She looked at them and said, "It's a shame to put such beautiful wings in a stock pot."

The rest is history! My mother created the famous chicken wings now served all over the country! Wherever you go, when you mention chicken wings, you will remember about my mother, Teressa, and that famous night in Buffalo!"

# Buffalo-Style Chicken Wings

The actual recipe for the Anchor Bar's Buffalo Chicken Wings is kept a closely guarded secret by the family, but you will find that the following recipe tastes a lot like theirs.

*24 (about 4 pounds) chicken wings*

*Salt and freshly ground black pepper*

*4 cups vegetable oil*

*4 teaspoons butter*

*2 to 5 tablespoons hot pepper sauce or to taste*

*1 tablespoon white vinegar*

*Blue Cheese Dressing (recipe follows)*

*Celery sticks*

1. Make Blue Cheese Dressing first and refrigerate 1 hour before using.

2. Cut off the tip of each chicken wing and discard it. Cut the wing in half (cutting at the joint) to make two pieces. Wash and dry the chicken wings (they need to be very dry to be fried crisp). Sprinkle with salt and pepper.

3. In a deep fryer or large pot, add oil and heat to 400°, or until it starts to pop and sizzle. *(Note: The oil should be able to cover the wings and still maintain the same temperature. If using an electric fryer, set the temperature to 425°.)* Add half of the chicken wings and cook 10 to 15 minutes or until golden and crisp, stirring occasionally. When done, remove from hot oil and drain on paper towels (do not pile the wings in a bowl, because the fat will cool and congeal before it runs off). Repeat with remaining chicken wings.

4. In a large saucepan over medium heat, melt butter. Add hot sauce and vinegar; stir well and remove from heat immediately. Add drained and cooled chicken wings and mix together. Using tongs, take chicken wings out of sauce and let the excess sauce drain off. Place the wings on a hot grill or in a 350° oven for 2 to 3 minutes to bake on the sauce. Serve with Blue Cheese Dressing and celery sticks.

Makes 4 to 6 servings.

## BLUE CHEESE DRESSING

*1 cup mayonnaise*

*2 tablespoons finely chopped onion*

*1 clove garlic, minced*

*¼ cup finely chopped fresh parsley leaves*

*½ cup sour cream*

*1 tablespoon lemon juice*

*1 tablespoon white vinegar*

*¼ cup crumbled blue cheese*

*Salt and freshly ground pepper to taste*

*Red (cayenne) pepper to taste*

In a large bowl, combine mayonnaise, onion, garlic, parsley, sour cream, lemon juice, vinegar, blue cheese, salt, pepper, and cayenne pepper. Cover and refrigerate for at least 1 hour before serving.

Makes 2½ cups.

# California Roll

**Long ago an old man and his wife charitably left some rice in the nest of an osprey living near their house. Later they found fish in the nest, ate it, and were delighted by the intriguing flavor their left-over rice had imparted to the fish as it underwent natural fermentation.**

*—Japanese legend about ancient sushi preparation*

Sushi, cold rice dressed with vinegar and garnished with raw fish or shellfish, is perhaps Japan's best-known contribution to world cuisine, but it has only been popular in the United States for the past twenty years or so. Today, in California and Hawaii, and in other states as well, sushi reigns supreme.

During the 1970s, a smart unknown California chef, realizing that many Americans did not like the thought of eating raw fish, created the now famous California Roll, made with crab, avocado, and cucumber. Since then, American sushi chefs have created many variations with unique names such as Spider Roll, Philadelphia Roll, and Rainbow Roll. Most people in Japan have never heard of the California Roll, though, and I would advise not trying to order one there.

Contrary to popular belief, *sushi* does not mean "raw fish," but "with rice." Sushi preparation is a highly developed skill that requires years of apprenticeship under a master chef, as it is considered an art form. The method of preparation, shape, and taste differ somewhat depending on the locality. In America, two kinds of sushi are most common, nigiri and maki sushi. Nigiri sushi is the Japanese version of an open-faced sandwich. The rice and topping are hand formed into bite-size pieces and served in pairs. Maki sushi is the Japanese rendition of a rolled up sandwich. A regular roll has nori (seaweed) wrapped around the rice filling. A reverse roll has rice on the outside.

Japanese sushi has a history and tradition more than two thousand years old, beginning as a way of preserving fish. It was not until 1824 that sushi became standardized, when Hanaya Yohei of Japan conceived the idea of sliced, raw seafood to be served on small fingers of vinegar-coated rice.

## California Roll

6 tablespoons rice vinegar

2 tablespoons sugar

2 teaspoons salt

3 cups uncooked short or medium grain rice

4 cups water

1 large English cucumber

2 to 3 avocados

Fresh lemon juice

Cooked snow crabmeat or imitation crab sticks*

5 sheets of sushi nori (seaweed in big squares)**

Wasabi (Japanese horseradish)

Soy sauce

Pickled ginger

\* Imitation crab sticks are the easiest to use. They can be found in Asian grocery stores.

\*\* You will need a bamboo sushi-rolling mat to assemble the California Rolls. The mats are often sold in Asian grocery stores.

**1.** In a small saucepan over medium heat, combine rice vinegar, sugar, and salt. Heat mixture just until the sugar dissolves. Remove from heat and let cool.

**2.** Wash rice, stirring with your hand, until water runs clear. Place rice in a saucepan with water; soak 30 minutes. Drain rice in a colander and transfer to a rice cooker; add 4 cups water. If you don't have a rice cooker, place rice and water into a large heavy saucepan over medium-high heat; bring just to a boil, reduce heat to low, and simmer, covered, for 15 minutes. Turn off heat and leave pan covered for 15 additional minutes.

**3.** Wash, peel, and seed cucumber. Slice in half lengthwise, then cut into long, slender strips. Cut the avocados in half lengthwise, then remove the pit; cut each section in half again (lengthwise), and carefully remove the peel. Cut the sections in long slender strips. Sprinkle the sliced avocado with lemon juice to keep from discoloring. If you are using snow crab, remove the crabmeat from the thicker portion of the legs and cut in half lengthwise. If you are using imitation crab sticks, remove the plastic wrapping and cut each in half lengthwise. Place the cucumber slices, avocado slices, and crab slices on a plate; cover with plastic wrap and refrigerate until you are ready to use.

4. When rice is done cooking, transfer to a large bowl; loosen rice grains gently with a wooden spatula or spoon by cutting and folding (do not stir, as this will crush the rice). Sprinkle the vinegar mixture over the rice, mixing together as you sprinkle. Add enough dressing to coat the rice but not make it damp. You may not need to use all the vinegar dressing. Spread the hot rice on top of a large sheet of aluminum foil and let it cool.

5. Lay the bamboo sushi-rolling mat on a cutting board with bamboo strips going horizontally from you. Place a sheet of plastic wrap on top of the bamboo mat. Place the nori (shiny side down) on top of the plastic wrap. Spread a thin layer, ¾ to 1 cup, of rice over ¾ of the nori leaving approximately one inch of uncovered nori at each end (it helps to wet your fingers with cold water when you are patting the rice onto the nori).

6. Arrange strips of avocado and cucumber along the center of the rice; top with crabmeat. Placing your fingers on the ingredients, carefully bring the bottom end of the rolling mat and the plastic wrap up and over the ingredients (tucking the end of the nori to start a roll). Pull back the rolling mat with plastic wrap, as necessary, so it does not get rolled into the sushi. Continue rolling the sushi and pulling back the rolling mat and plastic wrap, as necessary, until

you have approximately 1 to 2 inches of the top of the nori showing. Rub a small amount of cold water on the edge of the nori and bring the nori around so that it completes the sushi roll. Gently squeeze the rolling mat around the sushi roll until it is firm and forms an even roll (be careful not to squeeze too hard, as you may crush the ingredients or squeeze them out). Wrap the plastic wrap around the roll and set aside until ready to cut or refrigerate for longer storage. Repeat with remaining 4 nori sheets to make additional rolls.

7. Place rolls on a flat cutting board and remove plastic wrap. Using a sharp knife, cut each roll into 8 pieces (wet the knife between each cut to make it easier to cut and keep the rice from sticking to the knife). Arrange California Rolls on a platter and serve with wasabi, soy sauce, and pickled ginger.

Makes 40 California Rolls.

# Cheese Curds

**Cheese curds, booyah and beer,**
**That's what I like to hear**
**I may be kinda pokey,**
**But I say "okey-dokey!"**
**To cheese curds, booyah and beer.**

—from the musical comedy Belgians in Heaven,
   by Frederick Heide and James Kaplan

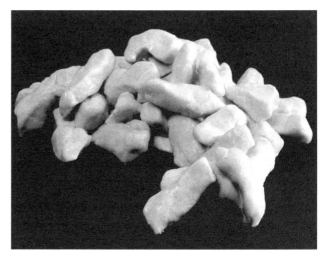

Fresh cheese curds—the appetizer of choice for Cheeseheads.
©2001 Wisconsin Milk Marketing Board, Inc.

The people of the state of Wisconsin love their cheese so much that they even wear funky Styrofoam cheese hats at Green Bay Packers football games. They call themselves "cheese-heads" and like to nibble on deep-fried cheese curds. Cheese curds, a uniquely Wisconsin delicacy, are formed as a by-product of the cheese-making process. They are little nubs of cheese, which, if very fresh, squeak when you bite down on them. Unlike aged cheese, curds lose their desirable qualities if refrigerated or if not eaten within a few days. The squeak disappears, and they turn dry and salty. If you find them in supermarkets, they are probably a few weeks old and inedible. Cheese curds have become so popular that many Wisconsin cheese factories make the curds daily to meet the demands of cheese curd lovers.

Every restaurant and bar in Wisconsin seems to serve them. They are usually a monster-sized appetizer, and they compete with french fries as a side order with sandwiches. They are also a favorite at local fairs, festivals, and fishing lodges. It is said that the folks in Wisconsin crave their curds.

Wisconsin is the leading producer of cheese in the United States, with much of Wisconsin's cheese made at small, family-owned and -operated cheese factories. Cheese making began in Wisconsin around 1840, when word of Wisconsin's rich farmland spread throughout Europe and the United States. Settlers from the eastern dairy states of New York and Ohio, as well as immigrants from Switzerland, Germany, and other countries in Europe, brought their traditions of cheese making and secret recipes to Wisconsin. By 1922, there were more than 2,800 cheese factories in the state. Wisconsin produces over 2 billion pounds of cheese per year, and its cheese is considered among the best in the world.

## Deep-Fried Cheese Curds

Vegetable oil (for frying)*

1 egg, beaten

1 tablespoon vegetable oil

1 cup milk or beer

1 cup all-purpose flour

1 teaspoon sugar

¼ teaspoon salt

1 teaspoon baking powder

1 (9-ounce) package fresh cheese curds, room temperature

* Use enough vegetable oil to completely cover cheese curds while frying.

1. In a deep fryer or large pot, heat vegetable oil (375° to 385°). In a medium bowl, combine egg, 1 tablespoon vegetable oil, and milk or beer until well blended. Add flour, sugar, salt, and baking powder; mix until smooth. Drop cheese curds in batter. Using a spoon, turn cheese curds to coat thoroughly.

2. A few at a time, drop the coated curds into the hot vegetable oil; fry approximately 1 minute or until brown and puffed, turning to coat all sides (do not overcook, or the cheese will begin to melt and ooze through the coating). Remove from hot oil and drain on paper towels. Allow fried cheese to cool a couple of minutes before eating.

Serves many.

# Chiles Rellenos

**They eat it with such appetite that their mouths froth and tears come to their eyes.**

—*Father Ignaz Pfefferkorn (1725–1795), German Jesuit, from Sonora: A Description of the Province.*

While Texans argue over the perfect chili con carne, all southwesterners search out the perfect chiles rellenos. Chiles rellenos (stuffed chile peppers) are normally filled with cheese, but they can be stuffed with practically anything—meat, seafood, or bean fillings. A restaurant's reputation can be made or broken on its chiles rellenos. In late summer, when the fresh crop comes in, nothing tastes better than stuffed chiles.

Chile terminology is confusing: pepper, chili, chile, chilli, aji, paprika, and capsicum are used interchangeably. In Mexico, Central America, Texas, Arizona, and especially New Mexico, the peppers are called chiles.

In New Mexican cooking, the chile pepper is king. Chiles have played a prominent role in New Mexico's culture and cuisine since the early 1600s, when the Spanish first planted them in the fertile Rio Grande Valley (now called Hatch Valley). Today the Hatch Valley is known as New Mexico's Chile Belt. Every Labor Day weekend, the normally pacific town of Hatch is transformed into relative pandemonium, with its festival celebrating the local chile harvest. Hundreds of "chile heads" arrive with 40-pound burlap bags to buy the famous chiles. Although chile peppers are now grown worldwide, New Mexico grows the best and tastiest chile peppers.

The hotness level, or heat index, of chiles is determined by pepper size, growing conditions, and genetics. Generally, smaller varieties taste hotter than larger ones. This is because smaller peppers have less flesh in proportion to the amount of veins and seeds, where the heat is concentrated. Growing location also affects the heat index. Those chiles grown in cooler, wetter climates tend to be milder than ones produced in hot, dry climates.

## Chiles Rellenos

*12 whole fresh green chiles (poblanos or Anaheim chiles), roasted and peeled\**

*1 pound sharp Cheddar or Monterey Jack cheese, cut into strips as long as the chiles*

*1 cup all-purpose flour*

*½ teaspoon baking powder*

*½ teaspoon salt*

*6 eggs, separated, at room temperature*

*Vegetable oil*

\* To roast chiles: Lay whole chiles directly on a barbecue grill, under a broiler, or on a stove top grill, or hold chiles over a gas flame with tongs. Cook, turning frequently, until the chile skins are evenly blackened and charred all over, but the flesh is still crisp. Put the chiles in a paper bag and seal the bag for 20 to 30 minutes to cool and steam the chiles (this helps to loosen the skins). When cool enough to handle, the skins will slide off easily. Leave stems on and pat chiles dry with paper towels. *(Note: Wear rubber gloves and be careful not to touch your eyes when preparing chiles.)*

1. Make a slit in the side of each roasted chile with a sharp knife, starting at the larger end and going down a couple of inches. If desired, remove veins and seeds, being careful not to rip the chile. Stuff with cheese (do not pack too tightly, as the cheese expands when it melts). If chiles are loose and open, fasten with toothpicks; set aside.

2. In a pie plate, combine the flour, baking powder, and salt. In a large bowl, beat egg whites until stiff peaks form. In a small bowl, beat egg yolks; fold into beaten egg whites.

3. Hold the prepared chile pepper by the stem, dip in flour, then dip in egg mixture until well coated (a rubber spatula can be used to spread batter if it does not cover the entire chile pepper).

4. In a large frying pan over medium-high heat, heat approximately ¼ inch of vegetable oil to 375°. Fry each coated chile pepper until golden brown, slowly rotating the chile pepper. Remove from heat and drain on paper towels. Serve immediately.

Makes 4 to 6 servings.

# Crabmeat Hoezel

This tasty appetizer is truly a Pittsburgh specialty. Stories say that John Hoezel was president of the Pittsburgh Screw and Bolt Corporation as well as a member of the Duquesne Club in Pittsburgh, Pennsylvania. During the 1940s, he visited a childhood friend there every Saturday. The two men would experiment with the recipe, changing ingredients and amounts. The finished recipe was given to the then-executive chef, Abel Rene Bomberault, sometime in the fall of 1948, who placed it on the menu of the Duquesne Club, calling it Crabmeat Hoezel. The crabmeat appetizer was served in special dishes, with Melba toast accompanying it to help scoop up the delicious crab.

The original recipe called for only tarragon vinegar. Later variations used cider vinegar to cut the tartness of the tarragon. Several restaurants in the Pittsburgh area now carry their own version of this dish, some with a combination of vinegars, others with only tarragon.

## Crabmeat Hoezel

Cynthia Bowan, a Pennsylvania food columnist, freelance writer, and lecturer, offers this version of the dish.

¼ cup tarragon vinegar

¼ cup cider vinegar

½ teaspoon salt

1 teaspoon freshly ground black pepper

¼ cup extra-virgin olive oil

1 pound flaked crabmeat*

1 teaspoon chopped fresh chives

Melba toast

* Lump crabmeat is best.

1. In a small bowl or jar, combine tarragon vinegar, cider vinegar, salt, and pepper; add olive oil and stir well. Cover and refrigerate 24 hours before using.

2. Place the crabmeat in a chilled serving dish. The crabmeat should be mounded, not spread out. Stir the dressing well in order to blend the flavors; ladle over the crabmeat. Sprinkle with chives and serve with Melba toast.

Makes 4 to 6 servings as a first course.

# Frito Pie

What is a puzzlement to Yankees and an icon for Texans? It is the Frito Pie, a Texas comfort food and a mainstay at football and basketball games there. Both Texas and New Mexico have claimed invention of the Frito Pie. New Mexico legend says that a Woolworth's department store employee, Teresa Hernandez, concocted the first Frito Pie in 1960 when business was lagging at the new store in Santa Fe. The manager of the store had challenged the workers to come up with something special to attract customers. Teresa is known in Santa Fe as the Frito Pie Lady.

The most logical claim and the one the Frito-Lay Company touts, occurred in 1932. Daisy Dean Doolin, mother of the company founder, Elmer Doolin, invented it in her San Antonio home. She poured leftover chili over Fritos corn chips. In 1952, Frito-Lay put together a cookbook that included the recipe for Frito Pie.

## Friday Night Frito Pie

This is the Friday night high school football game variation of Frito Pie. Proper etiquette requires that you not worry about a plate and that you eat it with a plastic spoon.

*Fritos corn chips*

*Hot canned chili*

*Shredded sharp Cheddar cheese*

*Chopped onion*

Open the bag of Fritos corn chips down the back seam (not the top), then add chili, Cheddar cheese, and onion (in that order). Eat and enjoy as you watch the game.

## Frito Pie

*3 cups Fritos corn chips, divided*

*¾ cup diced onion, divided*

*1 cup shredded mild Cheddar cheese, divided*

*1 (15-ounce) can chili (with no beans)*

Preheat oven to 350°. In a large ungreased baking dish, spread 2 cups corn chips. Sprinkle half of the onion and half of the Cheddar cheese over the top. Pour chili over the onion and cheese. Sprinkle the remaining onion and cheese over the chili. Top with remaining 1 cup corn chips. Bake 15 to 20 minutes or until cheese is bubbly. Remove from oven and serve hot.

Makes 4 to 6 servings.

# New York Knish

**You don't have to be Jewish to like Jewish food.**

*—New York saying*

Y ou can't write about New York City foods and not include the famous knish (pronounced kuh-NISH). Knishes are still as much in vogue today as a street food (sold from pushcart vendors) and as a quick meal as they were in the 1900s. In New York City, knishes are as much a part of the snack food scene as the hot dog.

The knish is a pastry of Jewish origin consisting of a piece of dough that encloses a filling of seasoned mashed potatoes—basically a mashed potato pie. It makes a great snack, appetizer, or side dish. Eat it as is, hot or cold, as an on-the-go lunch, or dipped in mustard sauce. According to New Yorkers, knishes are good anytime. There are arguments as to which is the best way to prepare a knish: baked or fried. Most knishes sold by street corner vendors are fried and square shaped. The baked ones typically are round and made at home or at knish bakeries.

Eastern European Jews developed the knish. During the early 1900s, when hundreds of thousands of Eastern Europeans migrated to America and settled in New York City, they brought with them their family recipes for knishes.

Knishes traditionally were made at home until Yonah Schimmel, a rabbi from Romania, began to sell them at Coney Island in New York City, and also from a pushcart on the Lower East Side. In 1910, he opened his original knish bakery located on East Houston Street.

## New York Potato Knish

Trying to reproduce the New York knish was been quite a challenge for me. The following recipe comes as close as you can to "fast food" knishes without frying them and without having a machine to shape them. My brother-in-law, Jim Arroyo, grew up in New York and is a knish lover. He verifies that the following recipe is pretty close to the original.

*3 large baking potatoes, peeled and quartered*

*4 tablespoons butter*

*1 medium onion, finely chopped*

*2 eggs, beaten*

*2 tablespoons finely minced fresh parsley leaves*

*1 teaspoon salt*

*½ teaspoon ground black pepper*

*¼ teaspoon garlic powder*

*1 (17.3-ounce) package of puff pastry sheets\**

*Egg wash (1 egg beaten and ¼ teaspoon water combined)*

*Yellow cornmeal*

\* Can be found in the frozen foods section at your local grocery (each package contains two dough sheets)

1. In a large pot, boil potatoes 15 to 20 minutes or until tender; remove from heat and drain. Mash or rice potatoes until fine. In a large frying pan over medium-low heat, melt butter; add onions and sauté until soft. Remove from heat. In a food processor or blender, add mashed or riced potatoes, cooked onions, eggs, parsley, salt, pepper, and garlic powder. Process until well mixed; chill thoroughly in the refrigerator.

2. Preheat oven to 375°. Lightly grease a baking sheet. On a cutting board or counter covered with a sheet of wax paper (use a new sheet of wax paper each time), place one sheet of puff pastry dough, keeping the remaining unused sheet covered with plastic wrap (this will prevent the sheet from drying out). Roll the puff dough as thin as possible. Using a sharp knife, cut dough into 3 x 6-inch rectangles.

3. Place approximately ¼ cup of potato filling in the center lower half of each rectangle; gently spread out and flatten the filling. Fold down the top part of the dough over potato filling (the knish will be square-shaped now). Brush egg wash over each knish. Using your fingers or a small knife edge, bring edges of dough up and over until sealed. Brush seams with additional egg wash. Gently press down on potato filling to spread out closer to the sealed edge. Trim and discard any excess dough around the edges, and gently press down on the seams. Sprinkle ¼ teaspoon cornmeal over each knish. Place onto prepared baking sheet. Repeat with remaining puff pastry sheet. Bake 20 to 25 minutes or until golden brown. Remove from oven and let cool slightly before serving. (Note: Knishes can be stored in the refrigerator, covered, for up to 1 week or frozen, covered, for up to 1 month.)

Makes 12 to 14 knishes.

# Oyster Cocktail

**You needn't tell me that a man who doesn't love oysters and asparagus and good wines has got a soul, or a stomach either. He's simply got the instinct for being unhappy.**

—*Saki, pen name of Scottish writer Hector Hugh Munro (1870–1916)*

The oyster cocktail, a popular West Coast appetizer, originated in a San Francisco restaurant around 1860 by a miner back from the gold fields. The miner was loaded down with gold nuggets bigger than ballpark peanuts. Being hungry, the miner asked one of the restaurant's waiters to bring him a plate of California raw oysters with some ketchup, horseradish, vinegar, and Worcestershire sauce, and a whiskey cocktail. After drinking the whiskey, he put the oysters into the goblet, added salt and pepper, vinegar, Worcestershire sauce, horseradish, and ketchup.

The restaurant keeper looked on with interest. "What sort of mess do you call that, pardner?" he asked.

The miner responded, "That is what I call an oyster cocktail."

The next day a sign appeared in the restaurant's front window: OYSTER COCKTAIL—FOUR BITS PER GLASS. Within a week, every restaurant in San Francisco was serving the new dish.

Oysters were popular with the gold miners because most of the miners thought that rich people always ate oysters. They figured that what was good enough for the rich swells back East was certainly good enough for them! During the gold rush era, there was a great demand for oysters in San Francisco, and stories were told of oysters being paid for with gold. Originally local oysters were harvested, but it took only a short time to over harvest and deplete the beds in San Francisco Bay.

Starting in 1850, large numbers of native oysters, also known as Olympia oysters, were harvested from Willapa Bay In northwestern Washington State and shipped live to San Francisco by large oyster schooners. Nearly 200,000 bushels of oysters were shipped annually to California.

The native beds of oysters, several feet thick, were heavily harvested, and nothing was done to help them replenish themselves. The oyster trade continued until around 1870, when both the numbers of oysters in the Willapa Bay began to diminish due to over harvesting and the first transcontinental railroad reached San Francisco, bringing East Coast oysters. By early twentieth century, 85 percent of the oysters sold in California were from the East Coast.

Oysterville, a small town on the Long Beach peninsula, was the center of the burgeoning oyster industry. For a time Oysterville was the wealthiest town in Washington, earning it the nickname "the Baltimore of the West."

## Oyster Cocktail

*1 teaspoon prepared horseradish or to taste*

*4 tablespoons tomato ketchup*

*Dash of hot pepper sauce or to taste*

*2 teaspoons fresh lemon juice*

*12 small, shucked oysters*

*Lemon wedge*

In a small bowl, combine horseradish, ketchup, hot sauce, and lemon juice; refrigerate for several hours before using. Place 3 oysters in each serving dish. Spoon 2 to 3 tablespoons of sauce over the oysters in each dish. Serve with lemon wedges for squeezing juice over the cocktail.

Makes 4 servings.

# Pemmican

**Of all foods I am acquainted with, pemmican is the only one that, under appropriate conditions, a man can eat twice a day for three hundred and sixty-five days in the year and have the last mouthful taste as good as the first. . . . It is the most satisfying food I know.**

*—Admiral Robert Edwin Peary (1856–1920), Arctic explorer, from his book* Northward over the Great Ice, *1898*

The food that crossed the North American continent, helped open up the exploration of the Far Northwest, and fed the men who made the first successful attempts to reach the North and South Poles was pemmican. You might say that pemmican is the original trail food or power bar. Pemmican is still considered a power food and is just as important to Native Americans today. Native Americans, hikers, mountain climbers, and explorers are still using modern versions of the recipe.

While recipes varied in the past as much as they do today, the method of making pemmican is basically the same. It was originally made with bison (buffalo meat) cut into thin strips, dried in the sun or next to the campfire, then pounded between two stones and reduced to a powder. This powder was then mixed with a range of wild fruits, berries, and seeds, according to the region. The mixture was placed in animal-hide bags and topped with melted grease, then the bag was sewn shut. Before the contents became hard from cooling, the filled bags were walked upon to flatten to about 6 or 7 inches.

A single sack or "piece" weighed close to ninety pounds. It has been figured, based on individual tribes' recipes, that each pound of pemmican was the same as three pounds of buffalo steak. Some tribes used less fat and claimed that a pound equaled five pounds of fresh meat. Pemmican, made this way, could last for many years.

Native Americans throughout the country developed and used this nutritious, high-energy food for thousands of years. It was the staple food, especially during long winter months and periods of poor hunting.

Not a better food could be found, as it required no campfires to prepare. A small amount would go a long way, and it could be eaten for weeks at a time to sustain energy and health. People forced to live solely on salted meats, bread, and cereals suffered and died from scurvy, a disease that results from the lack of vitamin C. Those who lived on pemmican had no scurvy.

In eastern Canada (present-day Saskatchewan), the Pemmican War of 1816 was fought between the Métis (first generation descendants of Canadian fur traders and Native American women, and French for the term "mixed blood") Nation and the Hudson Bay Company. During the late 1700s and early 1800s, the Métis Nation established itself as the processors and suppliers of pemmican to the New World.

It was called the Pemmican War because the Hudson Bay Company was trying to displace the Métis people from their homeland and cut them off from their supply of pemmican; thus, threatening the economic livelihood of the Métis people.

## Modern Pemmican

*½ pound jerky (buffalo or beef), chopped*

*2 cups chopped dried fruit (any combination of your choice, such as chokeberries, cranberries, cherries, apples, dates, apricots, or raisins)*

*1 cup chopped unsalted sunflower seeds or nuts (peanuts, cashews, walnuts, hazelnuts)*

*1 cup rendered beef suet or melted butter*

**1.** In a blender or food processor, mince jerky as fine as possible; pour into a large bowl. Stir in dried fruits and nuts.

**2.** Pour melted beef suet or butter over top, using only enough to hold the mixture together (may not use all of the butter). Allow to cool slightly. Spread mixture, approximately ½-inch thick, onto a baking sheet. Cover with plastic wrap or wax paper and allow to cool completely. When cool, cut into bars about 1 inch wide and 3½ inches long. Store in resealable plastic bags. For long-term storage, store in freezer.

*Makes 26 bars.*

# Pine/Pinyon Nuts

Pine nuts are considered a gourmet item to most Americans. Few realize, however, that in the southwestern United States, pine nuts have been a staple food for thousands of years. The pine nut was to the people of the Great Basin what the buffalo was to the people of the Plains. Pine nuts were not only an important food product for the early Americans (Washo, Shoshones, Paiutes, and Hopi) but was also a part of their spiritual life. They placed great focus on the nuts in ceremonies and dancing, as the nuts provided both food and shelter for them. Most Southwest Native Americans held nut-gathering regions to be sacred ground. Thought to bring good luck to the tribes, the pinyon tree, the source of pine nuts, was called the manna of the desert regions.

Harvesting pine nuts is relatively difficult and requires a substantial group effort. Because harvesting time was the last big food-gathering opportunity of the year before winter came, picking was considered an occasion for a village outing to gather cones. The nuts were roasted by piling the cones on a sagebrush fire or in a hot rock oven, then eaten directly from the shell or ground into a thick soup. Sometimes this soup was fed to babies in lieu of milk.

Today, two types of pine nuts are harvested for eating in the United States. The hard shell, commonly called pinyon nuts, is found mainly in Arizona, Colorado, New Mexico, and Utah. Of the two nuts, this is the more popular variety. The shells of pinyon nuts are hard, and you will need a nutcracker or a hammer to crack them open. The soft shell, commonly called the Nevada soft shell pine nut, is found mainly in Nevada and on the border with the surrounding states. This pine nut can be cracked using your teeth or fingers.

Pine nuts are expensive, but for good reason. The gnarled pines that produce the nuts yield a good crop only once every few years. It was not until the recipe for Italian pesto sauce became trendy about fifteen years ago that the general population really became interested in the pine nut. Pine nuts have become increasingly popular ever since.

# Popped Wild Rice

**Wild rice is the most nutritive single food which the Indians of North America consumed. The Indian diet of this grain, combined with maple sugar and with bison, deer, and other meats, was probably richer than that of the average American family today.**

*—Dr. Albert E. Jenks (1869–1953), "Wild Rice Gatherers of the Upper Lakes: A Study in American Primitives Economies," 19th Annual Report of the Bureau of American Ethnology, 1898*

It looks like rice and it cooks like rice, but in fact it is a long-grain marsh grass (a tall aquatic grass). Wild rice is naturally abundant in the cold rivers and lakes of the Great Lakes region, notably Minnesota, and it grows wild in shallow lakes and ponds, although commercial rice paddies are now found in parts of Minnesota. It is also known as Indian or Tuscarora rice.

To most people, wild rice remains a gourmet delicacy that we enjoy on rare occasions. To the Ojibwa of the Great Lakes area, wild rice is considered a sacred food and one that has sustained them for over 2,500 years. Wild rice once played a central role in tribal life. Its discovery was passed down in legends and was endowed with spiritual attributes. Popped wild rice, rice that is popped like corn, is eaten at modern Native American celebrations such as powwows, thanksgiving feasts, and numerous other ceremonies held during the year.

Wild rice was such an important food for the Sioux and Chippewa (Ojibwa) that they fought many battles for hundreds of years over control of the wild rice fields. Those who controlled the shallow lakes and rivers where wild rice grew were stronger and survived the long, hard winters better than those who did not. French explorers were probably the first Europeans to enjoy this delicacy as guests at the Indian sugar camps. For winter travel, the popped rice was crushed and shaped into cakes with deer or bear fat, maple sugar, and dried berries. This made a lightweight and nutritious food that could be eaten without the benefit of a campfire. Not all wild rice will pop successfully. The best variety to use is hand-processed rice that usually has more moisture left in each kernel, which will then expand when heated.

To this day, wild rice is harvested by hand. Native growers glide along in canoes through the tall growing rice and shake off the grains right into the canoe. Mainly the women of the tribe do this job.

## Popped Wild Rice

Most Native American tribes who live in the wild rice areas have tribal enterprises that sell their hand-harvested rice. Look for this rice to make popped wild rice.

*Vegetable oil*

*¼ cup uncooked wild rice\**

*Salt to taste*

\* To test the rice, place some vegetable oil in a frying pan, sprinkle in a little rice, and stir so it doesn't burn. If it slowly puffs, it is good rice.

1. In a large, heavy skillet over medium-high heat, place a flat-bottomed strainer and add ½ inch of vegetable oil. Heat until temperature of oil reaches 450° or until a kernel of wild rice placed in the strainer and dropped in the oil sizzles and expands to about double its length and width in fewer than 5 seconds.

2. Add 1 tablespoon of rice at a time to the oil. When all the kernels have expanded (which constitutes the popping), remove the strainer from the heat and empty popped rice onto paper toweling, pat any excess oil with paper towels. Repeat process until all rice is popped. Season with salt to taste. May be stored in a sealed container for several weeks.

## VARIATION

**Maple Popped Rice:** After rice is popped, toss with ¼ cup melted butter and 2 tablespoons maple sugar, maple syrup, or brown sugar.

Makes about 2 cups.

# Rocky Mountain Oysters

**I had a ball at the Testicle Festival.**

*—motto of the annual Testicle Festival held in Clinton, Montana*

Anything that walks, swims, crawls, or flies can be eaten. It just takes an open mind and a willing stomach. Of course, there are some people who will eat anything. Rocky Mountain oysters—also known as prairie oysters, Montana tendergroins, cowboy caviar, swinging beef, and calf fries—are true Western delicacies.

What are Rocky Mountain oysters? They are that part of the male cow that is removed in his youth so that he may thereby be more tractable, grow meatier, and behave less masculine. When the calves are branded, the testicles are cut off and thrown in a bucket of water. They are then peeled, washed, rolled in flour and pepper, and fried in a pan. They are considered to be quite a delicacy. Like other organ meats, testicles may be cooked in a variety of ways—deep fried whole, cut into broad, thin slices, or marinated. At roundups in the old West, cowboys and ranch hands tossed the meat on a hot iron stove. When the calf fries exploded, they were done!

Eating animal genitalia dates back to ancient Roman times, when it was believed that eating a healthy animal's organ might correct some ailment in the corresponding human organ of the male person eating it. Because of this belief, the practice continues to the present day, especially in Asia, where animal genitalia are considered an aphrodisiac.

The rugged folks of the Rocky Mountain region are not squeamish. Testicle festivals are held every spring and fall in Montana. The Rock Creek Lodge in Clinton, Montana, is home to one of the most famous testicle festivals every year. More than 15,000 visitors dine on over 2½ tons of Rocky Mountain oysters. These festivals can be very rowdy and may not be the best place to bring your children. If you can't get to a festival, many restaurants and bars in Montana, Idaho, and Kansas serve Rocky Mountain oysters all year long and with less fanfare.

## Rocky Mountain Oysters

I have not personally tried this recipe. (I haven't worked up my courage yet!)

*2 pounds calf testicles\**

*2 cups beer*

*2 eggs, beaten*

*1½ cups all-purpose flour*

*¼ cup yellow cornmeal*

*Salt and ground black pepper to taste*

*Vegetable oil\*\**

*1 tablespoon hot pepper sauce*

\* Be sure to ask your butcher for calf testicles, not bull testicles. Calf testicles are the size of a walnut and are much more tender than the larger bull testicles.

\*\* Use enough vegetable oil to fill your frying container halfway to the top (to allow for bubbling up and splattering) and to completely cover calf testicles while frying.

1. With a very sharp knife, split the tough skinlike muscle that surrounds each testicle. Remove the skin (you can remove the skin easily if the testicles are frozen, then peel while thawing). Slice each testicle into approximately ¼- to ½-inch-thick ovals. Place slices in a large pan or bowl with enough beer to cover them; cover and let sit 2 hours.

2. In a shallow bowl combine eggs, flour, cornmeal, salt, and pepper. Remove testicles from beer, drain, and dredge thoroughly in the flour mixture. In a large, deep pot, heat oil to 375°. Deep fry 3 minutes or until golden brown (will rise to the surface when done). Drain on paper towels. Serve warm with your favorite hot pepper sauce.

# Spam Musubi

**We had lost our most fertile, food-bearing land— the Ukraine and the Northern Caucasians. Without Spam, we wouldn't have been able to feed our army.**

*—Nikita Krushchev (1894–1971), premier of the Soviet Union, from his autobiography* Krushchev Remembers, *1970.*

Spam is considered the food that changed the course of history. Hawaiians have a love affair with Spam—they eat it as a delicacy, adding it to soups and stews, treating it as a side dish for breakfast, and enjoying it as the main event for lunch and dinner. Residents of Hawaii consume more Spam than populations anywhere else in the world: More than four million cans every year, or an average twelve cans of Spam per person per year.

A favorite Hawaiian way to eat Spam is in the form of a musubi (pronounced *moo-soo-bee,* with no accent). It is a fried slice of Spam on rice pressed together to form a small block, then wrapped with a strip of seaweed. A special kitchen gadget, known as the Spam Musubi Maker, is responsible for the proliferation of this treat. It is a special plexiglas mold with the outline of a single Spam slice. The Spam musubi is eaten as a sandwich, and it is perhaps the Island's favorite "to go" or snack food. Spam musubi is literally everywhere in Hawaii, including local convenience stores, grocery stores, school cafeterias, and even at the zoo. Eating a Spam musubi seems to serve as a rite of passage for newcomers anxious to attain "local" status.

The Hormel Company developed America's first canned ham in 1926. After the ham's were cut, the company was left with thousands of pounds of nearly worthless pork shoulder. Jay C. Hormel, son of Hormel founder George A. Hormel, developed the idea of using the pork shoulder in a new product called "Hormel Spiced Ham." Since the name was rather uninspiring, a contest was held at a New Year's Eve party for a new name with a $100 prize to the winner. The winning name was the name it goes by today—Spam. Kenneth Daigneau, an actor and the brother of a Hormel vice president Ralph Daigneau, won the contest.

During World War II, sales of Spam soared. In part because it requires no refrigeration, Spam was perfect for the military and became a standard K-ration for U.S. soldiers. Military personnel introduced it in Hawaii and elsewhere.

*One variation of Spam Musubi, perhaps the most unusual of all of Hawaii's local foods.*
Les Drent photo, courtesy coffee@coffeetimes.com.

# Hawaiian Spam Musubi

*3 cups uncooked short- or medium-grain rice*

*4 cups water*

*5 sheets of sushi nori (seaweed in big squares)*

*1 (12-ounce) can Spam luncheon meat*

*¼ cup soy sauce*

*¼ cup sugar*

*¼ cup rice wine (mirin)*

*Water*

1. Wash rice, stirring with your hand, until water runs clear. Place rice in a saucepan with water; soak 30 minutes. Drain rice in a colander and transfer to a rice cooker; add 4 cups water. If you don't have a rice cooker, put rice and water in a large, heavy saucepan over medium-high heat; bring just to a boil, reduce heat to low, and simmer, covered, for 15 minutes. Turn off heat and leave pan, covered, for 15 additional minutes.

2. Cut nori in half widthwise. Place cut nori in a resealable plastic bag to keep from exposing the nori to air (exposing the nori to air will make it tough and hard to eat).

3. Cut Spam into 8 rectangular slices approximately ¼ -inch thick. In a large, ungreased frying pan over medium heat (Spam has plenty of grease to keep it from sticking), fry slices until brown and slightly crispy. Remove from heat, drain on paper towels, and set aside.

4. In a small saucepan over high heat, add soy sauce, sugar, and rice wine; bring just to a boil, then remove from heat. Add fried Spam slices to soy sauce mixture, turning them to coat with the sauce; let Spam slices sit in marinade until ready to use.

5. In a small bowl, add some water to use as a sealer for the ends of the nori wrapper; set aside. Using a Spam musubi press, place a piece of nori on a plate. Position press on top of the nori so the length of the press is in the middle of the nori (widthwise). The press and the width of the nori should fit exactly the length of a slice of Spam. (Note: If you don't have a musubi maker, you can use the empty Spam can by opening both sides, creating a musubi mold.)

6. Spread approximately ¼ cup cooked rice across the bottom of the musubi maker, on top of the nori; press rice down with flat part of the press to compact the rice until it is ¼ inch thick (add more rice if necessary). Place a slice of Spam on top of the rice (it should cover most of the length of the musubi maker). Cover with an additional ¼ cup cooked rice; press until ¼-inch thick. Remove the musubi from the press by pushing the whole stack down (with the flat part of the press) while lifting off the press. Fold one end of nori over the musubi and press lightly onto the rice. Wet the remaining end slightly with water, then wrap over musubi and other piece of nori; press down on the other end. Cut log into 4 pieces. Repeat with the other 7 Spam slices, making sure to rinse off musubi maker after each use to prevent it from getting too sticky. Do not refrigerate musubi, as they will get dry and rubbery.

Makes 32 musubi.

# St. Louis Toasted Ravioli

St. Louis, Missouri, known as the Capital of Toasted Ravioli, seems to be the only city in the United States to produce this specialty. Toasted ravioli are a local favorite that are tremendously popular, particularly during the Christmas holidays. During the holidays, nearly 400,000 ravioli a day (about one for every person in the city) are produced.

Toasted ravioli are breaded and deep fried, not toasted, and are usually served with a rich marinara sauce for dipping. Technically, they're served as an appetizer, but four large ravioli could easily constitute dinner. Originally, toasted ravioli were handmade, but today most restaurants buy them frozen and personalize them with a signature sauce.

The story of toasted ravioli is probably more legend than fact. In 1942, a restaurant cook accidentally dropped a ravioli in a pan of bubbling oil. When the ravioli was pulled out of the hot oil, it still looked good. To cover up his mistake, the cook put some Parmesan cheese on it and served it.

## St. Louis Toasted Ravioli

1 (16-ounce) package ravioli*

1 cup all-purpose flour

1 cup dry bread crumbs

2 tablespoons milk

1 egg

Vegetable oil

1 cup prepared spaghetti or pizza sauce

Freshly grated Parmesan cheese

* Ravioli can be homemade or store bought and can have any filling that you prefer.

1. Preheat oven to 300°. In 3 shallow dishes, put flour in one, bread crumbs in another, and combine milk and egg in the third. Dust ravioli with flour, dip in egg mixture, then coat with bread crumbs.

2. In a large, heavy pot, heat 2 inches of vegetable oil to 350°. Fry ravioli, a few at a time, 1 minute per side or until golden. Remove from oil, drain on paper towels, and transfer to an ovenproof platter. Keep the ravioli warm in a preheated oven while frying the remainder.

3. In a small saucepan over medium heat, add spaghetti or pizza sauce and heat. To serve, sprinkle ravioli with Parmesan cheese and serve with warm sauce for dipping.

Makes 4 servings.

# Shave Ice

Shave ice can be found everywhere in the Hawaiian Islands—in coffee shops, mom-and-pop stores, shave ice stands, lunch wagons, crack seed stores, and especially at any and all public events. In Hawaii, shave ice is thought of as a snack and a thirst quencher.

Mainlanders call them snow cones, but locals in Hawaii call it shave (not shaved) ice. Unlike a mainland snow cone, shave ice is not ground ice. The shave ice is so fine that flavorings are absorbed into the ice rather than settling to the bottom of the cup as with a snow cone. In other words, it is the gourmet's snow cone in tropical flavors. An authentic shave ice starts with a block of ice that is spun across a razor-sharp blade (which shaves the ice creating a soft snow-like texture). Then it is packed into a paper cone, and flavored syrup is poured over the ice.

Usually you can choose up to three flavors, or add a scoop of vanilla ice cream in the bottom of the cone to create a delicious treat. The ultimate shave ice is with a mochi coating (a rice cake). In the 1950s, children would order their shave ice by color only, knowing what flavor each color represented. A mix of colors was called kalakoa, Hawaiian for "calico."

Japanese plantation workers who migrated to Hawaii around 1920 to 1930 to work in the sugar and pineapple fields brought shave ice to Hawaii. The workers enjoyed it as a refreshing break in the hot, tropical climate. The pickers would use their machetes to shave flakes of ice from a large block of ice into cups, then pour different fruit juices over the top. The ice treats remain popular in Japan, which is the source of most shave ice machines.

*Shave ice is a refreshing Hawaiian treat for children and adults alike. Les Drent photo, courtesy coffee@coffeetimes.com.*

# Soups
# & Stews

# Brunswick Stew

**I would like to find a stew that will give me heartburn immediately, instead of at three o'clock in the morning.**

—*John Barrymore (1882–1942), American actor*

This famous dish was originally a game stew, not a domestic meat stew as it is today. Because Native Americans were making stews with wild game long before the first European settlers arrived, there were Brunswick stews (though known by various other names) long before there were any Brunswick counties. Cherokee women, for example, were excellent cooks and regularly concocted delicious stews of venison, squirrel, and rabbit.

The American naturalist William Bartram (1739–1823) wrote of his travels in 1774 through the southeast colonies and described the culture of both the Seminoles and Creek Indians. He recorded a Creek Indian feast that he attended: "The repast is now brought in, consisting of venison stewed with bear's oil, fresh corn cakes, milk and hominy; and our drink, honey and water, very cool and agreeable."

The first settlers, living off the land in the woods, probably made this stew with whatever ingredients they had on hand, such as birds, squirrels, rabbits, and a variety of vegetables. Everyone seems to make it a little differently, but it is thought that it was originally made with squirrel. According to the U.S. Food and Drug Administration, something cannot be called Brunswick stew unless it has two meats in it. The standard stew is now made with chicken, pork, and sometimes beef as the major ingredients. The vegetables usually included are corn and lima beans.

It is generally believed that Brunswick stew was named for Brunswick County, Virginia, by Thomas Jefferson. Counties by the same name in North Carolina and Georgia also lay claim to the stew.

According to one story, Brunswick stew began as a squirrel stew that was first created by "Uncle" Jimmy Matthews, an African-American camp cook for Dr. Creed Haskins. In 1828, Dr. Creed Haskins, a member of the Virginia State Legislature, wanted something special for a political rally he was sponsoring for the Democratic presidential candidate, Andrew Jackson. He persuaded Matthews to make up a giant batch of his special stew. The event was a success, Jackson was elected, and Brunswick County's name became associated with the stew. For many years, the stew remained one of the main attractions at political rallies conducted by both the Whigs and the Democrats.

It is also said that many of the early Brunswick stew cooks were Methodist ministers, who took their stew pots along with their Bibles when they were assigned new parishes. They were as passionate about their stew making as they were about their preaching. It is thought that Brunswick stew money paid for many a choir robe.

# Brunswick Stew

Recipe from *What's Cooking America*, by Linda Stradley and Andra Cook.

½ pound beef round steak, cut into 1-inch pieces

1 whole chicken breast, boneless and skinless, cut into 1-inch pieces

1 large pork chop, cut into 1-inch pieces

1 small veal chop, cut into 1-inch pieces

1½ teaspoons salt

Water

2 (14½-ounce) cans stewed tomatoes, undrained

1 (15¼-ounce) can whole kernel corn, undrained

1 cup coarsely chopped potatoes

1 (10-ounce) package frozen lima beans

½ cup chopped onion

1 teaspoon salt

¼ teaspoon ground black pepper

Red (cayenne) pepper to taste

1. In a large pot or Dutch oven over medium-high heat, put steak, chicken, pork, veal, and 1½ teaspoons salt. Add just enough water to cover; bring to a gentle boil. Reduce heat to low and simmer 2 hours or until meats are tender (add more water as necessary to keep meat covered).

2. Add tomatoes, corn, potatoes, lima beans, and onion; stir gently. Add 1 teaspoon salt, pepper, and cayenne pepper. Simmer another 2 hours or until soup is thick and well blended. Remove from heat and transfer to individual serving bowls.

Makes 8 to 10 servings.

# Burgoo

**Whatever didn't make it across the road the night before.**

*—popular Kentucky joke regarding the meat in burgoo*

Burgoo is Kentucky's answer to Virginia's Brunswick stew. The two dishes are very similar, but you can get into arguments from citizens of both states on the subject. Burgoo is also considered a "must have" dish on Kentucky Derby Day in Louisville. Any occasion—a political rally, a church supper, a horse sale, or a horserace—can become a burgoo event.

Burgoo is more of a concept than a recipe—there are as many different ways to prepare burgoo as there are people to eat it. Today, it is most often cooked in enormous iron kettles outdoors over an open flame, with cooking taking as long as thirty hours. The hot stew is then dished into tin cups to feed the crowd.

Most historians believe that burgoo was created during the nineteenth century with the bounty from hunting trips. Like Brunswick stew, burgoo once featured squirrel as the main ingredient.

Burgoo is also said to be a version of a stew served to Confederate soldiers during the Civil War. Around 1810, Colonel Gus Jaubert, a member of Confederate General John Hunt Morgan's militia, is credited with introducing the term in Kentucky. Jaubert used the word *burgoo* to describe the meat in the stew, which was prepared for the troops in massive quantities from field rations.

## Kentucky Burgoo

1 (3- to 4-pound) whole roasting chicken, cut into quarters

2 pounds beef (preferably beef shanks), bones included

1 pound lamb (preferably lamb shanks), bones included

Water

1 tablespoon salt

3 cups tomato puree

2½ cups shredded green cabbage

3 large potatoes, peeled and diced

2 medium green bell peppers, cored, seeded, and diced

2 large onions, chopped

4 carrots, sliced thin

3 celery ribs, diced

3 cloves garlic, minced

¼ cup red wine vinegar

1 tablespoon A-1 Steak Sauce or 3 tablespoons Worcestershire sauce

2 teaspoons freshly ground black pepper

¾ to 1 teaspoon red (cayenne) pepper or to taste

2½ cups okra (fresh or canned)

2 cups corn kernels (fresh, frozen, or canned)

1. In a large stockpot over medium-high heat, place chicken, beef, and lamb. (If using a beef shank, cut some of the meat off the bone to fit it in the stockpot.) Add enough water to cover the meats. Add salt and bring to a boil. Reduce heat to medium-low and simmer, uncovered, 1½ to 2 hours or until meat is cooked and falling off the bone. Remove from heat and let cool. When meat is cool enough to handle, remove from broth and discard skin, fat, and bones; shred the meats into bite-size pieces.

2. Return shredded meats to stockpot over medium-low heat. Add tomato puree, cabbage, potatoes, bell peppers, onions, carrots, celery, and garlic; stir to combine. Mix in vinegar, A-1 Steak Sauce or Worcestershire sauce, pepper, and cayenne pepper. Continue to simmer for an additional 2 hours, stirring frequently. Add okra and corn; cook another 1 to 2 hours, adding water if needed. The longer you cook the stew, the better. The stew should cook down to the point where the ingredients are not individually distinguishable. Either serve immediately, or better yet, reheat and serve the next day for better flavor.

Makes 10 to 12 servings.

*Gehardt Taylor prepares to carry hot burgoo to the serving line at the Arenzville Burgoo. The village of Arenzville, Illinois, has held an annual burgoo festival for more than a hundred years and each year sells more than 2,000 gallons of the soup. For more details, see www.burgoo.org.*

# Cioppino

**Whoever tells a lie cannot be pure in heart—and only the pure in heart can make good soup.**

—Ludwig van Beethoven (1770–1827),
 German composer

Cioppino (pronounced chuh-PEE-no) is considered San Francisco's signature dish, and no trip to this West Coast city would be complete without a bowlful. Because of the versatility of the ingredients, there are numerous recipes for it. Cioppino can be prepared with a dozen kinds of fish and shellfish. It all depends on the day's catch or your personal choice.

This fish stew first became popular on the docks of San Francisco (now known as Fisherman's Wharf) in the 1930s. Cioppino is thought to be the result of Italian immigrant fishermen adding something from the day's catch to the communal stew kettle on the wharf. The origin of the word *cioppino* is something of a mystery, and many historians believe that it is Italian-American for "chip in." It is also believed that the name comes from a Genoese fish stew called cioppin.

## San Francisco Cioppino

The key to this recipe is experimentation. Be creative with this fish stew: Leave something out, or substitute something new. Serve cioppino with a glass of your favorite wine and hot sourdough bread.

¾ cup butter

2 medium onions, chopped

3 cloves garlic, minced

1 bunch fresh parsley leaves, minced

2 (14½-ounce) cans plum tomatoes, undrained and cut up*

2 (8-ounce) bottles clam juice

2 bay leaves

1 tablespoon dried basil

½ teaspoon dried thyme

½ teaspoon dried oregano

1½ cups dry red or white wine (whichever you prefer)

12 small hard-shell clams in shell

12 mussels in shell

1½ pounds raw extra-large shrimp, peeled and deveined**

1½ pounds bay scallops

1½ pounds fish fillets (halibut, cod, or salmon), cut into bite-size chunks

1½ cups flaked Dungeness crabmeat

Salt and freshly ground black pepper to taste

\* To easily prepare the tomatoes, use a sharp knife and cut the tomatoes while still in the can.

\*\* For additional flavor, place the shells of the shrimp in a saucepan and cover with water. Simmer over low heat approximately 7 to 10 minutes. Remove from heat and strain the broth, discarding shells. Add shrimp broth to soup broth.

1. In a large soup pot or Dutch oven over medium-low heat, melt butter; add onions, garlic, and parsley. Cook slowly, stirring occasionally, until onions are softened. Add tomatoes, clam juice, bay leaves, basil, thyme, oregano, and red or white wine; bring to a boil, then reduce heat to low, cover, and simmer 45 minutes to 1 hour. If sauce becomes too thick, thin with additional wine or water. *(Note: At this point, stock may be refrigerated, covered, up to 2 days before using. To use stock that has been refrigerated, reheat to boiling, then reduce heat to low, until broth is simmering gently.)*

2. Scrub clams and mussels with a small stiff brush under cold running water; remove beards from mussels. Discard any open clams or mussels. Cover with cold salted water; let stand 5 minutes.

3. Gently stir in the clams, mussels, shrimp, scallops, fish fillets, and crabmeat. Cover and simmer 5 to 7 minutes until clams open and shrimp are opaque when cut. *(Note: Do not overcook the seafood: Remember that the seafood continues to cook after it is removed from the pan.)* Remove bay leaves; season with salt and pepper to taste. Remove from heat, and ladle broth and seafood into large soup bowls and serve.

Makes 6 to 8 servings.

# Chicken Booyah

**The person cooking a stew is like a composer conducting his own orchestra—his only limitations are his own genius and the number and quality of the instruments at his command.**

*—author unknown*

Thanks to Belgian immigrants, northeastern Wisconsin has what no other region of the United States can offer: Chicken Booyah, a super "stick to your ribs" soup/stew made with chicken. While chicken soup is universal and variations of this dish can be found in many cultures worldwide, Wisconsin is the only place in the world where Chicken Booyah is found. Let your nose lead the way to the cauldrons of Chicken Booyah at the many festivals, church picnics, bazaars, and other large gatherings in the northeastern area of the state. Local restaurants have their own special recipes that they serve to Booyah lovers. Booyah is lovingly referred to as "Belgian penicillin."

It is believed that the word *booyah* comes from the word *bouillon*. The theory is that an unnamed Belgian could not spell *bouillon* and wrote it as he heard it. Another theory is that the word comes from the French *bouillir* meaning "to boil." For years people have been trying to figure out the origination of booyah and what makes it so special. The best thing to do is to eat and enjoy it.

The first Belgian immigrants arrived in Wisconsin in 1853. These immigrants, from French-speaking Brussels, had their own version of French called Walloon. Even today, the area settled by these immigrants is known as Walloon. The immigrants brought with them the traditions of Belgium, as they created ethnic communities where the Walloon language is still spoken today, where churches play their part as social and religious centers, and where farming techniques, recipes, and entertainment are expressions of their heritage.

## Chicken Booyah

This is one of those delicious recipes that makes a large quantity. Plan to have family and friends over to help you eat it.

*1 (4- to 5-pound) whole roasting chicken, cut into quarters*

*1 pound beef stew meat, bones included*

*1 pound pork stew meat, bones included*

*2 large onions, chopped and divided*

*4 quarts water, divided*

*6 carrots, diced*

*6 potatoes, peeled and diced*

*1 cup fresh or frozen peas*

*1 small bunch celery, diced*

*1 (28-ounce) can whole tomatoes, undrained and cut up\**

*Salt and freshly ground black pepper to taste*

\* To easily prepare the tomatoes, use a sharp knife and cut the tomatoes while still in the can.

**1.** In a large soup pot over medium-high heat, add chicken, beef, pork, ½ of chopped onions, and 2 quarts water; cover and bring to a boil. Reduce heat to low and simmer 20 to 30 minutes until chicken is tender and the meat falls from the bone; remove chicken from the pan to a large bowl and set aside to cool (when cool, take meat from the bone and cut into pieces). Continue to cook beef and pork approximately 1½ to 2 hours or until tender. Remove beef and pork from the pot to a large bowl and let cool (when cool, take meat from the bone and cut into pieces). Strain the stock, place in refrigerator, and let cool. When cool, remove fat from surface of stock.

**2.** Return cooled and strained stock to soup pot. Add remaining 2 quarts water; bring to a boil. Reduce heat to low and add remaining onions, carrots, and potatoes; simmer 10 to 15 minutes or until vegetables are tender. Add chicken, beef, pork, peas, celery, tomatoes, salt, and pepper; simmer until thoroughly heated. Serve in large soup bowls.

Makes 10 to 12 servings.

# Clam Chowder

**Chowder for breakfast, and chowder for dinner, and chowder for supper, till you began to look for fish-bones coming through your clothes.**

*—Herman Melville (1819–1891), American novelist, from his book* Moby Dick, *1851*

What is traditional clam chowder? The true or traditional chowder is a matter of debate. There are numerous varieties, and each has its loyal following. Just bring up the subject of chowder and most likely a debate will ensue as to which style is the true, authentic clam chowder. True chowder lovers delight in their pursuit of the perfect chowder, from creamy white to clear and briny to tomato based. Even in New England, known for the Boston or New England style, you can find different types of clam chowder.

In Maine, those living on one side of Penobscot Bay like their clam chowder made with tomatoes, while those living on the other side like it made with milk and no tomatoes. Western Rhode Islanders prefer clear chowder, while others swear by adding tomatoes. Farther down the Atlantic coast to Virginia and North Carolina, the broth is made with clam juice and is clear. New Yorkers insist on tomatoes in their chowder and call it Manhattan clam chowder. Cookbook writer and chef James Beard described Manhattan clam chowder as "a vegetable soup that accidentally had some clams dumped into it." In fact, Maine tried to prohibit, by law, tomatoes in clam chowder.

The first chowders were brought by French fishermen to Canada, then drifted down the coast to New England. Fish chowders were the forerunners of clam chowder. The chowder originally made by the early settlers differed from other fish soups because it used salt pork and ship's biscuits. Today most chowders do not include biscuits, but generally have crackers sprinkled on top.

On the West Coast, milk or cream is the key. The debate there is whether the chowder should be thick or thin.

Beyond the debate of whether creamy, clear, or tomato-based clam chowder is best, St. Augustine, Florida, has its own famous hopped-up version called Minorcan clam chowder. Hopped up, it is! This tomato-based, Manhattan-style chowder has one very potent ingredient: datil pepper. Long lines of diners at local restaurants attest to the popularity of this fiery chowder. Most historians, when writing about clam chowder, fail to mention Minorcan. Maybe it's because they don't know about it, or because the datil pepper used in this chowder is grown only in the St. Augustine area. In the late 1700s, colonists from the Mediterranean island of Minorca were brought to St. Augustine as indentured servants. They brought their own spices and cooking traditions with them, and the key ingredient was the datil pepper. Just as in New England, chowder was an easy food to make, it could be cooked in one pot, and it would feed many hungry people. It was a meal made from necessity using fish that was plentiful and their own familiar seasonings.

Chowder is derived from the French word *cauldron,* meaning "cooking kettle." Vegetables or fish stewed in a cauldron thus became known as chowder in English-speaking nations, a corruption of the name of the pot or kettle in which they were cooked.

# Pacific Coast Clam Chowder

Because there are so many types and styles of clam chowder, and because I'm extremely prejudiced about the chowder served on the Pacific Coast, I've included my favorite family clam chowder recipe. To me, this recipe resolves the clam chowder debate.

*5 bacon slices, cut into ¼ -inch pieces*

*¼ cup butter*

*1 medium onion, chopped*

*¼ cup all-purpose flour*

*Salt and pepper to taste*

*4 cups milk*

*1 to 2 large potatoes, peeled and cut into ¼-inch pieces (or as many potatoes as you prefer)*

*2 (6½-ounce) cans minced clams, undrained*

*Saltine crackers*

**1.** In a large soup pot over medium heat, sauté bacon until crisp and golden brown. Remove bacon with a slotted spoon; drain on paper towels (drain off fat from soup pot). Set aside.

**2.** Reduce heat to low and add butter, stir until melted. Add onion and sauté until soft. Add flour, salt, and pepper, stirring constantly until well blended. Gradually add milk, stirring constantly until sauce comes to a boil and thickens.

**3.** Add potatoes and simmer 10 to 15 minutes or until potatoes are soft. Add bacon and clams with their juice; simmer until thoroughly heated. Season to taste with additional salt and pepper. Remove from heat and serve in soup bowls. Serve with saltine crackers.

Makes 8 servings.

# Conch Chowder

**To make a good soup, the pot must only simmer, or smile.**

*—French proverb*

When traveling through the Florida Keys, you'll find the word conch (pronounced conk) almost everywhere you go. Conch can refer to the shells, seafood, houses, food, dialect, and more. Natives of Key West and the Bahamas proudly call themselves conchs. In the past, proud parents in Key West would place a conch shell on a stick at the front of their house to inform everyone of the birth of a baby.

Although conch may be served in different ways, the most popular dish is conch chowder, which is on almost every menu there. Along with key lime pie, it is considered the signature dish of the Florida Keys. Of course, like most foods, every resident and every restaurant seem to have their own version. It is traditionally made with a tomato base, but just like the controversy over New England versus Manhattan clam chowder, it can also be made with a cream base. Conch meat is delectably sweet, but tough as shoe leather if it isn't prepared and cooked just right.

Conch meat was a staple food of the early settlers in the Keys. In the early 1800s, people from the Bahamas began migrating there. These immigrants were called conchs because of the sea snails they liked to eat of the same name. By 1891, it is estimated that a third of the Key West population was Bahamian. This explains why the word conch is so much a part of the area's heritage.

The conch has become so popular and has been harvested to such an extent that it has become an endangered species in Florida and is now protected by state and federal law. In 1985, the Key's most famous shell and seafood was banned from being harvested in United States waters. It is still harvested elsewhere in the Caribbean with government controls. Any conch product eaten in the Keys is now being imported from the Bahamas and other Caribbean islands.

## Conch Chowder

This recipe comes from Jan Knowles Myers, formerly of Key West, Florida. Jan says, "My hometown is Key West, and I'm a fourth-generation Key West native or 'conch' and a fifth-generation Florida native. Back when I was young, Key West was a quaint little fishing village with nowhere near the level of tourism that currently exists. I truly loved my childhood and growing up in Key West. This chowder recipe was my father's. He was George Irving Knowles, Jr. (1915–1984), a third-generation Key West native. Much of my family came to Key West from the Bahamas, arriving as early as the 1840s, although my French great-great-great-grandfather, Odet Philippe, had traveled to the city in the 1820s."

*3 onions, finely chopped*

*2 to 3 cloves garlic, minced*

*1 green bell pepper, cored, seeded, and finely chopped*

*1 (14½-ounce) can whole tomatoes, undrained and cut up\**

*2½ to 3 pounds conch meat, cleaned and ground\*\**

*2 potatoes, peeled and finely chopped*

*2 quarts water (approximately)*

*Salt and freshly ground black pepper to taste*

\*  To easily prepare the tomatoes, use a sharp knife and cut the tomatoes while still in the can.
\*\* Because conch meat is very tough, you must grind it using a meat grinder or food processor.

In a large, heavy pot over medium-high heat, add onions, garlic, bell pepper, and tomatoes; cook until vegetables are soft. Reduce heat to low; add ground conch meat, potatoes, and enough water to make it soupy but not watery. Let simmer 1 hour. Add salt and pepper to taste. Remove from heat and serve in individual soup bowls.

Makes 6 to 8 servings.

# Frogmore Stew

Frogmore stew, also known as Lowcountry Boil and Beaufort stew, comes from the African-American Gullah culture of the Sea Islands. Gullah cuisine reflects the Lowcountry cooking of the Carolinas, especially the Sea Islands (the Sea Islands are a cluster of islands that stretch along the coasts of South Carolina and northern Georgia). These islanders are descended from the slaves brought from Africa in the eighteenth and nineteenth centuries to work in the rice fields.

Gullah or Lowcountry cuisine features rice as the main ingredient. This type of food is often served at social gatherings, such as the oyster roast and fish fry. Everyone joins in the cooking, then sits down at a communal table to eat.

Frogmore stew gets its name from the community of Frogmore on St. Helena Island, South Carolina. According to the Beaufort County Public Library in South Carolina, Frogmore stew was created on National Guard's Day in the 1950s by Richard Gay of Gay Seafood Company. Gay was preparing a cookout for his fellow guardsmen with leftover sausage, corn, shrimp, and some spices. The recipe soon became popular in the area and has become one of the state's best known recipes. Gay campaigned to have Frogmore stew declared the "official seafood dish" of South Carolina. He didn't succeed, but the recipe remains an unofficial favorite.

Traditionally, the stew is served by first pouring off the extra liquid, then spreading the stew on a table covered with newsprint. The host and the diners determine the proper etiquette.

## Frogmore Stew

5 pounds smoked hot sausage, cut into 1-inch pieces

2 gallons water

1 (6-ounce) can Old Bay Seasoning or 4½ tablespoons Seafood Boil (recipe follows)

5 pounds new potatoes, halved

2 pounds small onions, peeled and quartered

6 cloves garlic, minced

2 pounds whole baby carrots

½ cup cider vinegar

15 ears of corn on the cob, shucked and cut into 2-inch lengths

5 pounds raw extra-large shrimp, peeled and deveined

Salt to taste

Cocktail sauce

Lemon wedges

1. In a large frying pan, brown sausage; remove from heat and set aside.

2. In a very large pot, add water and Old Bay Seasoning (or Seafood Boil) and bring to a boil. Add potatoes, onions, garlic, and carrots; boil for 20 minutes. Add the sausage (with drippings) and vinegar; cook another 15 minutes. Add corn and shrimp; cook an additional 4 to 5 minutes or until the shrimp turn pink and are opaque in center (cut to test). Taste and adjust salt. Remove potatoes, sausage, corn, and shrimp. Serve in large bowls with cocktail sauce and lemon wedges.

Makes 20 to 25 servings.

## SEAFOOD BOIL

¼ cup mustard seeds

2 tablespoons peppercorns

Red pepper flakes to taste

6 bay leaves

1 tablespoon celery seeds

1 tablespoon coriander seeds

1 tablespoon ground ginger

¼ teaspoon ground mace

¼ cup salt

In a blender or food processor, place all the ingredients and blend until fine. Store in a covered jar.

# Gumbo

**One cannot think well, sleep well, love well, if one has not dined well.**

—*Virginia Woolf (1882–1941), British novelist and critic*

Gumbo has been called the greatest contribution of Louisiana kitchens to American cuisine. When the first French settlers came to Louisiana, they brought their love for bouillabaisse, a highly seasoned fish stew. Having none of the usual ingredients necessary to make a typical French bouillabaisse, they substituted local ingredients. After about a century, with the Spanish, Africans, and Natives of the region offering their contributions of food, the stew was no longer recognizable as bouillabaisse and became gumbo. What started out as second best became better than the original. The word gumbo is derived from African words for okra (*guingombo, tchingombo,* and *kingombo*), a podlike vegetable introduced by black slaves and often used to thicken the stew.

Gumbo is a classic Cajun one-pot, communal stew that is especially important around Mardi Gras (the Mardi Gras season officially begins twelve days after Christmas, on January 6, and culminates on the Tuesday before Ash Wednesday, the start of Lent). In some rural areas of Louisiana, masked and costumed horseback riders participate in what is called the Courir de Mardi Gras, which means "run of Mardi Gras." They ride up to a farmhouse along the route to ask permission for the group to come up to the house. When permission is granted, the riders charge toward the house, where they sing, dance, and beg until the owner offers them an ingredient for making their gumbo. Often the owner will throw a live chicken into the air that the riders will chase, like football players trying to recover a fumble. Today, people come from all over to watch the riders start their Courir de Mardi Gras. They also are there to greet the riders after the run and to help cook a large gumbo with the food that was collected.

There is only one rule that remains constant in making gumbo: First you make a roux. The roux, a flour and oil or butter mixture, which acts as a thickening agent, is the gumbo's base. There are no other hard-and-fast rules for the ingredients used in making gumbo—anything that flies, crawls, creeps, or lies still may end up in the gumbo pot. There are as many recipes for gumbo as there are cooks in Louisiana. The making of gumbo draws out the competitive streak in most Louisianans, and most cooks closely guard their recipes.

# Shrimp Gumbo

3 tablespoons vegetable oil

3 tablespoons all-purpose flour

1 large onion, diced

1 green bell pepper, cored, seeded, and diced

2 to 3 cloves garlic, minced

½ teaspoon black pepper

1 bay leaf

½ teaspoon red (cayenne) pepper

¼ teaspoon salt

2 cups water or chicken stock

½ cup clam juice

½ cup dry white wine

½ cup tomato sauce

1 pound smoked sausage, cut into ¼-inch rounds

1 pound raw extra-large shrimp, peeled and deveined *

Hot cooked long-grain white rice

Hot pepper sauce to taste

\*   To add flavor, place the shells of the shrimp in a saucepan and cover with water. Simmer over low heat approximately 7 to 10 minutes. Remove from heat and strain the broth, discarding shells. Substitute shrimp broth for water or chicken stock.

1. In a thick, heavy pot over medium heat, heat vegetable oil until hot; add flour gradually, stirring or whisking to combine. Reduce heat to low and cook, stirring frequently, about 45 to 60 minutes or until roux is desired color and has a nutlike odor (it will be very thick and pasty). *(Note: This process takes some time, depending on how high the heat is. The slower, the better, but be ready to remove skillet from heat and stir more rapidly if the roux appears to be burning.)*

2. When the roux has reached the desired color, turn off the heat. Add onion, bell pepper, and garlic, stirring constantly until the roux has cooled. Stir in pepper, bay leaf, cayenne pepper, and salt; set aside.

3. In a large pot over medium-high heat, add water or chicken stock, clam juice, white wine, and tomato sauce; heat until it comes to a slow boil. Spoon in the roux/vegetable mix, stirring to completely dissolve between each addition. Add sausage and simmer for 10 minutes. Taste and adjust seasonings.

4. Add shrimp and cook 4 to 5 minutes or until shrimp are opaque in center (cut to test). Remove from heat and remove bay leaf. Serve in large soup or pasta bowls. To serve, mound rice in bowls; ladle gumbo over the top and serve with hot pepper sauce.

Makes 4 servings.

# Jambalaya

**Jambalaya and a crawfish pie and fillet gumbo
'cause tonight I'm gonna see my ma cher amio.
Pick guitar, fill fruit jar and be gayo,
son of a gun, we'll have big fun on the bayou.**

—Hank Williams, Sr. (1923–1953), country singer and
songwriter, chorus from his song "Jambalaya"

Jambalaya could be a second cousin of gumbo—
the recipes are similar with the exception of
cooked rice. In gumbo, the rice is cooked separately and the gumbo ingredients are ladled over
the rice. In jambalaya, the rice is slowly cooked
in the same pot with the rest of the ingredients.
Jambalaya is a rice dish that is highly seasoned and
strongly flavored with combinations of beef, pork, poultry, smoked sausage, ham or tasso (lean chunk of highly
seasoned ham), or seafood. It is a very adaptable dish
often made from leftovers and ingredients on hand, and
thus traditionally a meal for the Cajun rural folks rather
than their wealthier town cousins, the Creoles.

It is thought that the word *jambalaya* comes from
the French world *jambon* meaning "ham," the French
words *a la,* meaning "with" or "in the manner of," and
the African word *ya,* meaning "rice." Put the words
together and they mean "ham with rice." The dish is a
takeoff from the Spanish paella and is also amazingly
similar to the West African dish called jollof rice.
Jambalaya is a one-pot dish—most cooks prefer to cook
it in cast-iron pots.

There is one rule in cooking jambalaya. After the
rice has been added, jambalaya should never be
stirred. Instead, it should be turned, as this prevents the
grains of rice from breaking up. Most cooks turn jambalaya only two or three times after the rice is added,
being sure to scoop from the bottom of the pot to mix
rice evenly with other ingredients. Shovels are used
when cooking outdoors in large cast-iron kettles.
Jambalaya is a favorite at church fairs, political rallies,
weddings, family reunions, and any other affair with an
excuse to serve food.

In Gonzales, Louisiana, the Jambalaya Festival and
World Champion Jambalaya Cooking Contest is held
annually. This event attracts participants who have
spent years perfecting the art of cooking and seasoning
this wonderful stew.

# Shrimp Jambalaya

6 bacon slices, chopped

1 large onion, chopped

2 cloves garlic, minced

½ cup chopped celery

1 green bell pepper, cored, seeded, and chopped

2 sprigs of fresh thyme leaves or ⅓ teaspoon dried thyme

2 teaspoons salt

6 drops of hot pepper sauce or to taste

1 teaspoon red (cayenne) pepper

¼ teaspoon ground cloves

1 bay leaf

1 (15-ounce) can whole tomatoes, undrained and cut up*

1 (8-ounce) bottle clam juice

2 cups water

1½ cups uncooked long-grain rice

1½ to 2 pounds raw extra-large shrimp, peeled and deveined**

2 teaspoons chopped fresh parsley leaves

\* To easily prepare the tomatoes, use a sharp knife and cut the tomatoes while still in the can.

\*\*To add flavor, place the shells of the shrimp in a saucepan and cover with water. Simmer over low heat approximately 7 to 10 minutes. Remove from heat and strain the broth; discarding shells. Substitute shrimp broth for water.

1. In a large, heavy pot over medium heat, fry the bacon until it begins to turn brown. Add onion, garlic, celery, and bell pepper; sauté 8 to 10 minutes or until vegetables are soft. Stir in thyme, salt, hot pepper sauce, cayenne pepper, cloves, bay leaf, and tomatoes.

2. Stir in clam juice and water; bring mixture to a boil. Add rice, cover, and turn heat to low; cook 30 minutes or until the rice has absorbed almost all of the liquid and is cooked through. Gently turn the jambalaya, then add shrimp and parsley, tossing lightly to distribute them evenly; cook 6 to 7 minutes until shrimp is opaque in center (cut to test). Remove from heat and serve immediately.

Makes 4 to 6 servings.

# Posole Stew

The word *posole* has two meanings. It refers to large corn kernels that have been treated with lime, then cooked (also known as hominy). Posole is also the name of a New Mexico specialty, a spicy Mexican/Indian stew-type dish with posole corn as the main ingredient. Today's version of this popular stew represents a cross between the Mexican posole that originated in Jalisco (in Mexico's Pacific Coast region), and the posole stew of the Pueblo Indians who live in the Rio Grande Valley.

The Pueblo Indians have been making their version of this stew for generations as a staple winter dish. Posole stew traditionally is served on Christmas Eve and always served on New Year's Eve, as it represents good luck for the new year. To the Pueblo Indians, it is a ceremonial dish for celebrating life's blessings.

Like Texas Chili con Carne (page 44), the posole of New Mexico is usually made in large quantities and with much ritual. Restaurants and cooks throughout the Southwest all seem to have their favorite version of this delicious popular stew.

In making posole stew, the posole corn or hominy is mixed with other ingredients such as chicken or pork with garlic and chiles, then cooked until the kernels burst. When this happens, each kernel opens up like a flower. Traditional recipes call for hours of cooking, particularly if using dried posole corn. It is a thick, hearty stew that is served in a bowl with cool salad toppings and a squeeze of lime juice. It is usually served with warm flour or corn tortillas.

According to Mexican-Americans, this stew can be served without the traditional pork rinds and pigs' feet, but it will not be authentic. They have a saying: "The main difference between everyday posole and feast-day posole is how much of the hog gets in." Since most people in today's society are squeamish about eating unusual parts of the pig, pork roast is generally used in most recipes.

# Posole Stew

1 pound dried posole or 2 (15-ounce) cans hominy, rinsed and drained

¼ cup vegetable oil

2 onions, diced

5 cloves garlic, minced

1 red bell pepper, cored, seeded and chopped

3 pounds pork roast, cut into bite-size pieces

2 cups chicken broth or water

½ cup red (cayenne) pepper or to taste

2 (3-ounce) cans diced green chiles or to taste

2 teaspoons ground cumin

Salt and pepper to taste

Lime wedges

Flour or corn tortillas

Toppings (suggestions follow)

1. If using dried posole, wash well until water runs clear; place in a large pot with 8 quarts of water. Over medium-high heat, bring to a boil and cook, covered, for 3 hours or until the majority of the kernels blossom (expand) and are almost tender. Remove from heat, strain, rinse well, and set aside.

2. In another large pot over medium-high heat, heat vegetable oil. Add onions, garlic, red bell pepper, and pork; sauté 6 to 7 minutes or until vegetables are tender and pork is browned. Cover with chicken broth or water; add cayenne pepper, green chiles, cumin, salt, and pepper. Bring to a boil, then reduce heat to low and simmer slowly for 30 minutes or until meat is cooked. Add cooked posole or hominy and simmer an additional 15 to 20 minutes to blend flavors.

3. Preheat oven to 350°. Wrap stacked tortillas in aluminum foil and heat in oven 15 minutes or until hot. To microwave, wrap a stack of tortillas lightly in paper towels and warm on high for 6 or 7 seconds per tortilla.

4. To serve, ladle the posole stew into individual soup bowls. Serve with lime wedges, warmed flour or corn tortillas, and toppings.

Makes 8 to 10 servings.

## TOPPINGS

Chopped fresh cilantro leaves, shredded iceberg lettuce, shredded Cheddar cheese, chopped green onions, diced avocados

# Oyster Stew

Native Americans living near the Chesapeake Bay had been eating oysters for thousands of years. The European colonists learned from them how to gather oysters and many believe that the Native Americans taught the settlers to make oyster stew with different combinations of vegetables and grains. The oysters were abundant in supply with some measuring as long as a man's foot. In 1607, Captain John Smith reported seeing oysters that were the size of dinner plates, and the Dutch settlers, in the middle and late 1800s, were astonished by both the abundance and size of the giant oysters.

By 1820, every large town on the eastern seaboard had oyster parlors, oyster cellars, oyster saloons, oyster bars, oyster houses, oyster stalls, and oyster lunchrooms. New York City was one of the major markets for oysters. Oyster boats, known as arks, brought more than six million oysters a day to wholesale dealers. Raw oysters were devoured by the bushel, and nineteenth-century hostesses required appropriate tableware on which to serve them.

The harvesting of oysters was a huge business, particularly after the Civil War. Men actually fought over oyster beds in the Chesapeake Bay. The great popularity of the oyster led to overfishing, which depleted the oyster beds along the northeastern coast and bays. In recent years, the population of the eastern oyster has declined dramatically, with only 1 percent of its historic population remaining.

## New England Oyster Stew

*2 pounds or 2 (1-pint) jars shucked oysters, undrained*

*4 tablespoons butter*

*3 cups milk (for a richer sauce, substitute some cream for the milk)*

*1 or 2 dashes hot pepper sauce (optional)*

*Salt and freshly ground black pepper to taste*

*3 tablespoons finely chopped fresh parsley leaves or chives*

*6 teaspoons butter*

**1.** Drain the oysters, reserving their liquid. In a large pan over medium heat, melt butter. Add oysters; simmer very gently 2 to 4 minutes or until the edges of the oysters curl.

**2.** Meanwhile, in a medium saucepan over low heat, slowly heat the milk (and/or cream) and oyster liquid (do not boil). Slowly add the milk to the oysters, stirring gently. Season with hot pepper sauce, salt, and pepper. Remove from heat. Serve in warm soup bowls, and garnish each bowl with parsley or chives and a teaspoon of butter.

*Makes 4 to 6 servings.*

## Did You Know?

Giovanni Giacomo Casanova (1725–1798), Venetian adventurer and author, and touted as the world's greatest lover (this myth was created by Casanova and comes from his unreliable twelve-volume autobiography *The Story of My Life*), supposedly ate fifty raw oysters every morning with his mistress of the moment in a bathtub designed for two.

# Saimin

**Food is our common ground, a universal experience.**

—James Beard (1903–1985), American chef and author

The favorite local fast food of the Hawaiian Islands (also considered the national dish of Hawaii) is saimin, an inexpensive noodle and broth soup. It is considered the supreme comfort food of the Islands, eaten at any time of day. You can find this soup at snack bars, coffee shops, and even on the McDonald's menu (in Hawaii only).

A few ambitious home cooks will make this noodle soup from scratch, but most people just rip open the ready-mix instant packages that can be found in all stores and is manufactured in Honolulu. Saimin is basically the same thing as ramen, a Japanese noodle soup. In Hawaii, you will get the real thing, fresh, thin white noodles in a clear broth with green onions, kamaboko (fish cakes), and sometimes ham or char siu (pork). Some people add chicken, eggs, shrimp, and whatever else is desired. The saimin is eaten very hot with chopsticks or spoons, and the broth is then drunk from the bowl. Do not be afraid to slurp, as there is simply no quiet way to eat saimin.

Japanese immigrants consider saimin to be Chinese, and the Chinese consider it to be Japanese. Because Hawaii is made up of an incredible mix of cultures—Hawaiian, Chinese, Japanese, Filipino, Thai, and many others—it could have originated from anywhere, then combined into this very tasty and popular soup. Each new wave of immigrant workers adapted their native cuisine to fit the Islands' available ingredients.

## Saimin

4 quarts water

1 tablespoon salt

1 (8-ounce) package dried Japanese soba noodles*

4 cups chicken broth

1 tablespoon grated fresh ginger

2 tablespoons soy sauce

Toppings (suggestions follow)

*   Soba noodles can be found in the Asian foods section of most grocery stores or in Japanese food specialty stores.

1. In a large pot over medium-high heat, add 4 quarts of water and salt; bring to a boil. Add soba noodles and boil 4 to 6 minutes until al dente. Remove from heat, drain, and rinse under warm, running water.

2. In a large pot over medium-high heat, add chicken broth and ginger; bring to a boil. Reduce heat to low. Add soy sauce and your favorite toppings; simmer for 5 minutes longer or until toppings are cooked. Remove from heat. Place cooked soba noodles in a large soup bowl; spoon broth mixture over the top and serve.

Makes 3 to 4 servings.

## TOPPINGS

(pick and choose your favorite)

Sliced Spam, baked ham slices, roast pork slices, sliced carrots, shredded green cabbage, chopped bok choy, sliced mushrooms, green peas, scrambled or fried egg, sliced green onions or scallions, cooked small shrimp, peeled and deveined

# Senate Bean Soup

Some people say that the government is full of beans—maybe bean soup is why. Senate Bean Soup, prepared with traditional early American ingredients of dried white pea beans, onions, and a ham bone, has been on the menu in the Senate Restaurant since the early twentieth century, possibly longer. It is the most popular item on the menu and is usually recommended by members of Congress when entertaining guests there for the first time.

Bean soup, a favorite of Speaker of the House Joseph G. Cannon of Illinois, was omitted from the menu one hot, humid day in 1904. When Speaker Cannon arrived for lunch and learned he could not order it, he was more than a little upset. "Thunderation!" roared the Speaker. "I had my mind set for bean soup. From now on, hot or cold, rain, snow, or shine, I want it on the menu every day." From that time on, Senate Bean Soup has appeared on the menu of the Senate Restaurant every single day, regardless of the weather. A resolution was introduced, and the Senate Rules Committee ordered that while the Senate is in session, no day shall pass without Senate Bean Soup.

## Did You Know?

In March 1998, while walking down the marbled steps near the Senate Restaurant, U.S. Representative John Spratt, Jr., of South Carolina slipped on spilled Senate Bean Soup and ended up with two small fractures in his right arm.

## Senate Bean Soup

*1 pound dried white pea beans*

*3 quarts water*

*1 (¼- to ½-pound) thick slice of ham or ham bone with meat*

*2 tablespoons butter*

*3 medium onions, finely chopped*

*4 stalks celery (including tops), finely chopped*

*3 cloves garlic, finely chopped*

*1 cup prepared mashed potatoes*

*1½ teaspoons salt*

*½ teaspoon white pepper*

*¼ cup finely chopped fresh parsley leaves*

**1.** Rinse and drain beans. Place beans in a large soup pot, cover with cold water, and let sit overnight. Drain and rinse beans. In the same soup pot over medium-high heat, bring the 3 quarts of water to a boil. Reduce heat to low, and add beans and ham bone or ham. Cover pot and simmer 1 hour.

**2.** In a large frying pan, melt butter. Add onions, celery, and garlic; sauté until vegetables are soft. Add vegetables and mashed potatoes to cooked soup and simmer an additional 1 hour or until beans are thoroughly cooked.

**3.** Remove ham bone or ham piece. Cut ham into small pieces, removing bone and fat; return to soup pot. Add salt and pepper. Serve in soup bowls and garnish with chopped parsley.

*Makes 6 servings.*

# She Crab Soup

The most famous dish of Lowcountry cooking is she crab soup, which is uniquely Charlestonian. This elegant soup helped put Charleston, South Carolina, on the culinary map and is considered the city's signature dish. Local restaurants offer their own version, and in many Charleston restaurants, the soup du jour is often she crab soup. The Scottish settlers who arrived in the Carolinas in the early 1700s are credited with bringing their famous seafood bisque recipe called partan bree, a crab and rice soup, to the area. With the abundance of blue crabs available in the coastal Carolina waters, this soup became very popular. In elegant society, terrapin, oyster, or crab soups were the accepted preliminary to a sumptuous banquet.

The addition of the crab roe, or crab eggs, is credited to William Deas, a butler and a cook to R. Goodwyn Rhett, mayor of Charleston. According to local legend, William Howard Taft (1857–1930), twenty-seventh president of the United States, was being "wined and dined" by Mayor Rhett at his home. The exact date seems to be lost in history, as President Taft visited the Rhetts several times between 1909 and 1912. Supposedly the Rhetts asked their butler to "dress up" the pale crab soup they usually served. The butler added orange-hued crab eggs to give color and improve the flavor, thus inventing the Charleston delicacy known as she crab soup.

She crab soup is a bisque-style soup made from the delicate meat of the blue crab with a little crab roe added for richness and flavor. It is a rich, smooth, and very elegant soup—often a midwinter treat, when the female blue crabs are full of roe.

Blue crab is a protected species. Whether the crab is a male called jimmy, or a female, called sook, it must measure at least 5 inches across the top or it must be released. If the eggs are showing on the female crab, a spongelike protrusion, she must be released regardless of size.

## She Crab Soup

2 tablespoons butter, divided

2 tablespoons all-purpose flour

1 cup milk

1½ cups half-and-half cream

4 teaspoons finely grated onion

¾ teaspoon Worcestershire sauce

Salt and white pepper to taste

¼ teaspoon ground mace

⅛ teaspoon red (cayenne) pepper

¼ teaspoon grated lemon zest

1½ pounds flaked blue crab meat*

¼ cup crab roe**

3 tablespoons dry sherry

1 tablespoon finely chopped fresh parsley leaves

\* If you live in parts of the country where blue crab is not available, other types of crabmeat such as Dungeness, snow, king, or rock crab may be substituted.

\*\* Two crumbled hard-cooked egg yolks may be substituted for the crab roe.

1. In a large, heavy pot over low heat, melt butter; add flour and blend until smooth. Slowly add milk and half-and-half cream, stirring constantly with a whisk. Cook until thickened. Add onion, Worcestershire sauce, salt, white pepper, mace, cayenne pepper, and lemon zest. Bring to a boil, stirring constantly. Add crabmeat and crab roe or crumbled hard-cooked egg yolks; simmer, uncovered, for 5 minutes (if the soup appears about to boil, remove the pan from the heat for a minute or so, then return). Remove from heat and add sherry, stirring to mix. Let sit for 3 to 4 minutes before serving.

2. To serve, pour the soup into individual heated soup bowls, dividing the crabmeat and roe equally into each bowl. Sprinkle with parsley and serve immediately.

Makes 4 servings.

# Texas Chili con Carne

In Texas, a bowl of chili con carne refers to beef chili without beans, as it literally means hot peppers with meat. True Texas chili con carne has no beans. Chili fans have caused national debates over the proper role of the pinto bean. This is a 150-year-old argument, one that is known to have led to a riot in an Oklahoma prison, a duel in Louisiana, and a series of barroom brawls in Texas. What everyone does agree on is that the finished dish must be deep red in color and should be hot enough to bring beads of perspiration to the cheeks and forehead.

The only thing certain about the origin of chili is that it did not originate in Mexico. It probably originated in the Southwest, near the Rio Grande, as that is where the wild ingredients are found. There are many legends and stories about where chili originated, and it is generally thought, by most historians, that the earliest versions of chili were made by the very poorest people, who would take the cheapest cut of meat, dice it into small pieces, and add an equal amount of peppers to make a little meat go a long way.

In the late 1600s and early 1700s, a handful of colonists arrived from the Canary Islands and settled in old La Villita just outside Mission San Antonio de Bejar (known today as the Alamo) to build churches and cathedrals. The women of the village would make Spanish stews, which are similar to chili. Around sundown, they would take their kettles into the plaza, spread red cloths on the ground, and build a small fire to keep the meal hot. Passersby were invited to dine and would sit on the ground and eat this chili from handmade earthen dishes.

Residents of the Texas prisons in the mid to late 1800s also lay claim to the creation of chili. Historians say that the Texas version of bread and water (or gruel) was a stew of the cheapest available ingredients (tough beef that was hacked fine, chiles, and spices) boiled in water to an edible consistency. The inmates would rate jails on the quality of their chili, and freed inmates often wrote for the recipe, saying what they missed most after leaving was a really good bowl of chili.

During the late 1800s, Latino women nicknamed "chili queens" sold stew they called chili made with dried red chiles and beef from open-air stalls at the Military Plaza Mercado. In those days, the word *chili* referred strictly to the pepper. They served a variation of simple, chile-spiked dishes (tamales, tortillas, chili con carne, and enchiladas). A night was not considered complete without a visit to one of these "chili queens."

So passionate are chili lovers that they hold competitions (some local, some international). The first known chili cook-off took place in 1967 in uninhabited Terlingua, Texas (once a thriving mercury-mining town of 5,000 people). It was a two-man cook-off between Wick Fowler (a Dallas and Denton newspaper reporter) and H. Allen Smith (humorist and author), which ended in a tie. The International Chili Society was formed and continued to hold its annual cook-off in Terlingua until 1975, when it moved to Rosamound, California. Chili competitions are still held each year in Terlingua.

## Did You Know?

Will Rogers (1879–1935), American humorist and actor, judged a town by the quality of its chili. He sampled chili in hundreds of towns, especially in Texas and Oklahoma, and kept a box score. He concluded that the finest chili, in his judgment, was from a small cafe in Coleman, Texas.

# Texas Chili Con Carne

I've won two local chili contests with this recipe, including one that had a Texan on the judging committee. If a Texan can give my chili a "thumbs up," it must be great! Remember, there are no beans in a true Texas chili.

2 pounds lean ground beef

6 cloves garlic, minced or finely chopped

1 large onion, chopped

1 tablespoon dried ground cumin

1 tablespoon dried oregano

2 tablespoons chili powder or to taste

1 teaspoon fresh ground black pepper

1 tablespoon salt

3 cups tomato puree, tomato sauce, or fresh tomatoes, coarsely chopped (or a combination of all three)

2 to 3 (14½-ounce) cans beef broth*

1 to 2 tablespoons molasses

2 to 3 tablespoons masa harina (optional)**

\*  Water or a combination of broth and water may be substituted for beef broth.

\*\* Masa harina is yellow corn flour. White corn meal or all-purpose flour may be substituted.

1. In a large skillet or Dutch oven over medium-high heat, sauté ground beef, garlic, onion, cumin, and oregano until the meat becomes gray in color. Add chili powder, pepper, salt, tomatoes, and beef broth. Reduce heat to low and simmer, covered, approximately 2 to 3 hours, stirring often. (Note: Additional beef broth or water may be added as needed.)

2. Add molasses to taste to cut down the acidity of the tomatoes. Add masa harina to thicken if desired. Continue to simmer another 30 minutes. (Note: During this last 30 minutes of cooking, do a lot of tasting and adjust seasoning to taste.)

3. For maximum flavor, cool chili and refrigerate overnight so flavors will mellow. To serve, remove top layer of solidified fat, reheat chili over low heat, and serve in large individual bowls.

Makes 4 to 6 servings.

*This batch of Texas chili con carne prepared for the Chilympiad is so hearty it's stirred with a paddle. Courtesy Chilympiad, San Marcos, Texas.*

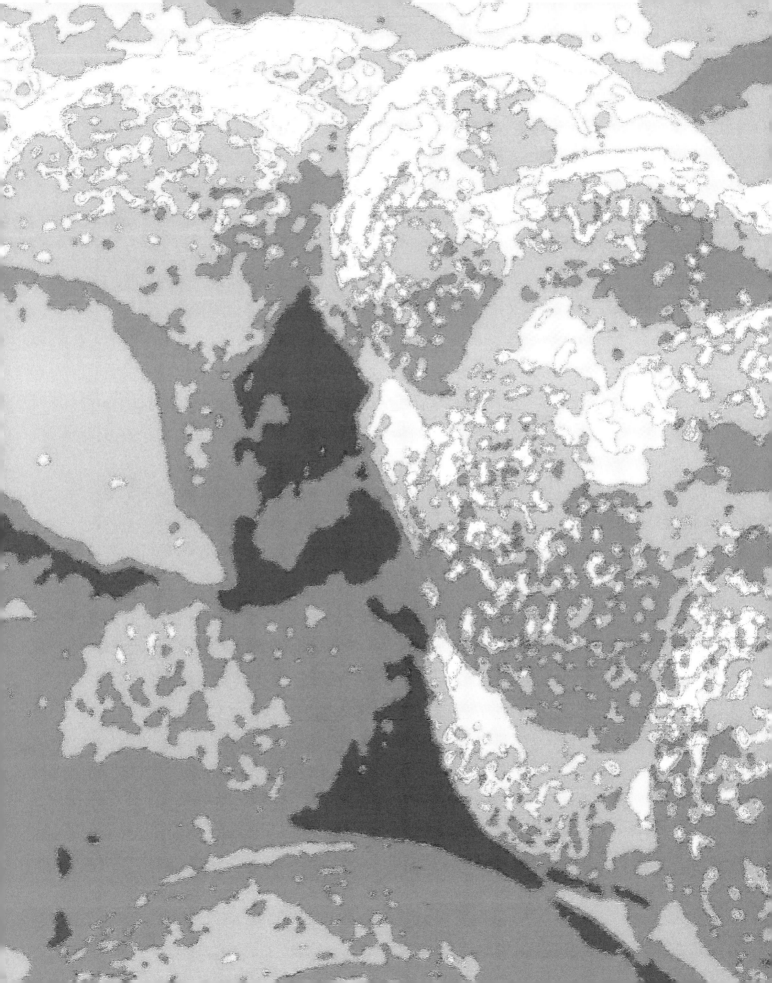

# Breads
# & Pastries

# Beignets

**Coffee is strong at the Café du Monde**
**Donuts are too hot to touch**
**Just like a fool, when those sweet goodies cool**
**I eat 'til I eat way too much**

*—Jimmy Buffett, American musician and songwriter, from his song "The Wino and I Know," on the album* Living and Dying in Three-Quarter Time, *1974.*

The word *beignet* (pronounced ben-YAY) comes from the early Celtic word *bigne* meaning "to raise." It is also French for "fritter." Beignets, a New Orleans specialty, are fried, raised pieces of yeast dough, usually about 2 inches in diameter or 2 inches square. After being fried, they are sprinkled with sugar or coated with various icings. It is like a sweet doughnut, but the beignet is square shaped and without a hole. Beignets are the forerunners of the raised doughnut. When you hear people in New Orleans say, "Goin' fo' coffee an' doughnuts," they mean coffee and beignets. In 1986, beignets became the Louisiana State Doughnut.

The French colonists of the eighteenth century brought the recipe and custom of making beignets to New Orleans. According to the 1901 *Picayune Creole Cook Book,* published by *The Picayune,* a leading New Orleans newspaper:

> The ancient French colonist brought the custom of serving sweet entremets and eatres, such as Beignets, Compotes, Souffles, Gelees, etc., from the old mother country to Louisiana. The Creoles applied these to the various delightful and refreshing fruits, which abound in Louisiana. . . . The custom of serving these sweet entremets spread from New Orleans to other portions of the United States, till now no fastidious chef would think of keeping a fashionable hotel or restaurant without including some of these in the daily bill of fare.

For many years, beignets were shaped into balls or squares and covered with mocha frosting. Later the beignet was cut in the shape of a doughnut, and the raised doughnut was born.

The original Café du Monde coffee stand was established in the New Orleans French Market in 1862 and still operates today. In fact, it is traditional to go there for dark roasted coffee with chicory and beignets when visiting the city.

# Beignets

1 cup lukewarm water (110° to 115°)

¼ cup sugar

½ teaspoon salt

1 egg, room temperature and beaten

2 tablespoons butter, softened

½ cup evaporated milk

4 cups bread flour or all-purpose flour

3 teaspoons instant active dry yeast

Vegetable oil*

Powdered sugar for dusting

\* Use just enough vegetable oil to completely cover beignets while frying.

1. Using a mixer with a dough hook, place water, sugar, salt, egg, butter, evaporated milk, flour, and yeast in the bowl. Beat until smooth. If using a bread machine, select dough setting and press Start. When dough cycle has finished, remove dough from pan and turn out onto a lightly oiled surface. Form dough into an oval, place in a lightly greased bowl, cover with plastic wrap, and refrigerate until well chilled (3 to 4 hours) or overnight.

2. To prepare dough, remove from refrigerator and roll out on a lightly floured board to ⅛-inch thickness. Cut into approximately 3-inch squares.

3. In a deep fryer or large pot, heat vegetable oil to 360°. Fry the beignets (2 or 3 at a time) 2 to 3 minutes or until they are puffed and golden brown on both sides, turning them in the oil with tongs once or twice to get them evenly brown; beignets will rise to the surface of the oil as soon as they begin to puff. (Note: If the beignets don't rise to the top immediately when dropped into the oil, the oil is not hot enough.) Remove from oil and drain on paper towels, then sprinkle heavily with powdered sugar. Serve hot. (Note: The dough can be kept for up to a week in the refrigerator—it actually improves with age; just punch down when it rises. Dough can also be frozen; cut and roll, or shape doughnuts before freezing.)

Makes 18 beignets.

# Bialys

*Fresh bialys and cream cheese.*

Outside of New York City, the bialy is little known. Bialys came to the United States from Bialystok, Poland, and they are sometimes known as Bialystok kuchen. In the early 1900s, hundreds of thousands of Eastern European Jews immigrated to America and settled in New York City. They brought with them their taste and recipes for bialys. While there were once dozens of bialy bakeries in New York, the number can now be counted on one hand. Bialys have long been a staple in New York delicatessens and a favorite of the Jewish community. True bialy lovers know where the best bakeries are. In fact, Manhattan's Lower East Side is lovingly called "Bialy Central."

A bialy is similar to a bagel, in that it is a round, chewy roll. But it is unlike a bagel in three important ways: One, it does not have a hole in the middle, but a depression; two, bialys never became popular outside of New York City; and three, bagels are boiled and bialys are baked. The indentation in the middle of the dough is filled with onion, garlic, or poppy seeds. Because the bialy has a very short shelf life, about 6 hours, they do not lend to being shipped around the country. They can be modest in size, 3 to 4 inches, or the size of a small pizza. Similar to the bialy is the onion pletzel and the onion board, popular Jewish breads from other countries.

Jessica (Jess) Selin of Chicago sent the following interesting story about her family's history with the bialy:

My great-great-great grandfather, Moshe Nosovich, was a baker in Bialystok, then part of the Russian empire, now part of Poland. Despite the extensive research we've conducted, we don't know how he became such a successful man—a Jew owning three bakeries in czarist Russia. It is perhaps doubly curious because the fashion in those days was for Jewish men to be pale and academic, while the women were more down-to-earth and worldly. But he did well as a baker. So much so, in fact, that family tradition holds him to be the inventor of the bialy, not a mere baker thereof.

Moshe had four children, three girls and a boy. Two of the girls became involved in the bakeries. My great-great-grandmother, Neshka, was one of those two girls. She worked at the bakeries because her husband, pale and academic, and not the man Moshe had picked out for her (thus defying custom), died young. She and her four children, all daughters, worked in the bakeries. On very cold nights, they slept there as well, warming themselves on the residual heat of the ovens. But we know they didn't live over the bakery, as poorer shop owners did. My great grandmother, Bella, talked about walking past the prison to get to the bakery.

Bella was the oldest of Neshka's four children and so started working fairly young. There was a lot of work to do as bialys were a central part of the Jewish diet in Poland, eaten at all three daily meals. Perhaps she tired of this work, because she immigrated to the United States in 1899 when she was seventeen years old. We don't know if she brought the family recipes for bialys or anything else.

After my family visited Bialystok in 1993, we confirmed where the family had lived and where the bakery had been. A number of stories, including this one, went from Bella to Ida to Nina, to me; but alas, no bialy recipes.

# Brooklyn Bialys

This recipe was sent to me by Bonni Lee Brown of Bradenton, Florida. Bonni grew up in New York City where her father owned a pharmacy in Brooklyn. Bonni says, "This is the closest recipe I've played with that approximates the fresh bialys my Dad would bring home on Sunday mornings. I was never a big bagel fan, but cream cheese and lox on a bialy I could go for anytime. My children think these bialys are the best they've had outside of New York City."

Cornmeal

Onion Topping (recipe follows)

2 cups warm water (110° to 115°), divided

1 package active dry yeast

2 teaspoons sugar

2¼ teaspoons salt

1¾ cups bread flour

3½ cups all-purpose flour

1. Cover two baking sheets with parchment paper and sprinkle lightly with cornmeal. Prepare Onion Topping; set aside.  In a large bowl combine ½ cup water, yeast, and sugar; let stand 10 minutes or until foamy. Add remaining 1½ cups water, salt, bread flour, and all-purpose flour. Knead by hand or with dough hook of mixer for 8 minutes until smooth (the dough will be soft). If you think the dough is too moist, add flour a tablespoon at a time. If the dough is looking dry and gnarly, add warm water a tablespoon at a time).

2. Form dough into a ball and place in a lightly oiled bowl, turning to oil all sides. Cover with plastic wrap and let rise 1½ hours or until tripled in bulk. Punch dough down in bowl, turn it over, cover with plastic wrap, and let rise another 45 minutes or until doubled in bulk. On a floured board or counter, punch dough down and roll into a cylinder shape. With a sharp knife, cut cylinder into 8 rounds. Lay dough rounds flat on a lightly floured board, cover with a towel, and let them rest 10 minutes. Gently pat each dough round into circles  (a little higher in the middle than at the edge), each about 3 to 4 inches in diameter.

Place bialys on prepared baking sheets, cover with plastic wrap, and let rise an additional 30 minutes or until increased by about half in bulk (don't let them over-rise).

3. Make an indention in the center of each bialy with two fingers of each hand, pressing from the center outward, leaving a 1-inch rim. Place approximately 1 teaspoon of Onion Topping in the hole of each bialy. Dust lightly with flour, cover with plastic wrap, and let rise 15 minutes.

4. Preheat oven to 425°. Bake on upper and lower shelves of the oven for 6 to 7 minutes, then switch pans and reverse positions of pans (front to back), and bake another 5 to 6 minutes until bialys are lightly browned. (Note: These are soft rolls, and it is important not to bake them too long or they will be very dry.) Remove from oven and let cool on wire racks. After cooling, immediately place in a plastic bag. This will allow the exterior to soften slightly. (Note: These rolls are best eaten fresh, preferably lightly toasted and smeared with cream cheese.) For longer storage, keep in the freezer.

Makes 8 bialys.

## ONION TOPPING

1 tablespoon vegetable or olive oil

1½ teaspoons poppy seeds

⅓ cup minced onion

½ teaspoon coarse kosher salt

In a small bowl, combine vegetable or olive oil, poppy seeds, onions, and salt; set aside.

# Hushpuppies

**So Jim he got out some corn-dodgers and butter-milk, and pork and cabbage and greens—there ain't nothing in the world so good when it's cooked right. . . .**

—Mark Twain, *from his novel* The Adventures of Huckleberry Finn, *1885.*

Hushpuppies are finger-shaped dumplings of cornmeal that are deep-fried and traditionally served with fried catfish. Also known as corn dodgers, they are especially popular throughout the South. There are several interesting stories of the origins of hushpuppies:

- The oldest story is that hushpuppies originated in the settlement of Nouvell Orleans (later called New Orleans, Louisiana), shortly after 1727. They were created by a group of Ursuline nuns who had come from France. The nuns converted cornmeal into a delicious food that they named croquettes de maise. The making of these croquettes spread rapidly throughout the southern states.

- An African cook in Atlanta is said to have given the name hushpuppy to this food. When frying a batch of catfish and croquettes, a nearby puppy began to howl. To keep the puppy quiet, she gave it a plateful of the croquettes and said, "hush, puppy." Since the name was cute, it stuck. This same story is also attributed to a Creole cook.

- Hunters and trappers could be on the trail for days at a time. At suppertime the hunting dogs would get hungry, so the hunters would mix a batter out of cornmeal or flour and cook it in grease on the campfire. Then they would throw the fried dough to the pups, telling them to be quiet, shut up, or "hush."

- Confederate soldiers would sit beside a campfire preparing their meals. If they detected Yankee soldiers approaching, they would toss their yapping dogs some of the fried cornmeal cakes with the command "Hush, puppies!"

- In the South, the salamander was often known as a "water dog" or "water puppy." These were deep-fried with cornmeal and formed into sticks. It is said they were called hushpuppies because eating such lowly food was not something a southern wife would want known to her neighbors.

## Hushpuppies

This recipe is from my friend Andra Cook of Raleigh, North Carolina. Andra says, "My mother-in-law, Belle Cook, would make these hushpuppies, cooking them in an iron pot over an open fire, at the Neuse River in North Carolina. They were delicious with fresh fish, cole slaw, french fries, and a big dose of fresh air. They never tasted so good!"

*4 cups vegetable oil*

*2 cups yellow cornmeal*

*1 cup all-purpose flour*

*1 egg, beaten*

*¾ teaspoon salt*

*¼ teaspoon baking soda*

*2 cups milk*

*1 cup water*

1. In a cast-iron skillet over medium-high heat, heat vegetable oil to 350° or until a small amount of batter dropped into the hot oil sizzles and floats. Do not let the oil get too hot or the center of the hushpuppies will not cook thoroughly.

2. In a large mixing bowl combine cornmeal, flour, egg, salt, baking soda, milk, and water. Mix until batter is smooth and free of any lumps. Batter should be stiff (if batter is too dry, add milk; if batter is too thin, add flour).

3. Using two spoons push a small amount of batter into hot oil (370° to 380°). After about 10 seconds, hushpuppies will float to the top and begin to brown. Fry for approximately 5 minutes, or until golden brown, turning to brown all sides. Remove from oil and place hushpuppies on paper towels; continue cooking the remaining batter. Fry in small batches, adding 4 to 6 hushpuppies to the oil at a time. They can be held in a 200° oven until serving time (approximately 30 minutes). Serve hot.

Makes 2 dozen hushpuppies.

**I'll Have What They're Having**

# Johnnycakes

Johnnycakes are the New England equivalent of tortillas. The simplest recipes call for nothing but cornmeal, boiling water, and a little salt. The batter should be fairly thin so that when fried on a hot griddle, the batter is no more than a quarter of an inch thick. Rhode Islanders take their johnnycakes so seriously that they hold baking and eating contests every year. In Rhode Island, traditionally, the cake is made only from fine white corn that has been ground by a water process.

The origin of the name johnnycakes (jonnycakes) is something of a mystery and probably has nothing to do with the name John. They were also called journey cakes because they could be carried on long trips in saddlebags and baked along the way. Some historians think that they were originally called Shawnee cakes and that the colonists slurred the words, pronouncing it as johnnycakes. Historians also posit that *joniken*, an American Indian word meaning "corn cake," could possibly be the origin.

The settlers of New England learned how to make johnnycakes from the local Pawtuxet Indians, who showed the starving Pilgrims how to grind and use corn for eating. When the Pilgrims landed at Plymouth in 1620, most of their wheat brought from England had spoiled on the long voyage. It is said that Myles Standish (1584–1656), the military leader of the Plymouth Colony, discovered a cache of corn stored by the Indians. An Indian named Tisquantum (1585–1622), also known as Squanto, was helpful in the settlers' survival during the winter of 1621. Tisquantum was one of five Indians taken to England in 1605 by Captain John Weymouth, who was employed by Sir Ferinando Gorges of the Plymouth Company and sent out to discover the Northwest Passage. In 1614, Tisquantum was brought back to America, assisting some of Gorges' men in mapping the New England coast.

Tisquantum lived out the rest of his life in the Plymouth Colony teaching the settlers how to grow corn, pound corn into meal, and how to cook with it. He also acted as interpreter and guide.

## Johnnycakes

*1 cup white cornmeal*

*¾ teaspoon salt*

*1 cup water*

*½ cup milk*

*Bacon drippings*

1. In a medium bowl, place cornmeal and salt. In a medium saucepan over high heat, bring water to a rapid boil; remove from heat. With the saucepan in one hand, let the boiling water dribble onto the cornmeal while stirring constantly with the other hand. Then stir the milk into the mixture (it will be fairly thick, but not runny).

2. Generously grease a large, heavy frying pan with the bacon drippings and heat. When pan is hot, drop the batter by spoonfuls. Flatten the batter with a spatula to a thickness of approximately ¼ inch. Fry until golden brown, turn, and brown on the other side (adding more bacon drippings as needed). Serve hot with butter, maple syrup, or applesauce.

Makes 4 servings.

# Kolache

Most people do not think of Czech food when they picture Texas, but during the nineteenth century, Czechoslovakian immigrants began arriving in Texas. They settled mainly in the rich Blackland Prairie, which stretches from just north of Houston to just north of Dallas.

Czechoslovakian cuisine includes wonderful baked goods such as the kolache. Kolaches are sweetened yeast dough formed into rolls and filled with fruit, cheese, or sausage. The kolache is the original Czech wedding pastry, and no true Czech wedding feast would be complete without a bountiful supply of kolaches on the dessert table.

The town of West was proclaimed the "Czech Heritage Capital of Texas" in 1998 by a State House resolution, which declared it the "home of the official kolache of the Texas Legislature." Caldwell, Texas, also holds an annual Kolache Festival in September featuring kolache-baking contests.

## Poppy Seed Kolache

This recipe is from Claudia Matcek of Caldwell, Texas. Claudia was the 1987 State Grand Champion Kolache Baker and the 1996 Burleson County Grand Champion.

*2 packages active dry yeast*

*¼ cup warm water (110° to 115°)*

*1 tablespoon sugar*

*2 cups milk*

*½ cup butter, room temperature*

*½ cup sugar*

*6¼ cups sifted all-purpose flour, divided*

*2 teaspoons salt*

*2 egg yolks, slightly beaten*

*Melted butter for brushing*

*Poppy Seed Filling (recipe follows)*

*Glaze (recipe follows)*

1. In a small bowl, dissolve yeast in warm water. Stir in 1 tablespoon sugar; set aside. In a medium saucepan over medium-high heat, heat milk until almost scalding; remove from heat. Stir in butter and ½ cup sugar; cool to lukewarm and add yeast mixture.

2. In a large bowl, combine 5¼ cups flour and salt; add milk mixture and mix. Mix in egg yolks and enough of remaining 1 cup flour for desired texture (should not be too sticky). Knead on floured board until smooth. Place into a lightly oiled bowl. Cover bowl with plastic wrap and place in a draft-free place to rise 1 hour or until the dough doubles in volume.

3. Lightly coat a large baking sheet with butter or vegetable spray; set aside. Roll out dough to about ½-inch thick and cut individual kolaches with a round biscuit cutter (approximately 4 inches in diameter). Place on prepared pan 2 inches apart. Brush with butter; let rise again, covered, approximately 20 to 30 minutes or until doubled in bulk.

**4.** Preheat oven to 375°. Prepare Poppy Seed Filling and Glaze. After rising, make indention in center of each Kolache with thumb. Spoon approximately 1 heaping teaspoon of cooled Poppy Seed Filling into each unbaked kolache. Bake 20 minutes or until lightly browned. Remove from oven and brush with softened butter, then Glaze. Kolaches are best the day they are made.

## POPPY SEED FILLING

*1½ cups milk*

*1¼ cups sugar*

*2 tablespoons all-purpose flour*

*1 cup ground poppy seeds\**

*1 teaspoon butter*

*1 teaspoon vanilla extract*

*\* If you cannot find ground poppy seeds, grind your own in a food processor, blender, or spice grinder.*

In a medium saucepan over medium-high heat, heat milk just until it starts to boil. Reduce heat to medium and add sugar, flour, and poppy seeds, stirring vigorously. Continue cooking, stirring constantly, until mixture thickens; remove from heat. Stir in butter and vanilla extract; let cool.

## GLAZE

*2 cups powdered sugar*

*½ teaspoon vanilla extract*

*2 tablespoons butter, melted*

*4 tablespoons milk*

In a medium bowl, combine powdered sugar, vanilla extract, butter, and milk. Drizzle over kolaches while still warm.

Makes 4 to 5 dozen (depending on size).

# Kringle

Racine, Wisconsin, is known as the "most Danish city in America." One of its favorite Danish treats is the kringle. There is a story about one resident, Lars Larson, who was on his deathbed in an upstairs bedroom. His doctor had said Lars would last for only a matter of hours. Lars woke from a deep sleep and sniffed. His wife must have just returned from the bakery, and the aroma of freshly baked kringles brought a spark to Lars. He whispered, "If I could just have a taste of kringle before I die, it would make my dying sweeter."

He mustered every ounce of strength and got out of bed. Slowly he made his way downstairs and into the kitchen. There he spied two kringles on the counter. Just as he was reaching out to take a piece, his wife swatted his hand away. "Stop that," she said. "We're saving these for the funeral."

Kringles are oval, butter-layered Danish pastries that were first introduced to Racine in the late 1800s by immigrant Danish bakers. They were originally pretzel-shaped, almond-filled coffee cakes called Wienerbrot (Viennese bread). Over the years, a variety of fruit and nut fillings were added, and the pretzel shape was changed to its present oval shape to eliminate the unfilled, overlapping parts.

True kringles are very labor intensive and can take up to three days to prepare, as they are made with up to thirty layers of delicate pastry dough. The challenge for a kringle baker is to roll butter thinly between several layers of yeast-raised dough. According to kringle bakers, you must roll very slowly to make the layers thinner. The traditional Racine bakeries offer a flat, oval kringle. The best places to enjoy kringles are in the bakeries in Racine.

*Mike, Dale, and Eric Olesen, partners of O&H Danish Bakery, Racine, Wisconsin. If you can't get to Racine, you can find them at www.ohdanishbakery.com or call them at 1–800–227–6665.*

# Kringle

Although this recipe does not require the tedious process of rolling out layers of butter and dough, as is done in Racine kringle bakeries, the result is similar.

*1 package active dry yeast*

*¼ cup warm water (110° to 115°)*

*½ cup cold butter*

*2 cups all-purpose flour*

*½ teaspoon salt*

*1 tablespoon sugar*

*½ cup warm milk (110° to 115°)*

*1 egg, beaten*

*Nut Filling (recipe follows)*

*Glaze (recipe follows)*

*2 tablespoons chopped pecans or walnuts*

**1.** In a small bowl, dissolve yeast in warm water. Using a pastry blender or two knives, in a large bowl, cut butter into flour and salt until particles are the size of small peas. Add yeast mixture, sugar, warm milk, and egg; beat until smooth (dough will be very soft). Cover and refrigerate at least 2 hours but not more than 24 hours.

**2.** When ready to use, remove from refrigerator. Punch dough down and divide in half; return other half to refrigerator. On a well-floured board, working quickly before dough softens, roll into a 15 x 10-inch rectangle, approximately ¼ to ½ inch thick (if dough gets too warm from handling, return to refrigerator).

**3.** Spread half of the prepared Nut Filling down the center of the rolled-out dough rectangle in a 2-inch strip. Fold sides of dough over filling, overlapping 1½ inches; pinch edges to seal. Shape into an oval; pinch ends together. Place seam side down on a large greased baking sheet. Repeat same process with remaining dough and filling. Cover and let rise in a warm place for 30 minutes or until double in size.

**4.** Preheat oven to 375°. Bake for 20 minutes or until golden brown. Remove from oven and let cool for 15 minutes. Spread prepared Glaze over kringles. Sprinkle with chopped pecans or walnuts. Serve kringles warm or at room temperature. To rewarm, preheat oven to 300°. Slide a whole, uncut kringle onto a baking sheet lined with aluminum foil. Cover loosely with a large piece of aluminum foil and heat for 12 to 15 minutes. Remove from oven and remove aluminum foil before slicing.

Makes 2 large kringles.

## NUT FILLING

*1½ cups finely chopped pecans or walnuts*

*1 cup firmly packed brown sugar*

*½ cup butter, room temperature*

In a large bowl, combine pecans or walnuts, brown sugar, and butter.

## GLAZE

*1 cup powdered sugar*

*5 teaspoons water*

*½ teaspoon vanilla extract*

In a medium bowl, combine powdered sugar, water, and vanilla.

# Lefse

According to legend, when St. Patrick was trying to chase Norwegian invaders out of Ireland, he stole all of their meat and replaced it with potatoes. This was no problem for the Norwegians, however; they just made lefse.

A Scandinavian tradition for decades, lefse (pronounced LEF-suh) is a Norwegian pastry made from potatoes, flour, butter, and cream. It is a delicious delicacy, whether served plain or with butter and sugar. If you have even a trace of Scandinavian blood in your veins, lefse can be very addictive, and there is no known cure.

In areas of Wisconsin and Minnesota settled originally by Norwegian immigrants, lefse is most often served through the months of November and December and associated with Thanksgiving and Christmas. It can be eaten as a dessert or as a side dish. The most common way to prepare lefse is to spread a thin layer of butter on the lefse, sprinkle it with sugar, roll it up, and eat it. Many people eat it with lutefisk, or dried codfish (see recipe page 74). Special lefse rolling pins are available at kitchen stores. Today you can find multicultural lefse stuffed with jalapeños, pesto, tofu, chocolate, and anything else you can think of.

## Lefse

Family friend Neil Sticha of Bloomington, Minnesota, persuaded one of his favorite Norwegian cooks, Shirley LaBissonniers, to share her recipe and techniques on the preparation of lefse.

*4 cups cooked (riced twice) potatoes*

*¼ cup butter or solid vegetable shortening, room temperature*

*6 tablespoons heavy cream*

*1½ teaspoons salt*

*2 cups all-purpose flour*

**1.** Refrigerate potatoes until thoroughly chilled. Add butter or vegetable shortening, cream, and salt, beating until well blended. Add flour and mix until smooth. Dampen hands with cold water and pinch off pastry the size of large eggs. Knead into balls and set aside in a baking dish or tray. Flatten balls one at a time into patties on a lightly floured pastry cloth. Using a lefse rolling pin, roll pieces of dough into very thin circles approximately 12 inches in diameter. *(Note: A lefse rolling pin has a grooved design on its roller. If you do not have a lefse rolling pin, you can use a regular rolling pin.)*

**2.** On an ungreased lefse griddle or large frying pan over medium-high heat, cook until golden; turn and brown other side. Remove from griddle. Stack lefse between two towels to cool. Serve with butter or sugar.

Makes 24 lefse.

# Malassadas

The most enduring culinary legacy of the Portuguese in Hawaii is the malassada, a warm, sugar-coated ball of fried egg dough. The malassada is considered the "king" of doughnuts and a cultural icon in the Hawaiian Islands. Malassadas have been embraced by everyone in Hawaii and are sold hot at bakeries and roadside stands, at fairs, and at community functions and fund-raisers all over Hawaii. Hawaiians seem to be in love with them, with approximately two thousand sold each day.

Leonard's Bakery in Honolulu was the first commercial outlet in Hawaii to make this Portuguese treat, and the bakery is credited with popularizing malassadas. The tradition began on Shrove Tuesday (the day before Ash Wednesday, which marks the beginning of Lent) in 1953, when bakery owner Leonard Rego first made a batch of malassadas using his mother's recipe and began selling them. Since the eating of something truly indulgent on Shrove Tuesday is a must, malassadas filled the need and made the reputation of Leonard's Bakery.

*Malassadas are one of the richest of Hawaii's local comfort foods.* Les Drent photo, courtesy coffee@coffeetimes.com.

*Mal* means "badly" and *assada* means "cooked." Thus, the literal translation of the word *malassada* is "badly cooked" piece of dough. Malassadas are sugary, yeasty doughnuts without a hole. Traditional malassadas have an egginess to them and can be a bit heavy. Many of today's versions are made with fewer eggs and as a result are lighter. Some pastry chefs are taking the traditional malassadas to a more "upscale" level, adding all kinds of fillings (cream, papaya, pineapple, chocolate, and more). This usually 50-cent treat can sell for as much as $9.00 apiece after it's been transformed into haute cuisine. Traditionalists say that the fillings take away from the quality and consider these newfangled malassadas to be sacrilegious.

## Malassadas

½ cup evaporated milk

½ cup lukewarm water (110° to 115°)

½ teaspoon salt

¼ cup sugar

3 eggs, room temperature and beaten

2 tablespoons butter, melted

4¼ cups bread flour or all-purpose flour

3 teaspoons instant active dry yeast

Vegetable oil

½ cup sugar

1. Using a mixer with a dough hook, place milk, water, salt, sugar, eggs, butter, flour, and yeast in a bowl. Beat until smooth. If using a bread machine, select dough setting and press Start. When dough cycle has finished, remove dough from pan and turn out onto a lightly oiled surface. Form dough into an oval, place in a lightly greased bowl, cover with plastic wrap, and let rise in a warm place 1 to 1½ hours or until doubled in size. Turn dough over, but do not punch down; cover and let rise an additional 1 to 1½ hours or until doubled in size.

2. In a deep fryer or large pot, heat vegetable oil to 360°. Drop golf ball-size pieces of dough into hot oil and cook for 3 to 4 minutes on each side (turning once) or until brown. (Note: Do not put too many in the hot oil at a time because the oil temperature will drop and the malassadas will come out greasy.) Remove from oil and drain on paper towels for 2 minutes to cool; roll balls in sugar or drop into a brown bag with sugar and shake. Serve warm.

Makes approximately 36 malassadas.

# Paczki

Paczki (pronounced poonch-key) are sometimes referred to as the "Cadillacs" of doughnuts. The word *paczki* (plural; singular is *paczek*) comes from the Polish word *pak*, which means "bud." Paczki are circular, like the buds on trees, and they also expand, or grow, when fried. They are fat, round, deep-fried rolls served either plain or filled with fruit or jelly, and then sugar coated. Properly made, they look like huge baseballs.

On Paczki Day, or Fat Tuesday (the last day of feasting before Lent), paczki lovers trek to their favorite bakeries for a taste of the sweet pastry. Before refrigerators, paczki were enjoyed as a last-minute fling and a way to use up perishables such as lard, eggs, and cream, which were prohibited during Lent.

Although paczki began as a Polish tradition and were brought to the Great Lakes region in the 1900s, their popularity has spread, and they are now a very trendy food served just once a year. Bakers work around the clock to make paczki for customers. Fans of paczki buy them throughout the week before Ash Wednesday, and they are especially popular on Fat Tuesday. They have crossed ethnic boundaries and are now loved by everyone.

## Paczki

*1½ cups lukewarm milk (110° to 115°)*

*½ cup butter, room temperature*

*½ cup sugar*

*1 egg*

*3 egg yolks*

*1 teaspoon salt*

*1 teaspoon light or dark rum*

*½ teaspoon ground nutmeg*

*5½ cups all-purpose flour*

*4 teaspoons instant active dry yeast*

*Vegetable oil\**

*Powdered sugar*

\*   Use just enough vegetable oil to completely cover paczki while frying.

1. Using your mixer with dough hook, place milk, butter, sugar, egg, egg yolks, salt, rum, nutmeg, flour, and yeast in a bowl. Beat until smooth. If using a bread machine, add the same ingredients and select dough setting; press Start. When dough cycle has finished, remove dough from pan and turn out onto a lightly oiled surface. Form dough into an oval, place in a lightly greased bowl, cover with plastic wrap, and let rise in a warm place 1 hour or until doubled in size.

2. After dough has risen, turn dough out onto a lightly oiled surface, cut the dough and roll into balls about the size of golf balls. Place balls on a lightly oiled baking sheet (allowing room between each for rising), cover with plastic wrap, and let rise until doubled in size.

3. In a large pot, heat vegetable oil to 375°. Fry a few paczki at a time, 3 to 4 minutes or until golden brown. Turn and fry other side about 3 minutes or until golden brown. Remove from hot oil; drain on paper towels. Dust the tops of paczki with powdered sugar.

Makes 1 to 2 dozen, depending on size.

**I'll Have What They're Having**

# Philadelphia Soft Pretzels

Philadelphia, the City of Brotherly Love, is pretzel crazy. Pretzels can be bought all over the city, from street vendors to small mom-and-pop stores. The earliest reference to pretzels in America is from 1652 in a tale told in Beverwyck, New York. It seems that Jochem Wessels and his wife, Gertrude, were arrested, then publicly humiliated, for selling pretzels to the local Indians, who would pay almost any price for them. The Wessels' crime was that they used good flour to make pretzels for the "heathens" while Christians were eating bread made with the remnants of the ground meal. In other words, the Indians were eating flour while the Christians were eating bran.

When Germans migrated to Philadelphia in the 1700s, they brought with them their trades and customs, including the art of pretzel baking. Today, the pretzel industry is still centered in Pennsylvania, where the first commercial pretzel bakery was founded in the small town of Lititz, in 1861.

There are two different stories on who baked the first pretzel in Pennsylvania. The first maintains that Jacob Geitner, a local Lititz baker and confectioner, baked the first pretzel for his customers around 1820.

The other story relates that in the late 1850s, a tramp or drifter passing through the village of Lititz, stopped at a bakery operated by Ambrose Rauch. In exchange for a free meal given him, he gave Rauch a recipe for pretzels. Rauch thought it was worthless and passed the recipe on to Julius Sturgis, an apprentice baker, who then opened the first commercial pretzel bakery in Lititz in 1861.

In those days pretzels were packed in large wooden barrels and shipped by horse and wagon. Just like the U.S. mail, nothing stopped the delivery of pretzels—regardless of hail, sleet, rain, snow, mud, or high water, the pretzels got through. In 1951, a bronze plaque was erected on the wall of Sturgis's bakery, marking it as the birthplace of the American pretzel industry.

## Philadelphia Soft Pretzels

*3 cups bread or all-purpose flour*

*1 tablespoon sugar*

*2 teaspoons salt*

*3 teaspoons instant active dry yeast*

*2 tablespoons butter, room temperature*

*1 cup warm milk*

*Water*

*2 teaspoons baking soda*

*Egg wash (recipe follows)*

*Coarse salt*

**1.** In a large bowl, sift together flour, sugar, salt, and yeast. Add butter and milk; stir or mix together until thoroughly combined and the dough forms a smooth ball. Remove from bowl and place on a floured board; knead 5 minutes. Place in a greased bowl; turn dough to grease top. Cover and let rise in warm, draft-free place for 40 minutes or until dough has doubled in size. Remove dough to a lightly floured cutting board; punch down the dough and divide into 8 equal pieces. Roll each piece into a rope, 18 to 20 inches long, and twist each rope into a pretzel (use a small amount of warm water to cement the joining points of the dough). Cover the pretzels with plastic wrap, and allow to rise for 30 minutes in a warm place.

**2.** Preheat oven to 400°. Lightly grease two large baking sheets. In a large pan over medium-high heat, fill with water, add baking soda, and bring to a boil; reduce heat to low and let simmer gently. With a slotted spoon or spatula, place pretzels into the boiling water; boil each one 30 seconds on each side. Remove immediately and place on prepared baking sheets. Brush tops of the pretzels with the prepared Egg Wash and sprinkle with coarse salt. On the top rack of your oven, bake 12 to 15 minutes until golden brown (watch carefully after 10 minutes so the bottoms do not overbrown). Serve hot or cold.

Makes 8 pretzels.

## EGG WASH

*1 egg*

*⅛ teaspoon water*

In a small bowl, beat together egg and water; set aside.

# Sourdough Bread

**Here's to the man on the trail.**
**May his dogs keep their legs,**
**May his grub hold out,**
**And may his matches never miss fire.**

*—toast to an "Alaskan Sourdough," written by Jack London*

Sourdough is really an international pioneer food, but San Francisco truly refined this highly developed and specialized bread, thereby earning its reputation as the sourdough capital of the United States.

The ancient Egyptians made sourdough bread, having discovered that fermented dough would rise in an oven. Thousands of years later, on the western frontier, a sourdough starter was the most important personal possession, something to be guarded at the expense of everything else. The famed California gold rush of 1849 not only started one of the greatest human stampedes, but also firmly established sourdough as the most popular and practical food for settlers and prospectors. Prospectors from around the nation came to San Francisco on their way to the northern California gold-mining country. Besides stocking up on mining supplies, they made sure to take with them a bit of sourdough starter from which to make their bread. These starters were carefully tended. The prospectors were nicknamed "sourdoughs" because of the sourdough starters that they usually had hidden in the tops of their sacks of flour or under their jackets to keep warm.

A French baker named Isadore Boudin established a bakery in San Francisco in 1849. He made sourdough bread, which he formed into traditional French loaves. In the early 1900s, the bakery delivered to homes by horse-drawn wagon. If a customer wasn't at home, the freshly baked bread would be left hanging on a nail by the front door. The Boudin Bakery continues to make their traditional sourdough French bread from their "mother dough" that dates back to Boudin's very first loaf.

During the Klondike gold rush of 1898, it was said that a real "Alaskan sourdough" would just as soon spend a year in the hills without his rifle, as to tough it through without his bubbling sourdough pot. Since food was scare, food provisions were more valuable than gold.

The American pioneers jealously guarded their sourdough starters, as freshly baked bread, biscuits, and pancakes often provided the only variety in the wilderness diet. They usually carried their starters in wooden pails, which became permeated with the culture and which would retain the life of the yeast even if the starter spilled. Many families handed down the starter through several generations, always passing with the starter the directions for its care and preservation.

## San Francisco–Style Sourdough French Bread

I've spent much time experimenting with sourdough to come up with a recipe that I feel can rival the famous San Francisco sourdough French bread.

*1 cup Sourdough Starter (recipe follows), room temperature*

*¾ cup lukewarm water (110° to 115°)*

*1 teaspoon salt*

*¼ teaspoon baking soda*

*3 cups bread flour or unbleached all-purpose flour*

*Cornmeal*

**1.** Prepare Sourdough Starter.

**2.** Using a mixer with dough hook, place Sourdough Starter, water, salt, baking soda, and flour in a bowl. Beat until smooth. If using a bread machine, add the same ingredients and select dough setting; press Start. *(Note: Do not be afraid to open the lid and check the dough. It should form a nice elastic ball. If you think the dough is too moist, add flour a tablespoon at a time. If the dough is dry and gnarly, add warm water a tablespoon at a time.)*

**3.** When the bread machine has completed the dough cycle, remove the dough from the pan to a lightly oiled surface. Knead the dough several times and shape into an oval; cover with plastic wrap and let rest for 10 minutes. Turn dough bottom side up and press to flatten. Form dough into either a large baguette or a round boule, and place on a baking sheet dusted with cornmeal. Cover with plastic wrap and place in a warm spot to rise until doubled in size, approximately 1 to 2 hours.

**4.** Preheat oven to 400°. After rising, slash the bread with a very sharp knife, making three ½-inch-deep diagonal slashes. Brush or spray the top of the bread with cold water and bake for 20 to 25 minutes or until nicely browned. (A good check is to use an instant thermometer to test your bread for doneness. The interior temperature should be between 200° and 210°.) Remove from oven and place the bread on a wire rack to cool.

Makes 1 large loaf.

## Sourdough Starter

*2 cups all-purpose flour*

*1 package active dry yeast*

*1½ cups lukewarm water (110° to 115°)*

**1.** In a ceramic bowl or crock, stir together flour and yeast. Add enough water to make a thick batter, stirring with a wooden spoon, only enough to break up the lumps. The starter will take at least 24 hours before it is ready to be used. You need to place the starter in a dark, warm place to promote the fermentation process. A good place is the oven. If you have a gas oven, the pilot light will create enough heat to warm the mixture. For an electric oven, turning on the light will supply warmth. Do not actually turn on the oven, however, because even the lowest setting will be too hot for the starter. If it is summertime and air temperatures are near 80° or above, you can simply keep the starter on the kitchen counter covered with a small hand towel or plastic wrap. When the bubbling subsides and you notice a yeasty, sour aroma, stir the starter and refrigerate it.

**2.** Sourdough Starter will keep for years if it is fed and kept properly covered in the refrigerator. Try to use the starter at least once a week. To use in recipes, stir Sourdough Starter well before use. Pour out required amount called for in recipe and use as directed. Always use the starter at room temperature in your baking. Always remember to

*Papa Steve displays traditional loaves of Boudin family sourdough bread.*
*Courtesy Boudin Bakery, San Francisco, California.*

replenish the starter you remove for cooking purposes by adding 1 cup lukewarm water and 1 cup flour. Stir slightly and let it activate for a least a day, before storing in the refrigerator.

# Main Dishes

Fish & Seafood
Meat & Poultry

# Crawfish Boil

**Kiss the blue crawfish and spare his life, and you will be blessed with good luck.**

*—Cajun saying*

What looks, tastes, and smells like seafood, but doesn't come from the sea? It's crawfish, a freshwater shellfish that is considered a Louisiana delicacy. Nothing else symbolizes the Cajun culture of Louisiana like crawfish. Crawfish have become synonymous with the hardy French pioneers who settled in the area after being forced by British troops to leave their homes in Nova Scotia.

According to Cajun legend, crawfish are descendants of the Maine lobster. After the Acadians (now called Cajuns) were exiled in the 1700s from Nova Scotia, the lobsters yearned for the Cajuns so much that they set off across the country to find them. This journey over land and sea was so long and treacherous that the lobsters began to shrink in size. By the time they found the Cajuns in Louisiana, they had shrunk so much that they hardly looked like lobsters anymore. A great festival was held upon their arrival, and this smaller lobster was renamed crawfish.

Most of the crawfish consumed in the United States are from Louisiana, although people from other states consider them a delicacy, too. Locals still hold the traditional crawfish boils, where friends and family gather to feast on pounds of crawfish. In the spring, families will go out fishing on the bayous or crawfish farms in an age-old tradition that thrives to this day.

Crawfish (or crayfish) resemble tiny lobsters. They are also known in the South as mudbugs because they live in the mud of freshwater bayous. They are more tender than lobsters and have a unique flavor. Today, crawfish are raised commercially and are an important Louisiana industry.

The local Indians are credited with harvesting and consuming crawfish before the Cajuns arrived. They would bait reeds with venison, stick them in the water, then pick up the reeds with the crawfish attached to the bait. By using this method, the Indians would catch bushels of crawfish for their consumption. By the 1930s, nets were substituted, and by the 1950s, the crawfish trap was used.

## Crawfish Boil

*23 pounds live crawfish*

*2 cups salt*

*2 (3-ounce) boxes crawfish or crab boil seasoning or 2 cups liquid crab boil\**

*Salt*

*4 lemons, sliced in half*

*8 bay leaves*

*10 cloves garlic, whole*

*8 small onions, peeled*

*5 pounds small red or new potatoes, unpeeled*

*8 ears of fresh corn on the cob, shucked and broken in half*

*Old Bay Seasoning*

\* Crawfish or crab boil seasoning can be found in the seasoning or seafood section of any grocery store.

1. Rinse the crawfish in a large container with enough changes of water for the water to run reasonably clear. Add additional water to cover the crawfish, then add 2 cups salt (salt will cause the crawfish to purge themselves of impurities and will also clean their outer shells); stir for 3 minutes only (if the crawfish are allowed to soak in the salt water too long, they will die). Remove crawfish from the water, then rinse in clear water again.

2. In a large (18- to 20-gallon) pot over high heat, add enough water to fill a little more than halfway. Add crawfish or crab boil seasoning, ½ cup salt for each gallon of water used, lemon halves, bay leaves, and garlic. Cover pot and bring water to a boil; boil 2 to 3 minutes to allow the spices to mix well.

3. Using a large wire basket that fits into the pot, add onions and potatoes. Maintain a boil and cook 10 minutes or

until potatoes are tender. Add corn and crawfish to the wire basket; cook an additional 4 to 5 minutes (being careful not to overcook). Remove wire basket from pot.

4. To serve the traditional way, cover a table (preferably out-doors) with thick layers of newspaper. Spill the contents of the basket (onions, potatoes, corn, and crawfish) onto the center of the newspaper-covered table. Serve with shakers of Old Bay Seasoning.

Makes 10 servings.

## EATING INSTRUCTIONS

Crawfish are eaten with your hands (don't ask for utensils; you will only be laughed at).

1. Hold the body of the crawfish in one hand and grasp a claw, pulling up and down until it snaps off. Repeat the same process with the other claw. With your teeth or between your fingers, crack open the shell. Suck out the meat inside each claw.

2. Next, hold the head between the thumb and forefinger of your left hand. With your right hand, grab the tail, placing your thumb under the belly of the tail, and wrap your forefinger over the top of the tail. Then twist and pull with both hands—the tail should then pop off. Crack and peel away the shell of the tail, and pull the meat out with your teeth or fingers.

3. The part that shows if you are a true Cajun or not is the head. Using your hands, split the head down the middle. Find the yellowish fat inside (this is what most Cajuns consider the best part of the crawfish), and either remove with your fingers or suck it out (the most popular way).

# Calabash-Style Seafood

All through the Carolinas you will find restaurants boasting "Calabash-style seafood." Calabash restaurants serve generous quantities, or all-you-can-eat, of freshly caught deep-fried seafood. The seafood is usually accompanied by creamy cole slaw and hushpuppies.

The original and most authentic Calabash-style seafood comes from the town of Calabash, a small port town on the border of North and South Carolina at the mouth of the Calabash River. Many of the restaurants have docks where local fishermen bring the daily catch right to the door. Calabash is known as the "Seafood Capital of the World" and boasts a large number of seafood restaurants.

The Calabash-style seafood tradition started in the 1930s, when fishermen would bring in their boats with the fresh catch. As in most fishing communities, a communal fish feed was cooked in large pots on the docks to feed the fishermen. Locals started buying leftovers, and Calabash-style seafood was born. These open-air cookouts were the beginning of a number of area restaurants.

# Hangtown Fry

Hangtown fry could possibly be the first California cuisine. It consists of fried breaded oysters, eggs, and fried bacon, cooked together like an omelet. In the gold-mining camps of the late 1800s, Hangtown fry was a one-skillet meal for hungry miners who struck it rich and had plenty of gold to spend. Live oysters would be brought to the gold fields in barrels of sea water after being gathered in and around San Francisco Bay. Such a meal cost approximately $6.00, a fortune in those days.

During the late 1800s, Hangtown (known as Placerville today) was a base of supply for the mining region in California. It was originally known as Old Dry Diggins, but was shortly labeled Hangtown after three desperadoes had been hanged there on the same day and from the same large oak tree.

Legend has it that the Hangtown fry originated in the saloon of the El Dorado Hotel, now the site of the Cary House Hotel, across the street from the Hangman's Tree. *Mountain Democrat* newspaper columnist Doug Nobel wrote this interesting and charming story of how the event could have taken place:

A prospector rushed into the saloon of the El Dorado Hotel, announcing that right there in town, along the banks of Hangtown Creek, he had struck it rich and had every reason to celebrate. Untying his leather "poke" from his belt, he tossed it on the bar where it landed heavily, spilling its shining contents of gold dust and nuggets. Turning to the bartender, he loudly demanded, "I want you to cook me up the finest and most expensive meal in the house. I'm a rich man and I'm going to celebrate my good luck."...

The cook, looking the prospector in the eye, said, "The most expensive things on the menu are eggs, bacon and oysters. The eggs have to be carefully packed to travel the rough roads from over on the coast; the bacon comes only by ship, 'round the horn from back East; and the fresh oysters we have to bring up each day on ice from the cold waters of San Francisco Bay. Take your choice. I can cook you anything you want, but it will cost you more than just a pinch of that gold dust you have there." The prospector said, "Scramble me up a whole mess of eggs and oysters, throw in some bacon, and serve 'em up. I'm starving. I've been living on nothing much more than canned beans since I got to California, and at last I can afford a real meal." The cook did just that, cooking up a full plate of the mixture. Thus the Hangtown Fry was invented.

However it came to be, ordering a Hangtown fry became a mark of prosperity for gold-rich miners, the status symbol of the day. The recipe swept the entire Northwest Territory, from California to Seattle, in the mid-1800s. A few drinks and a Hangtown fry were considered a gentleman's evening.

The Hangtown fry is the official dish of both the city of Placerville and the county of El Dorado. There is also a group known as the "Hangtown FRYers" trying to promote the dish as the "Official Dish of the Great State of California," according to Doug Noble. Doug said, "The state legislature is cool on the subject, as they have no sense of humor. We actually got some support from a restaurant in Sydney, Australia. They love Hangtown fry."

# Blue Bell Café Hangtown Fry

The Blue Bell Café (no longer in business) on Placerville's Main Street made this version of the Hangtown fry for many years.

*3 eggs, divided*

*1 teaspoon milk*

*¼ cup saltine cracker crumbs*

*¼ cup dry bread crumbs*

*3 shucked medium-size oysters*

*2 tablespoons butter*

*2 bacon slices*

1. In a small bowl, beat 1 egg and milk together. In another bowl, combine cracker crumbs and bread crumbs. Dip the oysters in the egg and milk mixture, then in the cracker and bread crumbs.

2. In a large nonstick frying pan over medium-high heat, melt butter; add prepared oysters and fry 1 to 2 minutes per side or until ¾ cooked (turning once). In another large frying pan, fry the bacon until just before it becomes crisp.

3. In a small bowl, beat the 2 eggs lightly. In a non-stick frying pan over medium-low heat, place the bacon parallel to one another and off-center (this is because you are basically making an omelet and need to be able to fold or overlap the eggs over the top). Pour some of the beaten eggs over the bacon. Place the oysters on top of the bacon, and pour the remaining beaten eggs over the top. Cook until eggs are semi-firm but still moist, then fold or overlap the omelet over the oysters. Place a lid over the pan and continue to cook 1 to 2 minutes more. Remove from heat and serve on individual plate.

Makes 1 serving.

*A traditional Hangtown fry as served up by Chuck's Restaurant in Placerville, California. Courtesy Chuck's Restaurant.*

# Door County Fish Boil

**Many go fishing all their lives without knowing that it is not fish they are after.**

—Henry David Thoreau (1817–1862),
 American essayist and poet

In the 1800s, the Great Lakes area was settled largely by people from Sweden, Norway, and Finland. These settlers, who included fishermen and lumberjacks, discovered that fish boils were an easy, practical, and tasty way to serve hungry men. Door County, Sturgeon Bay, in particular, is the home of the famous Door County Fish Boil. A fish boil traditionally is an outdoor cooking event—a dish prepared in a large heavy kettle over an open fire. Churches and civic groups have been holding fish boils for many years, and a local festival would not be complete without one. The fish boil creates a festive atmosphere with thousands of tourists flocking to Door County during the summer and fall to experience these cooking events.

Today, restaurants and fishing lodges throughout the Great Lakes area feature outdoor fish boils, and no visit to Door County is complete without the experience of one. Great food and showmanship have made this dining tradition famous throughout the country. The showmanship comes after everything is cooked to perfection. The chef completes the cooking ritual with the "boil over," when kerosene is splashed on the fire to make the pot boil over, thus washing the fish oil into the fire. The flash and roar of the "boil over" announce that the food is ready. When the fire subsides, the baskets of fish and vegetables are then lifted out and carried to the hungry crowd or into the restaurant with great ceremony. Whitefish and lake trout are normally used for the fish boil, but restaurants sometimes use salmon, cod, or even lobster to vary the dish.

## Door County Fish Boil

Not everyone has easy access to a large cauldron for an outdoor event, so your fish boil can be done indoors. You can do everything but the traditional "boil over," as it would be difficult and dangerous to duplicate this event in the house.

A public fish boil held on the waterfront in Ephraim, Wisconsin, as a part of their Fyr Bal Festival. Courtesy Door County Chamber of Commerce, www.doorcountyvacations.com.

3 gallons water

2 cups salt, divided

20 small red or new potatoes, unpeeled

20 small white onions, peeled

7½ pounds of firm fish (whitefish, trout, steelhead, salmon, cod, or pike), cut into 2-inch chunks

Melted butter

Lemon wedges

1. In a large, deep pot over medium-high heat, add water and 1 cup salt; bring to a boil. (Note: Water should remain at a constant boil throughout the entire cooking process.) Add potatoes and boil for 15 minutes or until potatoes are slightly firm. Add onions and boil an additional 5 minutes.

2. Add remaining 1 cup salt. Using a removable strainer, add fish; boil 8 to 10 minutes or until fish flakes easily with a fork. Skim any oil from surface of pot with a spoon while fish is cooking. Lift strainer with fish from water; let drain. Using a strainer, lift potatoes and onions from water; let drain. Place fish on individual serving plates along with 2 potatoes and 2 onions; pour melted butter over the top and garnish with lemon wedges.

Makes 10 servings.

# Fried Catfish

Fried catfish is considered a quintessential southern dish along with southern fried chicken, sweet tea, and hushpuppies. Once considered the "food of the poor," chefs around the country are now inventing new ways to cook and eat this fish. Small-town restaurants in the South feature fried catfish on their menus. Most urban dwellers have never tasted good catfish and tend to scorn it as a fish of lowly social status. But rural fish lovers, especially in the southern states, dote on the sweet flavor of catfish. It is the most widely eaten American fish. Catfish can be used in any recipe calling for a non-oily white fish, but most southerners prefer it dredged in cornmeal and fried. In the South, hushpuppies (see page 52) are considered an absolute must to serve with fried catfish, along with coleslaw and ketchup.

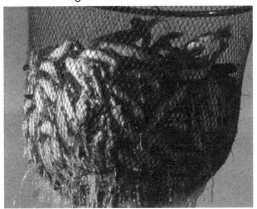

Farm-raised catfish are harvested in seines (large weighted nets) when they are about eighteen months old and average 1 to 1½ pounds.
Courtesy The Catfish Institute.

Catfish are not beautiful to look at, with their odd whiskers and big, gaping mouths. But beauty is not important when it comes to choosing fish that is flavorful. Catfish have skin that is similar to that of an eel, which is thick, slippery, and strong. All catfish should be skinned before cooking. The easiest method to skin a catfish is to nail the head of the dead fish to a board, hold on to its tail, and pull the skin off with pliers.

Channel catfish are farmed in Mississippi, Louisiana, and Arkansas. Mississippi is the world's leading producer of pond-raised catfish. Of all the catfish grown in the United States, 80 percent comes from Mississippi, where more than 102,000 acres are devoted to catfish farms. Humphreys County, Mississippi, produces about 70 percent of the catfish consumed in the United States and is called the "Catfish Capital of the World." Each spring the streets of downtown Belzoni, in Humphreys County, are transformed into a large carnival during the World Catfish Festival.

## Fried Catfish

Peanut oil*

4 medium freshwater catfish fillets**

1 cup cold milk

1 cup yellow cornmeal

2 to 3 teaspoons salt

1 teaspoon freshly ground black pepper

1 teaspoon red (cayenne) pepper

* Use enough peanut oil to completely cover fish while frying.
** To clean a whole catfish, remove skin from the catfish, then slice the fillet across to a thickness of no more than ¼-inch. The secret to frying catfish is using thin fillets less than ¼-inch thick.

1. In a large pot or deep fat fryer, preheat peanut oil to 375°. Preheat oven to 200°. Rinse the fillets under cold water and dry thoroughly with paper towels. In a pie plate, lay fillets and pour milk over the top. In another pie plate, combine cornmeal, salt, pepper, and cayenne pepper.

2. Remove the fillets one at a time from the milk and roll in the cornmeal mixture to coat evenly; place on a large platter to dry, leaving space between them. Let dry at least 5 minutes. Place 4 to 6 pieces of catfish at a time in the hot oil to fry (don't crowd the fryer or the oil temperature will drop too much). Fry 6 to 7 minutes per side or until the catfish fillets are a light golden brown and the meat flakes easily with a fork. A simple test for properly fried catfish is to pick up a fried fillet by one end and not have it bend or wilt.

3. Remove from the oil and place on paper towels to drain. After draining, place the fillets on another platter covered with paper towels; place in preheated oven to keep warm while frying the remaining fillets. The fillets will remain hot and crisp for as long as 35 minutes.

Makes 4 servings.

# Sturgeon

**There was a guy who hitched his plow horse to a big sturgeon in hopes of yarding it onto the banks of the Columbia, but instead the monster fish dragged the horse into the river, never to be seen again.**

*—Northwest sturgeon legend*

Sturgeon is one of the Northwest's best-eating fish. When properly cleaned, it is a gourmet's delight, whether you bake, barbecue, broil, or smoke it. Sturgeon tastes a bit like pork or chicken breast. Because sturgeon has a high oil content, the meat will cook very well by either grilling or broiling. One of the favorite ways of Pacific Northwest chefs to prepare sturgeon is with a hazelnut breading.

Sturgeon resemble a prehistoric creature, but they are actually the modern relics of an ancient group of fish with fossil records dating back 100 million years to the Cretaceous period. These fish can run up to 10 feet in length and weigh more than 300 pounds. Many fish of 800 to 1,000 pounds or more were caught around the turn of the twentieth century, but by the 1920s, the biggest sturgeon were gone. The biggest recorded sturgeon in the Columbia River was a 1,500-pound fish caught in 1928. Because they have no scales, a sturgeon's age is determined by removing and examining a small portion of its fin rays. Like rings on a tree, a count is made of the layers of cartilage that are developed each year.

The sturgeon has no skeletal structure. When removed from the water, all the fish's weight lies on its internal organs. They are bottom feeders, constantly rubbing against rocks. Sturgeon are found in many coastal river estuaries and in the Pacific Ocean (to a depth of about a hundred feet) from the Aleutian Islands in Alaska to Monterey, California. In Oregon, state fishing regulations require that any sturgeon shorter than 42 inches in length (called shakers) or longer than 60 inches (called bruisers) must be released unharmed.

## Hazelnut Sturgeon

*3 egg whites, divided*

*1 cup finely chopped toasted hazelnuts\**

*¾ cup dry bread crumbs, divided*

*1 tablespoon finely chopped fresh parsley leaves*

*⅛ teaspoon black pepper*

*¼ teaspoon salt*

*¼ teaspoon grated orange peel*

*2 teaspoons dry vermouth*

*2 tablespoons milk*

*4 sturgeon fillets (about 1 inch thick)*

*2 tablespoons butter, melted*

*¼ cup dry white wine*

*Lemon wedges*

\* To toast hazelnuts: Spread shelled hazelnuts in a shallow ungreased pan. In a preheated 250° oven, bake 7 to 10 minutes, stirring occasionally.

1. Preheat oven to 350°. Lightly grease a large baking dish. In a medium bowl, add 1 egg white and beat lightly; stir in hazelnuts, 1 tablespoon bread crumbs, parsley, pepper, salt, orange peel, and vermouth; set aside.

2. Place remaining bread crumbs on a large plate suitable for dredging. In a shallow pan or pie plate, lightly beat remaining egg whites and milk together. Dip sturgeon fillets, one at a time, into egg whites to coat well, then press each side of the fillets into bread crumbs to coat well.

3. Lay prepared fillets, well apart, in prepared baking dish; crumble the hazelnut mixture over the top of each fillet. In a small bowl, combine melted butter and white wine; drizzle over the top of the fillets. Bake 7 to 10 minutes, uncovered, or until fish is opaque in center of thickest part. Remove from oven and transfer to individual serving plates. Serve with lemon wedges.

Makes 4 servings.

# Hazelnuts/Filberts

In western Oregon, hazelnuts are the nut of choice. They are to Oregon what pecans are to the South and macadamias are to Hawaii. Oregonians use them in everything from cookies and pies to breading for their famous salmon, sturgeon, and halibut. Originally called filberts in Oregon, the growers renamed them hazelnuts when they first started talking to international markets about exporting them— European chefs thought they were a new variety of nut, not the hazelnuts that they were accustomed to using in their cooking. So, for marketing reasons, the Oregon growers now refer to the regionally grown nuts as hazelnuts.

An English sailor planted the first hazelnut tree in the United States in 1857 at Scottsburg, Oregon, and this original tree is still alive today. Around 1878, Frenchman David Gernot sent to France for seeds of the thin-shell variety. Fifty trees produced from these seeds were planted in Oregon's Willamette Valley. They

Hazelnuts are a tasty snack whole, or delicious when chopped or ground for use in recipes. *Courtesy Hazelnut Marketing Board.*

thrived with little attention, providing food for the settlers and the surrounding wildlife. The hazelnut tree grows naturally in shrub form, but in the Willamette Valley the shrubs are pruned into trees to make harvesting easier.

Unlike other fruit- or nut-bearing trees, the hazelnut blooms and pollinates in the middle of winter. The nuts mature during the summer and are harvested in October. They fall from the tree when ripe and are then swept into windrows to be picked up by harvesting machines.

A mere 3 percent of the world's total hazelnut crop but 99 percent of the United States' total are grown in the Willamette Valley. Those grown in Oregon are considered to be larger and tastier than those grown in other parts of the world. Whether this is due to the region's frequent rain and mild winters, its rich soil, or the growers' pruning, the crop's excellence is no surprise to Oregonians. They are among the most elegant of nuts and are highly prized in American cuisine.

# Lutefisk

**It is said that about half the Norwegians who immigrated to America came in order to escape the hated lutefisk, and the other half came to spread the gospel of lutefisk's wonderfulness.**

*—Norwegian-American saying*

Lutefisk (pronounced LEWD-uh-fisk) is dried cod that has been soaked in a lye solution for several days to rehydrate it. It is then boiled or baked and served with butter, salt, and pepper. The finished lutefisk usually is the consistency of Jello. It is also called lyefish, and in the United States, Norwegian-Americans traditionally serve it for Thanksgiving and Christmas. In many Norwegian homes, lutefisk takes the place of the Christmas turkey. In Minnesota and Wisconsin, you can find lutefisk in local food stores and even at some restaurants. It is a food that you either love or hate, and, as some people say, "Once a year is probably enough!"

During the fall in Wisconsin, people watch their local newspapers for announcements of lutefisk suppers, which are usually held in Norwegian churches. Usually every Norwegian church will host at least one lutefisk supper between October and the end of the year. The dinners have become so popular that lovers of the special dish drive great distances, and these are not just people of Scandinavian descent.

The history of lutefisk dates back to the Vikings. On one occasion, according to one legend, plundering Vikings burned down a fishing village, including the wooden racks with drying cod. The returning villagers poured water on the racks to put out the fire. Ashes covered the dried fish, and then it rained. The fish buried in the ashes thus became soaked in a lye slush. Later, the villagers were surprised to see that the dried fish had changed to what looked like fresh fish. They rinsed the fish in water and boiled it. The story is that one particularly brave villager tasted the fish and declared it "not bad."

Norwegian-Americans believe that lutefisk was brought by their ancestors on the ships when they came to America, and that it was all they had to eat. Today the fish is celebrated in ethnic and religious celebrations and is linked with hardship and courage.

## Lutefisk

Family friend Neil Sticha of Bloomington, Minnesota, persuaded one of his favorite Norwegian cooks, Shirley LaBissonniers, to share her recipe for lutefisk.

1. "First of all, invite brave people over for dinner who do not have misconceptions about this wonderful fish! Next, go to a store that carries the freshest of fish and seafood. Ideally, you would get the lutefisk that they pull out of a barrel (most stores hate those barrels a lot and don't do that anymore). Second best, it comes skinless and 'trimmed' and packaged in a plastic bag. Purchase the lutefisk a day before you want to serve it. Take it out of the plastic bag, put it in a large bowl, and cover with ice water. Change this water two or three times and keep in the refrigerator (if your family will let you). This firms up the fish.

2. "Put the lutefisk in a glass baking dish and season with salt and pepper. Put in a preheated oven at 375° for 25 or 30 minutes. The fish is done when it flakes easily with a fork. Do not overcook it or it will look like white Jello! It will not be brown.

3. "In Minnesota, we allow at least a pound of lutefisk per person, served with hot melted butter. The two side dishes are riced potatoes and very small cooked frozen peas—no exceptions. And, of course, you must have lefse (see recipe page 58). This is a ritual which we try to repeat as often as possible and as long as we can get the fresh lutefisk."

# Scrod

Contrary to popular belief, the name scrod, which is found on numerous restaurant menus throughout New England, is not a specific type of fish. Scrod is often used as a general label for other members of the cod family, including pollack, haddock, hake, and whiting. In most New England restaurants, scrod is loosely defined as "catch of the day," which allows them to offer whatever fish is available.

Some historians think that scrod is a contraction of Sacred Cod, the name of the 4-foot-tall wooden sculpture that has been in the Massachusetts State House since 1748. Others think that Boston's famous Parker House Restaurant coined the word as a generic term for their "fish of the day," not knowing in advance what to print on their menus.

Much of the fish that is caught in the waters of Narragansett Bay and Rhode Island Sound is sold to local seafood restaurants directly from the pier. Fish and chips made with scrod are a specialty at many restaurants. It seems that diners are divided into two distinct culinary regions regarding what to serve with their fish and chips. East of Narragansett Bay and into Massachusetts, the norm is to sprinkle cider vinegar over the fish and chips. The citizens of the coastal towns west of Narragansett Bay prefer New England tartar sauce and lemon wedges.

## Fish and Chips

3 medium-size potatoes, unpeeled

4 cups vegetable oil

1 egg

1 cup milk

1 pound fresh cod, haddock, or flounder

1 cup all-purpose flour

Salt and black pepper to taste

Caper Tartar Sauce (see recipe page 79)

Lemon wedges

**1.** Slice the potatoes lengthwise into small french fry–sized strips. In a large pot or electric frying pan, heat vegetable oil to 375°. Soak the potatoes in cold water and cover for 30 minutes before frying (soaking removes the starch so potatoes will be crisp when fried).

**2.** In a medium bowl, combine egg and milk. Cut the fish into serving-size slices and place in the bowl; allow to stand 10 minutes.

**3.** Combine flour, salt, and pepper in a large resealable plastic bag; add fish slices, seal bag, and shake to coat with flour mixture. Remove fish from bag and shake off any excess flour. Drop fish, a few at a time, into the hot oil and cook for 3 to 5 minutes or until golden brown. Remove fish and drain on paper towels; repeat until all fish are cooked.

**4.** When all fish have been cooked, reheat the oil to at least 375°. Drain the potatoes and pat dry with paper towels. Add a handful of potatoes. Cook 5 to 6 minutes or until light brown. Remove from oil and drain on paper towels; repeat until all potatoes are fried. Fry the potatoes again for 1 to 2 minutes for added crispness. Serve with Tartar Sauce and lemon wedges.

Makes 2 to 3 servings.

# Oysters Rockefeller

**He was a bold man that first eat an oyster.**

—*Jonathan Swift, from his book* Polite Conversation, *1738*

Antoine Alciatore, the original owner of Antoine's Restaurant in New Orleans, made a specialty dish of snails called Snails Bourgignon, which was very popular during the mid-1800s. When Antoine's son, Jules Alciatore, took over the business in 1899, the taste for snails had subsided. Wanting to use a local product to avoid any difficulties in procuring seafood, he chose oysters, adapting the snail recipe to use Gulf oysters. Jules Alciatore pioneered the art of cooking oysters (they were rarely cooked before this time).

In naming the dish, Alciatore wanted something to signify "the riches in the world." Because of the dish's green color (the color of money) and its rich taste, he named it oysters Rockefeller after John D. Rockefeller, one of the wealthiest men in the United States at that time. In the 1800s, the name Rockefeller was associated with the absolute pinnacle of wealth and position. No other American dish has received so much praise and attention as oysters Rockefeller.

The original recipe has never been shared by the restaurant, but it has been adapted and evolved in a host of ways. Jules Alciatore exacted a promise on his deathbed that the exact proportions be forever kept a secret.

Antoine's Restaurant is very likely the most famous restaurant in the United States, and to this day, oysters Rockefeller are the restaurant's specialty. Every order that goes out of the kitchen bears the number of its serving, now well into the millions. Nearly every other New Orleans restaurant has its own version of this dish, most with spinach, which is said to not be an ingredient of Antoine's original recipe.

## Oysters Rockefeller

Cocktail Sauce (recipe follows)

10 large oysters in shells

Rock salt

½ cup cooked fresh spinach leaves, drained and finely chopped

1 teaspoon fresh lemon juice

1 tablespoon Worcestershire sauce

¼ cup finely minced onion

½ teaspoon salt

2 cloves garlic, minced

2 tablespoons butter

¼ cup saltine cracker crumbs

5 bacon slices, partially cooked

Lemon wedges

**1.** Preheat oven to 350°. Prepare Cocktail Sauce. Scrub oyster shells thoroughly before opening. Open oysters, leaving them on the bottom half shell. Place shells on top of a thin bed of rock salt in an ungreased baking pan (the salt will keep the shells in place and hold the heat).

**2.** In a medium bowl, combine spinach, lemon juice, Worcestershire sauce, onion, salt, and garlic; stir in enough Cocktail Sauce to form a paste. Cover each oyster with approximately 1 tablespoon of the mixture.

**3.** In a small saucepan over medium heat, melt butter. Remove from heat and stir in cracker crumbs. Sprinkle the crumb mixture over each oyster. Cut each bacon strip into 8 pieces. Place 4 small pieces of bacon over each oyster. Bake, uncovered, 10 to 15 minutes or until edges of oysters begin to curl. Remove from heat and transfer onto a serving platter. Serve with additional Cocktail Sauce and lemon wedges.

Makes 2 servings.

*Antoine's Restaurant, home of oysters Rockefeller.*
*Courtesy Antoine's, New Orleans, Louisiana.*

# COCKTAIL SAUCE

*1¼ cups chili sauce*

*½ cup tomato ketchup*

*3 tablespoons prepared horseradish*

*1 tablespoon Worcestershire sauce*

*3 tablespoons fresh lemon juice*

*⅛ teaspoon hot pepper sauce*

In a medium bowl, combine chili sauce, ketchup, horseradish, Worcestershire sauce, lemon juice, and hot pepper sauce. Refrigerate and use as needed.

Makes 2 cups.

# Pan-Fried Smelt

To an old-timer living in the Pacific Northwest, smelt can bring back memories of glorious fish runs. For many families, annual smelt dipping was a social and recreational activity, and they came from miles around to net the smelt for frying and smoking. No one knew actually when the schools of smelt would come until someone spotted the first fish. When the announcement was made that "the smelt are running," everyone made a mad dash to the river.

The smelt runs were so large through the 1930s and 1940s, that there was the illusion the runs would be annual events. But the runs started becoming irregular and eventually stopped in some rivers, especially in the 1990s. No one knows what went wrong with the smelt runs. Among the possible reasons for the decline are the warm-water El Niño ocean conditions, water pollution from pulp mills, and the changes to the river estuary caused by channel dredging and construction of jetties and dams. This spirit of the smelt fever still continues whenever the fish decide to appear in the rivers of the Northwest.

My husband, Donald Stradley, writes about smelt fishing in the 1940s with his father, Lawrence Stradley, on the Sandy River, a tributary of the Columbia River near Portland, Oregon:

I remember, as a boy of twelve or thirteen, smelt fishing with my father on the Sandy River. We fished from a wooden float supported by oil drums and anchored to the bank where the

*Smelt fishing on the Cowlitz River.*
Courtesy Cowlitz County Historical Museum.

water ran 10 to 12 feet deep. Large nets, 2 feet in diameter and up to 4 feet long, attached to 16-foot-long poles, were dipped downstream to intercept the upstream migration of these thick schools of silvery fish.

Sometimes the schools were several feet in diameter moving in undulating fashion through the current, never following the exact same route more than a few seconds. The trick was to locate the school by the feel of the fish hitting the steel rim of the net and then rapidly stroking downstream to intercept as many as possible. On a good dip, as many as 50 pounds of fish could be intercepted, requiring more strength than I had to bring them to the surface.

Smelt, also called eulachon or oolichan by Native Americans, are small, silver fish the size of herring (approximately 6 to 10 inches long). Each spring they migrate in millions to coastal rivers from the Klamath River in northern California, north to the Nushagak River in Alaska, and to the Pribilof Islands in the Bering Sea. After spawning, most die, their carcasses decay, and they thus enrich the streams and estuaries. Another nickname is "candle fish." This nickname comes from the fact that the smelt are so full of oil that when dried, placed upright, and lit, the fish would burn from end to end like a candle.

To Native Americans, the return of the eulachon meant the beginning of spring and a renewed food supply, literally saving lives and earning them the name "salvation fish." These fish are almost 20 percent oil by weight, allowing a fine grease to be rendered from their bodies and creating a high-energy food source that could easily be transported and traded with other tribes farther inland. The name "Grease Trail" was given to these routes, because the most important trade item carried over them was the eulachon oil extracted from the tiny fish. These ancient "Grease Trails" later formed part of the Dalton Trail, a toll road that opened up the interior of Alaska to prospectors. Today parts of the ancient trail form the famous Alaskan Highway.

# Pan-Fried Smelt

Some macho folks will fry these silvery fish without benefit of cleaning, since the fish have eaten nothing since leaving the ocean some 80 miles away, but I have always preferred cleaning them as you would a trout and frying the cleaned smelt in butter until nearly crisp. Grabbing the tail and using a fork, neatly separate the backbone from the meat. This will leave about two good mouthfuls per fish. Most people will eat fifteen to twenty smelt before calling it quits.

Caper Tartar Sauce (recipe follows)

2 pounds whole fresh smelt, cleaned and heads removed

Salt and freshly ground black pepper to taste

½ cup all-purpose flour

½ cup fresh lemon juice

½ cup butter

2 lemons, cut into 8 wedges

**1.** Prepare Caper Tartar Sauce. Rinse cleaned smelt under cold running water and pat dry with paper towels. Sprinkle fish cavities with salt and pepper. Place flour in a shallow dish. In another shallow dish, pour the lemon juice; dip both sides of the smelt in lemon juice, then coat both sides with flour.

**2.** In a large frying pan over medium-high heat, melt butter; add the smelt and fry for 2 to 3 minutes, turning once or until fish is lightly browned and flakes readily when prodded with a fork. Remove from pan and drain on paper towels. Place smelt on a platter, garnish with lemon wedges, and serve immediately. Serve with Caper Tartar Sauce on the side.

Makes 4 servings.

# CAPER TARTAR SAUCE

This wonderful recipe was given to me by Leo Porter, manager of the Horseshoe Ranch in Fort Klamath, Oregon.

2 (⅛-inch) slices white or Spanish onion, diced and patted dry

3 tablespoons capers, drained, patted dry, then minced

1 tablespoon finely chopped fresh parsley leaves

1¼ cups mayonnaise

⅛ teaspoon red (cayenne) pepper or to taste

¼ to ½ teaspoon prepared horseradish or to taste

In a medium bowl, combine onion, capers, parsley, mayonnaise, cayenne pepper, and horseradish until well blended. Store, covered, in refrigerator until ready to use.

Makes 1½ cups.

# Smoked Salmon

**The number of dead Salmon on the shores and floating in the river is incredible to say—and at this season they have only to collect the fish, split them open and dry them on their scaffolds on which they have great numbers. . . . The waters of this river is clear, and a Salmon may be seen at the depth of 15 or 20 feet.**

—*October 17, 1805 journal entry of* Captain William Clark *(1770–1838), American explorer who served as co-leader with Meriwether Lewis of the Lewis and Clark Expedition (1804–1806)*

Smoked salmon is one of the most popular ways of using salmon in the Pacific Northwest. Originally, smoking (sometimes called "kippering") was the only way to preserve the bounty of salmon to last over the winter. To cooks, gourmets, and fishermen alike, the salmon is the king of the waters. The distinctive color of the flesh of a salmon is part of its attraction, varying from a very delicate pink to a much deeper shade, verging on red. In the Northwest, because of the various ethnic and cultural backgrounds, you can find different methods of smoking salmon. The Native American tradition for smoked salmon is jerky (also known as Squaw Candy), a common staple for the Inuits and the rural Alaskan settlers and their dogs. The Scottish tradition is simply barbecued salmon dotted with butter and lemon. Local cooks often use backyard smokers to cure salmon.

Most people in the United States know of salmon, but people living inland or even along the Atlantic Coast do not know salmon as the people of the Pacific states know it. It is as if the salmon are magical, as they have accomplished and provided great things. They are survivors of the Ice Age and have weathered many storms of nature, yet continue to thrive. Salmon is a saltwater fish that spawns in freshwater. The Columbia River and the Puget Sound are especially noted for their fine salmon. The life cycle of the salmon is an interesting one: Spawned in freshwater streams, the young salmon travel to sea early. Here they live and grow three to four years. In the spring after reaching maturity, the adult salmon return to their native streams to spawn. As salmon begin their journey home, they will stop eating and live mainly on the oils stored in their bodies. The salmon will leap over any obstacle in their way, including dams and waterfalls, hurling themselves many feet out of the water until they surmount the obstacle or die of exhaustion in the attempt; there is no turning back. Salmon always die after spawning is completed.

The Native Americans of the Pacific Northwest have always looked upon salmon with great reverence and have special rituals and legends for the yearly salmon run. Salmon is looked upon as life, as the salmon has nourished them physically and spiritually since their ancestors first came to this region. In the past, tribes would migrate to the Columbia River each year during the spring and fall spawning season, when the salmon hurled themselves upstream from the Pacific to lay their eggs. During that time, the Columbia River was so thick with the countless salmon that the Indians simply speared or clubbed them to death from their canoes or from the riverbanks. What was not eaten fresh would be dried in the river winds to create jerky.

Commercial fishing for salmon began shortly after the arrival of Europeans on the West Coast. The Hudson's Bay Company shipped salted salmon from Fort Langley to the Hawaiian Islands starting in 1835, and the first salmon cannery opened in 1876. By the turn of the twentieth century, seventy canneries were in operation. The first gill net fishing on the Columbia River took place in the mid-1850s, even before the states of Washington and Oregon were established, and before the Indian treaties were signed.

# Smoked Salmon

*2 large (2- to 3-pound) fresh salmon fillets*

*2½ tablespoons plain salt with 1 cup cold water for brine*

*2 tablespoons grated lime peel*

*6 tablespoons fresh lime juice*

*1 tablespoon chopped fresh herb leaves (basil, rosemary, or thyme)*

*1 teaspoon coarsely ground black pepper*

*1 teaspoon coarse kosher or coarse sea salt*

*1 to 2 tablespoons extra-virgin olive oil (depending on size of fillets)*

*1 lime for finish*

*Coarse kosher or sea salt*

**1.** Rinse the salmon fillets in cold water. Prepare brine. Place fish in brine for 15 to 20 minutes. Remove fish from brine. Discard brine and rinse fish with cold water; pat dry with paper towels.

**2.** Prepare the smoker according to manufacturer's instructions. Set temperature to high, then turn down when it is really smoking. *(Note: Keep the temperature of the smoker fairly low. Do not raise the lid of the smoker any more than you absolutely need to, as it reduces the temperature inside every time you do.)*

**3.** Place salmon fillets on sheets of aluminum foil and cut the foil around the fillets approximately ¼ inch larger. This keeps the fillets from sticking to the racks in the smoker.

**4.** In a small bowl, combine lime peel, lime juice, thyme (or other herbs), pepper, coarse salt, and olive oil; stir to mix. Rub the seasoning mix on the salmon fillets, coating them well. Place salmon fillets on the smoker rack. Smoke 1 hour or until fillets are slightly opaque in the thickest part (cut to test). Remember the salmon continues to cook after it is removed—do not overcook). Remove fillets from smoker. Cut lime in half and squeeze over cooked salmon fillets. Sprinkle lightly with additional coarse salt. Either serve immediately or cover with plastic wrap and refrigerate until ready to serve.

Makes 16 to 20 servings.

# Trout Hemingway

**A pan of fried trout can't be bettered, but there is a good and bad way of frying them.**

—*Ernest Hemingway (1899–1961),*
*American novelist and short story writer*

Trout Hemingway is a regional favorite in the Upper Peninsula of Michigan, and the dish is served at most fishing lodges there. It is named for Ernest Hemingway who liked to spend time at his cottage on Walloon Lake in Michigan. The Hemingway family summer cottage was built on the northwest side of Walloon Lake in 1899, the same year that Ernest was born. The cottage was the setting for his short story published in 1925 called "Big Two-Hearted River." Hemingway loved trout fishing and eating his catch. He considered himself a connoisseur of trout. According to him, the best way to fry fresh trout was to "coat the fish with cornmeal, then cook them slowly in bacon drippings until crispy outside but still moist inside."

With the hundreds of lakes in the Upper Peninsula area, it certainly does not take much to catch a large lake trout, brown trout, splake, or even rainbow trout.

## Trout Hemingway

*6 (8- to 10-ounce) whole fresh trout, cleaned with heads left on*

*Salt and freshly ground black pepper*

*3 green onions (tops included), finely chopped*

*2 tablespoons finely chopped fresh parsley leaves*

*½ cup all-purpose flour*

*2 tablespoons yellow cornmeal*

*¼ teaspoon salt*

*¼ teaspoon black pepper*

*½ cup fresh lemon juice*

*6 bacon slices*

*Lemon wedges*

**1.** Rinse the trout and pat them dry with paper towels. Sprinkle trout cavities with salt, pepper, green onions, and parsley. In a pie plate, combine flour, cornmeal, salt, and pepper. In another pie plate pour the lemon juice; dip both sides of the trout in the lemon juice, then coat both sides with seasoned flour mixture.

**2.** In a large frying pan over medium-high heat, cook bacon until crisp; remove bacon from pan and drain, leaving 2 to 3 tablespoons of the drippings in the pan. Add the trout and fry 3 minutes; gently flip the fish and fry the other side for an additional 3 minutes or until fish is lightly browned and flakes readily when prodded in thickest portion with a fork. Remove from pan. To serve, place a bacon strip into cavity of each fish and garnish with lemon wedges. Serve immediately.

Makes 6 servings.

*A freshly caught rainbow trout.*

# Chicago Deep-Dish Pizza

**When the moon hits your eye
Like a big pizza pie,
That's Amore.
When the world seems to shine
Like you've had too much wine,
That's Amore.**

*—from the song "That's Amore," by Harry Warren and
Jack Brooks, 1953. Recorded by Dean Martin (1917–1995),
American singer and actor*

Deep-dish pizza may be one of Chicago's most important contributions to American cuisine. Chicago is the home of deep-dish pizza. There are more than two thousand pizzerias serving the much beloved pie. What makes the Chicago deep-dish pizza so different from regular thin-crust pizzas is the thicker crust and the amount of ingredients topping it. It is almost like a casserole on bread crust.

The origin of this style of pizza is credited to Ike Sewell, who in 1943 created the dish at his bar and grill named Pizzeria Uno. The pizza was so popular that Sewell opened more restaurants to handle the crowds.

Pizza migrated to America with Italians in the latter half of the nineteenth century. It was introduced to Chicago by a peddler who walked up and down Taylor Street with a metal washtub of pizzas on his head, crying his wares at two cents a chew. This was the traditional way pizza was sold in Naples, in copper cylindrical drums with false bottoms that were packed with charcoal from the oven to keep the pizzas hot. The name of the pizzeria was embossed on the drum.

With the stationing of American soldiers in Italy during World War II came a growing appreciation of pizza. When the soldiers returned from the war, they brought with them a taste for pizza. It was not until the 1950s that Americans really started noticing pizza, however. Celebrities of Italian–American origin such as Jerry Colonna, Frank Sinatra, Jimmy Durante, and baseball star Joe DiMaggio all devoured pizzas.

## Chicago Deep-Dish Pizza

In Chicago you'll find deep-dish pizza with assorted ingredients—cheese, fresh spinach, and various meats and vegetables. The recipe here uses sausage.

*Tomato Sauce (recipe follows)*

*1 cup plus 1 tablespoon warm water (110° to 115°)*

*2 tablespoons extra-virgin olive oil*

*½ teaspoon salt*

*2 cloves garlic, minced*

*1 teaspoon dried basil leaves*

*1 teaspoon dried oregano leaves*

*3 cups bread flour or all-purpose flour*

*¼ cup semolina flour*

*3 teaspoons instant active dry yeast*

*Yellow cornmeal*

*1 teaspoon extra-virgin olive oil*

*12 ounces mozzarella cheese, shredded*

*½ cup freshly grated Parmesan cheese*

*½ pound sweet Italian sausage, casings removed*

*12-inch deep-dish pizza pan*

1. Prepare Tomato Sauce; set aside. Using a mixer with dough hook, place, water, olive oil, salt, garlic, basil, oregano, bread flour, semolina flour, and yeast in a bowl. Beat until smooth. If using a bread machine, add the same ingredients, select dough setting, and press Start. When the bread machine has completed the dough cycle, remove the dough from the pan to a lightly oiled surface. Once dough is ready by either method, knead the dough by hand several times, then form the dough into an oval ball and place in a greased bowl (turning to oil top); cover with plastic wrap and let dough rise in a warm place 1 to 1½ hours or until doubled in bulk.

2. Preheat oven to 450°. Oil bottom and sides of a 12-inch deep-dish pizza pan with olive oil; sprinkle bottom gener-

*Chicago deep-dish pizza ready to serve.*

ously with yellow cornmeal. Roll and stretch the dough into a 16-inch circle. Place in prepared pizza pan, pressing dough up sides of pan to form a 1- to 1½-inch edge. Prick bottom with a fork. Bake 4 minutes. Remove from oven and brush lightly with 1 teaspoon olive oil.

**3.** Top prebaked pizza crust with Tomato Sauce. Spread mozzarella and Parmesan cheese evenly over the top. Shape sausage into 1-inch rounds; flatten slightly and distribute evenly over cheeses. Bake 20 to 30 minutes or until crust is lightly browned and sausage is cooked through. Remove from oven and let cool 5 minutes before cutting and serving.

Makes 6 to 8 servings.

## TOMATO SAUCE

*1 (35-ounce) can Italian plum tomatoes, drained and chopped*

*2 tablespoons chopped fresh basil leaves or 1 teaspoon dried basil*

*1 teaspoon dried oregano*

*Salt and freshly ground black pepper to taste*

In a bowl, combine tomatoes, basil, oregano, salt, and pepper; set aside.

# Chicken-Fried Steak

**Yeah, I like my rice and gravy and my black-eyed peas.**
**Corn on the cob, I want a big glass of teas.**
**Some okra and tomatoes and some turnip greens,**
**I want some real soul food, do you know what I mean?**
**Well, I'm goin' on down to Ma and Pa's Café!**
**Mercy!**
**I want some taters and gravy with some chicken-fried steak!**

*—from the song "Taters and Gravy and Chicken-Fried Steak," by Kenny Bill Stinson, American country singer and songwriter*

In Texas, the reigning queen of comfort food or down-home cooking is chicken-fried steak, or as Texans affectionately call it CFS. Although not official, it's considered the state dish. According to the Texas Restaurant Association, some 800,000 orders of chicken-fried steak are served each day in Texas, not counting any prepared at home.

Each city, town, and village in the state prides itself on its version of CFS. Texans have a unique way of rating restaurants that serve it. Eateries are rated by the number of pickup trucks parked out front: Never stop at a one-pickup place, where the steak will have been frozen and factory-breaded. A two- or three-pickup restaurant is not much better. A four- or five-pickup place is a must stop, as the CFS will be fresh and tender with good sopping gravy.

You might be surprised to learn that there is no chicken in CFS. Instead, it's a tenderized round steak (a cheap, usually tough piece of beef) cooked like fried chicken with a milk gravy made from the drippings in the pan. In other parts of the South it is called country-fried steak. The traditional way to cook CFS is in a large cast-iron skillet with very little oil. Served with "the works" means accompanied by mashed potatoes, gravy, greens, black-eyed peas, and cornbread.

The origin of CFS is most likely German. Immigrants from Germany first settled in Texas about 1844. The first town surveyed and settled by German immigrants was New Braunfels, in 1845. When the town lots sold and new settlers came, the settlement spread northward into the surrounding countryside. The founding of New Braunfels had a major impact on the area and opened West Texas to further developments. It was a time of new beginnings but not much money.

Chicken-fried steak is probably a culinary cousin of wiener schnitzel, a German dish made with breaded veal cutlet. German immigrants probably adapted this popular dish to use the tougher cuts of beef available to them; thus, chicken-fried steak.

## Chicken-Fried Steak

*½ cup all-purpose flour*

*½ teaspoon salt or to taste*

*Freshly ground black pepper*

*1 large egg*

*2 tablespoons water*

*¾ cup buttermilk baking mix (such as Bisquick)*

*2 pounds bottom or top round steak (cut into four individual portions), pounded to tenderize*

*⅓ cup vegetable oil*

*Milk Gravy (recipe follows)*

1. In a shallow pan or plate, sift together flour, salt, and pepper. In another shallow pan, combine egg and water. In another shallow pan, place baking mix. Coat steaks in flour mixture, dip in egg mixture, then coat with baking mix.

2. Preheat oven to 150°. In a large frying pan over medium-high heat, add vegetable oil and heat until a drop of water sizzles. Add coated steaks, in batches, and fry 4 to 5 minutes per side or until golden brown and thoroughly cooked (add vegetable oil if needed). Remove from pan and keep warm in oven. Pour off all but 2 tablespoons of the cooking oil. Put the frying pan back over the heat and make the Milk Gravy.

*Makes 4 servings.*

## MILK GRAVY

*2 tablespoons pan drippings*

*1 tablespoon all-purpose flour*

*2 cups milk, heavy cream, or evaporated milk, room temperature*

*Salt and freshly ground black pepper*

**1.** In the same frying pan with 2 tablespoons pan drippings, over medium heat, sprinkle flour over the oil and blend with a wooden spoon or whisk until smooth. Whisking or stirring constantly, slowly pour in milk, cream, or evaporated milk; continue stirring, scraping loose browned bits from the bottom and sides of skillet, until the gravy begins to boil and thicken. Season with salt and pepper to taste.

**2.** Reduce heat to low and simmer, stirring occasionally, 5 to 8 minutes or until gravy is thickened to the desired consistency and the flour has lost its raw, pasty taste. Remove from pan and serve hot with the chicken-fried steak.

# Garbage Plate

Rochester, New York, is known for this unusual dish. The original Garbage Plate was created at Nick Tahou's fast-food restaurant more than fifty years ago. Tahou came to Rochester in 1937, selling hot dogs near the railroad depot. The Garbage Plate is considered a great late-night snack, and his restaurant is packed with diners from around midnight to 4:00 A.M.

There have been many imitations in Rochester and around the country, with names such as Sloppy Plate, Trash Plate, and Dumpster Plate. Young college men in Rochester, who like to have contests to see how much beer or food they can consume, consider the Garbage Plate a rite of passage from boyhood to manhood.

There are many different Garbage Plates, such as cheeseburger, hot dog, hamburger, egg, sausage, and steak. They all have the same base, though: Half the plate is piled with home fries, and the other half with a pile of macaroni salad. Then comes whatever you order, such as eggs or burgers, placed on top. Over everything are a couple spoonfuls of onions and a glob of mustard.

# Chimichanga

The Southwest is well known for its delicious Mexican food, and the residents of Tucson, Arizona, boldly proclaim their city the "Mexican Food Capital of the U.S." The city has its own version of Tex-Mex food, which it calls Arizona-Sonoran cuisine. Because southern Arizona was once part of the Mexican state of Sonora, this style is considered the "soul food" of Arizona.

The chimichanga, or "chimi," has achieved cult status in Tucson. A chimichanga is a burrito prepared with a choice of meat, vegetables, and spices, deep-fried to a golden perfection, and served on a bed of lettuce with cheese and mild sauce. The residents of Tucson take their chimis very seriously and prefer large, overstuffed versions. Every restaurant and mom-and-pop eatery has its own version of this favorite dish.

Culinary historians argue about exactly where chimichangas were invented. Several Tucson restaurants claim bragging rights. The strongest claim comes from the El Charro Cafe, the oldest Mexican restaurant in Tucson. Family legend says that Monica Flin, who started the restaurant in 1922, cussed in the kitchen when a burrito flipped into the deep fryer. Because young nieces and nephews were in the kitchen with her, she changed the swear word to *chimichanga,* the Spanish equivalent of "thingamagig."

*Chimichanga loaded with toppings and rice on the side.*
©1986–2001 Great American Stock.

## Chimichanga

*6 (12- to 14-inch) flour tortillas*

*1 pound ground beef*

*1 medium onion, chopped*

*½ cup red chile sauce or enchilada sauce*

*Salt and black pepper to taste*

*Vegetable oil*

*2 cups shredded Cheddar cheese*

*2 cups shredded iceberg lettuce*

*2 cups chopped green onions*

*Chopped tomatoes (optional)*

*Guacamole (optional)*

*Sliced black olives (optional)*

1. Preheat oven to 350°. Wrap stacked tortillas in aluminum foil, and heat in oven 15 minutes or until hot. To microwave, wrap a stack of tortillas lightly in paper towels and warm on high for 6 or 7 seconds per tortilla.

2. In a large frying pan over medium-high heat, brown beef; drain, leaving beef in the pan. Add onion, chile or enchilada sauce, salt, and pepper; cook 2 to 3 minutes or until onions are transparent.

3. In the center of each warm tortilla, spoon ⅙ of meat filling. Fold tortilla, tucking in the ends to make a secure fat tube, and fasten with wooden toothpicks. *(Note: Assemble only 2 or 3 at a time, as the tortilla will absorb liquid from the sauce.)*

4. In a large pot or deep fryer over medium heat, add at least 4 inches of vegetable oil. Heat oil (375° to 400°). Fry the chimichangas, 1 or 2 at a time, 3 minutes or until golden brown. Remove from oil, drain, and place on serving plates. Top with Cheddar cheese, lettuce, green onions, and any optional ingredients that you prefer.

*Makes 6 chimichangas.*

**I'll Have What They're Having**

# Chop Suey

The discovery of gold in California in 1849 brought tens of thousands of southern Chinese to the United States, most of them coming through San Francisco. Californians called the Chinese "Celestials," after the "Celestial Kingdom," a name by which the Chinese referred to their homeland. The gold rush in California (or "Gold Mountain" as the Chinese called California) occurred at the same time that famine hit Guangdong Province in southeastern China.

In the 1860s, a pattern of discrimination emerged that prevented the Chinese from working their own gold-mining claims, forcing them to take work as laborers and cooks for the transcontinental railway. Constrained by the lack of Asian vegetables, and trying to produce a Chinese dish palatable to Westerners, the Chinese cooks stir-fried whatever vegetables were handy. Thus chop suey, a mixture of odds and ends of large pieces of vegetables and meat, was born.

Chop suey was popular mainly with non-Chinese-Americans, especially in the 1920s. After World War II, it became as American as apple pie to the non-Chinese population.

The Chinese community introduced an improved method of cooking called "chowing" (vegetables cooked quickly and served while still crisp). The meals and diets of hundreds of California families were influenced by their Chinese cooks. Although the Chinese cooks were seldom permitted to prepare authentic meals, they held to their art of cooking and serving vegetables, contributing to the new cuisine of the West Coast.

## Cashew Chicken Chop Suey

2¼ cups water

1 teaspoon salt

1 cup uncooked long-grain white rice

3 teaspoons cornstarch

¼ cup cold water

3 tablespoons vegetable oil

2 chicken breast halves, boneless and skinless, cut into strips about ½ inch wide

1 medium green bell pepper, cored, seeded, and sliced into strips

½ cup thinly sliced celery

1 small onion, thinly sliced

1 cup sliced mushrooms

1½ cups bean sprouts

1 (5-ounce) can water chestnuts

3 tablespoons soy sauce

1 teaspoon grated fresh ginger

⅛ teaspoon black pepper

1 cup chicken broth

½ cup whole cashew nuts

**1.** In a large saucepan over medium-high heat, add 2¼ cups water, salt, and rice; bring to a boil. Reduce heat to low, cover, and cook for 20 minutes. Remove from heat and let sit 5 minutes before fluffing with a fork. If necessary, keep warm over very low heat with the lid cocked.

**2.** In a small bowl, add cornstarch and ¼ cup cold water; blend until cornstarch is dissolved. Set aside.

**3.** In a large frying pan or wok over medium-high heat, heat the oil. Add chicken and brown on all sides. Add bell pepper, celery, and onion; cover, reduce heat to low, and cook 10 to 15 minutes or until tender. Add mushrooms, bean sprouts, water chestnuts, soy sauce, ginger, pepper, and chicken broth; stir until blended. Increase heat to medium-high and bring liquid to a boil. Add cornstarch mixture, stirring until well blended; cook an additional 5 minutes or until thickened. Remove from heat. Serve on a large platter over hot rice; sprinkle with cashew nuts.

Makes 4 servings.

# Cincinnati Chili

Outside of the state of Texas, Cincinnati, Ohio, is the most chili-crazed city in the United States. Cincinnati prides itself on being a true chili capital, with more than 180 chili parlors. Cincinnati-style chili is quite different from its more familiar Texas cousin, and it has developed a cultlike popularity. What makes it different is the way the meat is cooked. The chili has a thinner consistency and is prepared with an unusual blend of spices that includes cinnamon, chocolate or cocoa, allspice, and Worcestershire sauce. This is truly the unofficial grub of Cincinnati.

The people of Cincinnati enjoy their chili spooned over freshly made pasta and topped with a combination of chopped onions, shredded Cheddar cheese, refried beans or kidney beans, and crushed oyster crackers. If you choose "the works," you are eating what they call Five-Way Chili. Make sure to pile on the toppings—that's what sets it apart from any other chili dish. To test a restaurant for authenticity, ask for a Four-Way. If the server asks you whether you want beans or onions, you know this is fake Cincinnati chili, since Four-Way always comes with onions.

Macedonian immigrant Tom Kiradjieff created Cincinnati chili in 1922. With his brother, John, Kiradjieff opened a small Greek restaurant called the Empress. The restaurant did poorly however, until Kiradjieff started offering a chili made with Middle Eastern spices, which could be served in a variety of ways. He called it his "spaghetti chili." Kiradjieff's "five way" was a concoction of a mound of spaghetti topped with chili, chopped onion, kidney beans, and shredded yellow cheese, served with oyster crackers and a side order of hot dogs topped with more shredded cheese.

## Cincinnati Chili

Recipe from *What's Cooking America*, by Linda Stradley and Andra Cook.

*1 large onion, chopped*

*1½ pounds lean ground beef*

*1 clove garlic, minced*

*1 tablespoon chili powder*

*1 teaspoon ground allspice*

*1 teaspoon ground cinnamon*

*1 teaspoon ground cumin*

*½ teaspoon red (cayenne) pepper*

*½ teaspoon salt*

*1 (15-ounce) can tomato sauce*

*1 tablespoon Worcestershire sauce*

*1 tablespoon cider vinegar*

*½ cup water*

*1 (16-ounce) package uncooked dried spaghetti*

*Toppings (see below)*

1. In a large frying pan over medium-high heat, sauté onion, ground beef, garlic, and chili powder until ground beef is slightly cooked. Add allspice, cinnamon, cumin, cayenne pepper, salt, tomato sauce, Worcestershire sauce, cider vinegar, and water. Reduce heat to low and simmer, uncovered, 1½ hours. Remove from heat.

2. Cook spaghetti according to package directions and transfer onto individual serving plates (small oval plates are traditional).

3. Ladle chili over spaghetti and serve with toppings. Oyster crackers are served in a separate container on the side. Cincinnati chili lovers order their chili by number. Two, Three, Four, or Five Way. Let your guests create their own final product.

| **Two-Way Chili:** | Chili served on spaghetti |
| **Three-Way Chili:** | Additionally topped with shredded Cheddar cheese |
| **Four-Way Chili:** | Additionally topped with chopped onions |
| **Five-Way Chili:** | Additionally topped with kidney beans |

Makes 4 to 6 servings.

## TOPPINGS

*Oyster crackers, shredded cheddar cheese, chopped onion, kidney beans (16-ounce can)*

*Skyline Chili's signature "3-Way."* Courtesy Skyline Chili.

# Country Captain Chicken

If you weren't raised in the South, it's very unlikely that you have ever eaten, or even heard of, this classic chicken dish. Country captain chicken, known throughout Georgia, dates to the early 1800s. It is thought that this dish was brought to Georgia by a British sea captain who had been stationed in India and who shared the recipe with some friends in the port city of Savannah, Georgia. Savannah was then a major shipping port for the spice trade. Another theory is that the dish was named for the native noncommissioned officers in India, called "country captains."

In the 1940s, President Franklin D. Roosevelt and General George S. Patton were served this dish in Warm Springs, Georgia, by Roosevelt's cook. Their praise of this dish helped to rekindle its southern classic status.

As with all chicken recipes in the South, country captain chicken varies with the cook. Some recipes call for a long cooking time, whereas others use quick-cooking chicken breasts. One thing is always certain, though: it is perfumed and slightly spiced with curry.

## Country Captain Chicken

½ cup all-purpose flour

Salt and freshly ground black pepper to taste

8 chicken breast halves, boneless and skinless

3 tablespoons vegetable oil

1 medium onion, coarsely chopped

1 large red bell pepper, cored, seeded, and thinly sliced into ¼-inch wide rings

2 cloves garlic, minced

1 (28-ounce) can plum or Roma tomatoes, crushed or 2 cups fresh chopped tomatoes

2 to 3 teaspoons curry powder or to taste

½ teaspoon salt

¼ teaspoon freshly ground black pepper

½ teaspoon dried thyme

½ cup currants or raisins

½ cup toasted slivered almonds

Hot cooked long-grain rice

**1.** Preheat oven to 200°. In a shallow dish, combine flour, salt, and pepper. Roll chicken in flour mixture to coat all sides. In a large nonstick frying pan over medium heat, heat vegetable oil. Add chicken and cook 5 minutes per side or until light brown. (Chicken should not be cooked through at this point.) Transfer chicken to an ovenproof dish and keep warm in the oven; reserving drippings in frying pan.

**2.** Reduce heat to medium low. To the pan drippings, add onion, bell pepper, and garlic; cook 5 minutes, stirring occasionally, until onions are transparent. Add tomatoes, curry powder, salt, pepper, and thyme; cover pan and simmer gently an additional 15 minutes. Add the browned chicken and currants or raisins; cover and simmer another 20 minutes, stirring occasionally, until the chicken is tender and cooked through. Remove from heat and transfer chicken to a deep platter. Spoon vegetables and sauce around the chicken and sprinkle with almonds. Serve with rice.

Makes 8 servings.

# Country Ham & Red Eye Gravy

Virginia, or Smithfield, hams are universally recognized as the country's finest, and serving these hams with red eye gravy is a southern specialty. Red eye gravy, also called bird-eye, poor man's, red ham, and muddy gravy, is well known in the South, but little known in the rest of the United States. These hams are very salty, and the gravy, often made from drippings and black coffee, packs a punch. Southern cooks continually debate whether the best red eye gravy is made with coffee or water.

There are several stories and legends on how red eye gravy got its name. One is that General Andrew Jackson, who later became the seventh president of the United States, asked his cook, who had bloodshot eyes as a result of drinking "moonshine," or corn whiskey the night before, to bring him some country ham with gravy "as red as his eyes." Some men nearby heard the general, and from then on, ham gravy became "red eye gravy."

Hams have been produced since the settling of Jamestown in the early 1600s. Pigs were not native to the Jamestown area, but were brought to the colonies from England and Bermuda. The climate of Virginia was perfect for raising pigs. They soon became so plentiful that they became a nuisance to the settlers. The settlers rounded up the pigs and transported them to an island in the James River, which became known as "Hog Island." The wild pigs became the principal food for new settlers, as well as Native Americans in the area. The local tribes, who had been curing venison long before Jamestown was established, taught the settlers to cure the meat with salt or "magic white sand."

In 1926, the Virginia General Assembly passed a law stipulating that only peanut-fed hogs, cured and processed in the town of Smithfield, could be labeled Smithfield hams. It was the practice at the time to let pigs roam the peanut fields, foraging for nuts missed during harvesting. Later, the peanut feed stipulation was dropped, and now the hogs are fed a variety of grains. Today, there are only four companies that can legally sell their products as Smithfield hams.

## Did You Know?

During the War of 1812, a New York pork packer named Uncle Sam Wilson shipped a boatload of several hundred barrels of pork to U.S. troops. Each barrel was stamped "U.S." It soon made the rounds that the "U.S." stood for "Uncle Sam," whose large shipment seemed to be enough to feed the entire army. This is how "Uncle Sam" came to represent the U.S. government.

## Country Ham and Red Eye Gravy

*1 large (½-inch thick) center-cut ham slice*

*½ cup hot, strong brewed coffee*

1. Do not trim fat off slice before frying (make a few cuts on the outer edge to ensure that the slice lays flat during cooking). Place ham slice in a medium-hot ungreased skillet, turning several times while frying. Do not overfry, as ham will become hard and dry. Remove ham from heat and transfer to a warm plate.

2. Pour coffee into hot skillet and stir with a wooden spoon, scraping up any brown bits on bottom of pan. Cook 2 minutes, remove from heat, and pour over ham. Serve with warm biscuits.

Makes 1 to 2 servings.

# Fajita

Texans would probably like to lay claim to the fajita, but history gives credit to Mexican ranch workers living in West Texas (along the Rio Grande on the Texas–Mexico border) in the late 1930s or early 1940s. When a steer was butchered, the workers were given the least desirable parts to eat for partial payment of their wages. Because of this, the workers learned to make good use of a tough cut of beef known as skirt steak.

The fajita is truly a Tex-Mex food (a blending of Texas cowboy and Mexican panchero foods). The Mexican term for grilled skirt steak is *arracheras,* and its American counterpart is *fajitas.* Today, the term *fajita* has completely lost its original meaning and has come to describe just about anything that is cooked and served rolled up in a soft flour tortilla. The only true faji-tas, however, are made from skirt steak.

In 1969, Sonny Falcon, often referred to as the "Fajita King," started a concession stand and sold grilled fajita at a festival in Kyle, Texas. His fajitas became a favorite at fairs and outdoor events all over Texas.

Around 1973, Ninfa Rodriguez Laurenzo opened her restaurant chain in Houston called Ninfa's and made fajitas a mainstay on the menu. Ninfa's version of the fajita was created at the suggestion of a customer who had just returned from a trip to Mexico City and asked the staff to slice a piece of steak into thin strips so he could make an upscale taco. Once the accompaniments were added—cilantro, onion, tomatoes, chilies, sour cream, and cheese—the new fajita dish became a house specialty.

*Fajita platter with tortillas and condiments on the side.*
©1986–2001 Great American Stock.

# Steak Fajita

Lime Marinade (recipe follows)

1½ pounds skirt steak

1 green or red bell pepper, cored, seeded, and thinly sliced

1 small onion, thinly sliced

3 tomatoes, chopped

Shredded Cheddar cheese

Sour cream

Guacamole sauce

Salsa

Flour tortillas

1. Prepare Lime Marinade. Lay the skirt steak on a cutting board and remove the outer membrane (grab the membrane with one hand and slide the knife beneath it, cutting as you go). Using a sharp paring knife, make a number of slits in the meat, cutting both with and against the grain of the meat (this cuts the muscle fiber and reduces any toughness).

2. In a large plastic bag with Lime Marinade, add skirt steak; reseal and marinate in the refrigerator at least 1 hour or overnight, turning steak occasionally.

3. Remove steak from refrigerator and bring to room temperature before cooking. Preheat barbecue. Drain steaks, reserving marinade. Place steak on hot grill and spoon some of the reserved marinade onto the steak. Close barbecue lid, open any vents, and cook 3 to 5 minutes for medium-rare. Remove from grill and transfer to a cutting board; cut on the diagonal into thin strips.

4. Preheat oven to 350°. Wrap stacked tortillas in aluminum foil and heat in oven 15 minutes or until hot. To microwave, wrap a stack of tortillas lightly in paper towels and warm on high for 6 or 7 seconds per tortilla.

5. While the skirt steak is cooking, grill the green pepper and onion slices 1 to 2 minutes or until soft; remove from grill and place on a serving platter. Place cooked steak strips onto the same platter.

6. For each fajita, fill a warm tortilla with cooked steak and desired amounts of green pepper and onion slices. Add tomatoes, Cheddar cheese, sour cream, guacamole, and salsa as desired; roll up like a burrito and enjoy.

Makes 4 to 6 servings.

## LIME MARINADE

Juice of 4 to 5 limes

¼ cup red wine vinegar

1 tablespoon soy sauce

1 tablespoon light molasses

1 tablespoon chopped fresh cilantro leaves

2 cloves garlic, minced

½ teaspoon ground cumin

½ teaspoon black pepper

In a large resealable plastic bag, combine lime juice, vinegar, soy sauce, molasses, cilantro, garlic, cumin, and pepper; set aside.

# Goetta

## Goetta

Check out this Cincinnati comfort food and breakfast favorite. Some believe goetta was created by the nineteenth-century German immigrants to the Cincinnati area. However, the Finke family of Covington, Kentucky, claims to have invented goetta around the turn of the twentieth century. The family owned a store that butchered meats for the old Covington Market and sold their oatmeal-sausage concoction as "Irish Mush." Goetta became so popular that packages were shipped across the Ohio River to Cincinnati markets, which began selling them to German immigrants.

Today, many local grocers and butchers make their own, and in Cincinnati, you can buy goetta ready-made in any meat department, packaged to look like sausage meat.

*Glier's Meats is the largest producer of goetta in the United States, with nearly one million pounds per year. Courtesy Glier's Specialty Haus, www.goetta.com.*

Goetta is often compared to scrapple, a Pennsylvania Dutch favorite. Everyone agrees that the goetta has to be made with pinhead oatmeal (pinhead oatmeal is made of whole oat kernels before they are flattened into rolled oats). If you cannot find pinhead oatmeal in your area, you can substitute steel-cut oats. Goetta is made by simmering pork (and sometimes beef) in water with onion, spices, and tiny pinhead oats. The mixture is cooked until it thickens, poured into pans or molds, and chilled. It is then sliced and fried.

Cold weather was eagerly anticipated as goetta season. Before refrigeration, goetta was relegated to the colder months so it could be kept cool. This is a hearty, delicious breakfast food when served with a couple of eggs. Goetta is equally at home at the dinner table. As it fries, it leaves enough residue to make a good gravy. Many people enjoy goetta sandwiches, or GLSs, for lunch. It also makes an excellent addition to soups, omelets, and casseroles. Any way it is prepared, it is a versatile, tasty, and nutritious product.

### Goetta

*6 cups water*

*1 tablespoon salt*

*2 teaspoons black pepper*

*2½ cups pinhead oats\**

*1 pound ground beef*

*1 pound spicy pork sausage*

*2 large onions, coarsely chopped*

*1 teaspoon dried sage*

*½ teaspoon dried thyme*

*4 bay leaves*

*¼ cup yellow cornmeal*

*All-purpose flour (optional)*

*Butter for frying*

\* If you cannot find pinhead oats in your area, substitute steel-cut oats.

1. In a large soup pot on high heat, add water, salt, pepper, and pinhead oats; bring to a boil. Reduce heat to low and simmer, covered, 1 hour (stirring frequently to keep oats from sticking to bottom of pan and burning). Add ground beef and pork sausage (break up well). Add onion, sage, thyme, and bay leaves, stirring to combine. Simmer for 3 hours, stirring frequently. Add cornmeal and cook, uncovered, another ½ hour. The mixture will be very thick when done. The saying is "The goetta is done if a wooden spoon stands upright when stuck in the center of it."

2. Pour into two or three loaf pans, or form into a roll and wrap securely in aluminum foil or plastic wrap. Can be stored up to 2 weeks in the refrigerator. For longer storage, place in the freezer.

3. To serve, slice into ¾-inch-thick patties. Dip both sides in flour if desired. Fry in a small amount of butter. Do not allow the slices to touch in the frying pan or they will run together. Brown each side until crusty.

Makes about 6 pounds of goetta.

# Loco Moco

**Hawaiians don't eat until they're full, they eat until they're tired.**

—*Hawaiian saying*

Loco Moco is a recipe unique to Hawaii. It is a comfort food, or "local grind," of the Hawaiian Islands. Local food is not the cuisine that is served in upscale hotels and restaurants of Hawaii. Its basic structure was established soon after World War II—the best fast food or mixture of cuisines from many Pacific Rim countries, with a special Hawaiian twist.

Loco Moco is a mountainous meal consisting of a heap of white rice topped with a hamburger patty and a sunnyside up egg, then smothered in gravy. This dish is popular for breakfast, lunch, or dinner and is a candidate for the Cholesterol Hall of Fame. Loco Mocos are served at almost every drive-in, fast-food, and mom-and-pop restaurant in the Islands.

There are many people who claim to have invented Loco Moco, but it is generally agreed that around 1949, either the Café 100 or the Lincoln Grill (both in Hilo, Hawaii) originated the first dish of Loco Moco. According to the story, the dish was created for teenagers who wanted something different from typical American sandwiches and less time-consuming than Asian food to eat for breakfast. The nickname of the first boy to eat this concoction was Loco ("crazy" in Portuguese and Hawaiian pidgin). *Moco* rhymed with *loco* and sounded great, so Loco Moco became the name of the dish.

## Loco Moco

*¼ pound ground beef*

*1 egg*

*½ cup cooked short- or medium-grain rice*

*Hot prepared gravy*

*Hot pepper sauce*

*Tomato ketchup*

*Soy sauce*

1. Form the ground beef into a patty. In a frying pan over medium-high heat, cook patty until cooked to your liking; remove from heat and set aside. Fry egg (sunnyside up or over easy) in the grease from the ground beef.

2. Assemble this dish by putting a bed of cooked rice in a large bowl, top with hamburger patty, fried egg, and 1 to 2 ladles of hot gravy. Add hot pepper sauce, ketchup, or soy sauce according to your preference.

Makes 1 serving for a very hungry person.

*The original Loco Moco to go from Café 100 in Hilo.*
Les Drent photo, courtesy coffee@coffeetimes.com.

# Kansas City Barbecued Ribs

**The pig, if I am not mistaken**
**Supplies us sausage, ham, and bacon.**
**Let others say his heart is big**
**I call it stupid of the pig.**

—*From the poem "The Pig" by Ogden Nash (1892–1971), from* Selected Poetry of Ogden Nash, *1995.*

Kansas City, which straddles Missouri and Kansas, is well known for its barbecue and jazz. Once considered the food of the poor, barbecue has become a fashionable Kansas City cuisine. In fact, barbecue is considered a regional art form that inspires lively debates over which method is best. The city is famous for its barbecue restaurants and dozens of annual national and international barbecue cook-offs. Each local restaurant has developed its own style and recipe. Amateur barbecue enthusiasts also abound in the area, with many entering one of the many competitions in hopes of becoming the next Kansas City barbecue legend.

The Kansas City barbecue (also called K.C. barbecue) phenomenon evolved during the 1920s and 1930s. Henry Perry, known as the "father of Kansas City barbecue," started barbecuing in an outdoor pit in an old trolley barn. He served slabs of barbecued ribs wrapped in newspaper for 25 cents a slab. Customers loved the ribs, and the barbecue trend was off and running. Others soon copied his technique, each adding their own flavor and style twist. Today, the restaurant Arthur Bryant's is the city's most famous barbecue establishment and also considered a Kansas City landmark.

Barbecue is different from regular outdoor grilling. Grilling involves fast cooking over high, direct heat. Barbecuing involves slow cooking with low, indirect heat. Usually the toughest cuts of meat, such as beef brisket or pork ribs, are smoked slowly over direct or indirect low heat. Cuts of meat may take up to fourteen hours to cook to perfection. Barbecuing is inherently communal because it is hard work. It is said that no one would go to all that trouble unless you intend to feed lots of people. Once you have gathered all your friends and family together, be prepared to wait and wait, because barbecue is rarely done on time. When the barbecue is ready, it is time to celebrate.

# Kansas City Barbecued Ribs

*Dry Rub (recipe follows)*

*Kansas City–Style Sauce (recipe follows)*

*4 slabs of loin ribs (also known as baby back pork ribs)*

**1.** Prepare Dry Rub and Kansas City–Style Sauce. Blot ribs with a paper towel to remove excess moisture. Sprinkle both sides of the ribs with the dry rub; rub in with your hands (really work it in on both sides). Let sit at room temperature 1 hour before cooking.

**2.** Prepare a barbecue grill to maintain a temperature of 250°. Arrange rib slabs on the grill and cook for 4 to 6 hours or until they gently pull apart. Remove from grill and transfer to a cutting board; allow to cool slightly before cutting and serving. Serve with Kansas City–Style Sauce on the side, or return individual cut ribs to the grill and bathe them in the sauce; cook another 10 minutes, turning ribs once.

Makes 4 servings.

## DRY RUB

*½ cup sugar*

*3 tablespoons ground paprika*

*2 tablespoons garlic salt*

*2 tablespoons celery salt*

*1 tablespoon onion salt*

*1½ teaspoons chili powder*

*1 tablespoon freshly ground black pepper*

*¼ teaspoon red (cayenne) pepper*

*2 tablespoons lemon pepper*

*1 tablespoon dried sage*

*¼ teaspoon dried thyme*

*½ teaspoon ground mustard*

In a medium bowl, sift sugar, paprika, garlic salt, celery salt, onion salt, chili powder, pepper, cayenne pepper, lemon pepper, sage, thyme, and mustard. Store in an airtight container until ready to use.

## KANSAS CITY–STYLE SAUCE

*3 tablespoons extra-virgin olive oil*

*2 cloves garlic, minced*

*1 cup tomato ketchup*

*¼ cup water*

*¼ cup cider vinegar*

*¼ cup firmly packed brown sugar*

*2 tablespoons ground paprika*

*1 tablespoon chili powder*

*Red (cayenne) pepper to taste*

In a large saucepan over medium-high heat, heat oil until hot; add garlic and sauté until brown. Add ketchup, water, vinegar, brown sugar, paprika, chili powder, and cayenne pepper; bring to a boil. Reduce heat to low and simmer, uncovered, stirring occasionally, 30 minutes. Remove from heat and set aside.

# North Carolina Pig Pickin'

**When asked to define the whole duty of a man in a political year, nine out of ten persons in the South or Middle West would say, "To holler right, vote straight, and eat as much barbecue as any other man in the country."**

—Harper's Weekly (1896), describing the
  barbecues in vogue at that time

Any month of the year is good for a pig pickin' in North Carolina. The barbecue style will vary according to what area you're in: In the eastern part of the state, the entire pig (split down the middle) is cooked, and the sauce is made with vinegar and pepper. In the western part, only pig shoulders are cooked, and a tomato-based finishing sauce is used. Unlike other food preparation in the South, which is usually dominated by women, barbecue is a male domain.

Before the Civil War, pigs were a food staple in the South because they were a low-maintenance and convenient food source. The pigs could be put out to root in the forest and caught when the food supply became low. These semi-wild pigs were tougher and stringier than modern-day pigs. Pig slaughtering

became a time for celebration, and other families would be invited to share in the eating. Out of these gatherings grew the traditional southern barbecue. Plantation owners regularly held large barbecues for their slaves. According to historians, southerners ate, on average, 5 pounds of pork for every 1 pound of beef.

In the nineteenth century, barbecues were an important feature of church functions and political rallies. Members of both political parties would come to the same gathering, with the leaders of each party competing with one another to supply the largest contribution of food and drink. Folks would gather from afar to reach the appointed place in time for the speeches, band concert, and all-important barbecue. The only accompaniments to the roast pig were thick slices of good bread, cucumbers (fresh and pickled), and whiskey. The saying "going whole hog" came out of these political rallies.

During the twentieth century, barbecue joints or pits flourished (a typical barbecue joint or pit was a bare concrete floor covered by a corrugated tin roof and walls). Restaurants grew out of a simple barbecue pit where the owner sold barbecue to take away. Many were open only on weekends, since the "pit men" worked on farms during the week. As the century progressed, barbecue joints grew and prospered.

# North Carolina Pig Pickin'

While visiting my friends Bill and Andra Cook, in Raleigh, North Carolina, a couple of years ago, Bill's father, Elbert Cook of New Bern, North Carolina, brought his homemade barbecue pit (which he has fixed on a trailer) to the Cook's home and carefully tended the pig. When done, we pulled the meat off the ribs with our fingers and ate (pig pickin').

1 (60- to 100-pound) dressed pig *

Coarse salt

60 pounds charcoal briquettes, divided

Secret Sauce (recipe follows)

\* A live pig weighing 90 to 130 pounds will dress out a carcass approximately the desired weight. (Dressed means that the pig is prepared for cooking.)

**1.** Split open the whole dressed pig and butterfly (slit the backbone to allow the pig to lay flat, being careful not to pierce the skin). Trim and discard any excess fat (excess fat may cause a flare-up during cooking). Sprinkle the cavity with salt, cover, and let pig sit overnight.

**2.** Place 20 pounds of charcoal in the barbecue pit or pig cooker (add charcoal as needed during cooking process). Pour charcoal lighter fluid on the briquettes and ignite. Let the charcoal burn until a fine white ash covers the briquettes. Place a heavy gauge wire screen or rack about a foot above the coals. Place butterflied pig on rack (skin side up) and season with additional salt. Close lid of the cooker and cook 7 to 8 hours or until the internal temperature of the pig reaches 170°. Raise temperature of cooker slowly. It should take up to 3 hours to get external temperature to 200° (meat will crust over if temperature is too high). Let external temperature rise to 250°. Carefully watch the temperature to maintain the 250° external temperature. When done, turn pig over (skin side down) and spread with Secret Sauce. Cover and cook an additional 1 hour until skin is crisp. Remove from cooker. Slice or chop the meat or allow guests to pull meat from the bones. Serve with additional Secret Sauce. Traditionally, cole slaw, baked beans, corn on the cob (see page 115), and hushpuppies (see page 52) are served with the meal; don't forget the sweet ice tea (see page 216).

# Secret Sauce

Most families and restaurants that are known for their barbecues make their own sauce. In fact, they'll tell you that the "secret is in the sauce." You would no more ask a barbecue man for his sauce recipe than you would for the use of his dog. Most people simply call their sauce "Secret Sauce."

1 gallon cider vinegar

½ cup crushed red pepper flakes (more or less to taste)

¾ cup firmly packed brown sugar

½ cup vegetable oil

1 (2-ounce) bottle Tabasco or other hot pepper sauce (more or less to taste)

Salt to taste

Pour 2⅓ cups vinegar into another container to save for another use. In a large saucepan over medium-high heat, combine remaining vinegar, red pepper flakes, brown sugar, vegetable oil, Tabasco, and salt; heat until sugar dissolves. Remove from heat and store in vinegar jug. Serve and use at room temperature. (Note: Make the sauce ahead of time, letting stand at least 12 hours before using.)

# Old Clothes/Ropa Vieja

How about telling your guests that the dinner entree is "old clothes." You may get some strange looks, but this classic Cuban beef dish is a sure winner. Ropa vieja is one of the best-loved dishes on menus at Cuban restaurants around the country, especially in Miami and the Tampa Bay area. It is an old favorite among Cuban-American cooks: the ingredients are readily available, the recipe is simple, and the results are wonderful. It is usually served with boiled or steamed white or yellow rice.

Ropa vieja was originally introduced to Cuba by Spanish sailors. The name "old clothes" takes a little imagination, but the dish is said to resemble old, tattered clothes or rags. It has also been called "dirty laundry."

## Ropa Vieja

1 (1½- to 2-pound) flank steak, beef brisket, or chuck roast, trimmed of excess fat

2 onions, finely chopped

4 cloves garlic, minced

1 bay leaf

Sofrito (recipe follows)

Yellow Rice (recipe follows)

1 (4-ounce) jar diced red pimientos, drained

**1.** In a large soup pot, lay the beef flat. Add the onions, garlic, and bay leaf. Add enough cold water to cover; bring to a boil over medium-high heat. Reduce heat to low, cover, and simmer for 1½ to 2 hours or until meat falls apart and shreds easily. Test by pulling a chunk of meat with a fork. If it pulls apart easily, it's ready.

**2.** Remove from heat and transfer cooked meat to a cutting board, reserving the broth for use in the Sofrito and discarding the bay leaf. Let the meat cool for approximately 20 minutes, then slice it across the grain into 2-inch-wide strips. Shred the strips into fine strands with two forks; place the shredded meat on a large serving dish and keep warm. *(Note: Meat may be refrigerated at this point up to 1 day ahead, storing the broth and beef in separate containers.)*

**3.** Prepare Sofrito. Add the shredded meat to the prepared Sofrito mixture. Simmer gently for 10 to 15 minutes. Prepare Yellow Rice. Serve over rice and garnish with diced pimientos.

Makes 8 servings.

## SOFRITO

*3 tablespoons extra-virgin olive oil (preferably Spanish olive oil)*

*2 onions, chopped*

*4 cloves garlic, minced*

*2 red bell peppers, cored, seeded, and chopped*

*1 (32-ounce) can diced or crushed tomatoes*

*1½ cups reserved braising liquid*

*¼ teaspoon ground cinnamon*

*¼ teaspoon ground cloves*

*Salt to taste*

*3 tablespoons capers, drained*

In a large soup pot over low heat, add the olive oil; add onions and garlic and sauté until soft. Add bell peppers, continuing to sauté until the peppers lose some of their crispness. Add tomatoes, reserved liquid, cinnamon, cloves, and salt; simmer for 10 to 15 minutes. Add the capers and simmer an additional 5 minutes.

## YELLOW RICE

*2 tablespoons extra-virgin olive oil*

*¼ teaspoon crumbled saffron threads*

*2 cups long-grain rice*

*4 cups water*

*¾ teaspoon salt*

In a large saucepan over medium-high heat, heat olive oil. Stir in saffron and rice; sauté, stirring 1 to 2 minutes or until rice is coated well. Stir in water and salt; boil rice 8 to 10 minutes, uncovered, until surface of rice is covered with steam holes and grains on top appear dry. Remove from heat and let rice stand, covered, 5 minutes. Fluff rice with a fork and serve.

# Southern Fried Chicken

**The North seldom tried to fry chicken and this is well: the art cannot be learned north of the line of Mason and Dixon.**

—*Mark Twain, American writer*

The quintessential southern dish is fried chicken. There are as many recipes for fried chicken as there are southern cooks, with most being passed down through generations. (If you are using this recipe, you must not have any southern relatives.) This classic American dish is thought to have developed in the latter half of the eighteenth century from the traditional fricassee or frigasee that was served in most homes in the South. Many early fricassee recipes called for the chicken to be fried in some kind of fat, most often lard, before being stewed.

The first published recipe for fried chicken was in Mary Randolph's cookbook *The Virginia Housewife* (1824). Her recipe is as follows:

Cut them (chicken) up as for the fricassee, dredge them well with flour, sprinkle them with salt, put them into a good quantity of boiling lards, and fry them a light brown; fry small pieces of mush and a quantity of parsley nicely picked, to be served in the dish with the chickens; take half a pint of rich milk, add to it a small bit of butter, with pepper, salt, and chopped parsley; stew it a little, and pour it over the chickens, and then garnish with the fried parsley.

Southern fried chicken was a seasonal treat, since a new crop of chickens was started in the spring. These "spring chickens" were used for frying when they weighed about 2 pounds, and the big event on the social calendar of any community was the year's first fried chicken dinner.

A cast-iron skillet seems to make the best southern fried chicken, but it can also be deep-fried. Most southern cooks have changed with the times and now use vegetable oil and shortening in place of lard. Pan gravy, which is traditionally served with fried chicken, is never poured over the chicken, but is used as an accompaniment to rice or potatoes. Some cooks add chopped, hard-cooked eggs to the gravy to flavor and thicken it.

# Southern Fried Chicken

*2 (2½- to 3-pound) whole frying chickens, cut up for frying*

*Salt and freshly ground black pepper*

*3 cups all-purpose flour*

*1½ cups lard or solid vegetable shortening*

*Cream Gravy (recipe follows)*

**1.** Place the chicken pieces in a basin of cold water and soak for a few minutes. Remove from water and drain well; pat dry with paper towels. Season generously with salt and pepper. In a large plastic bag, add flour; close the bag and shake to dust the inside of the bag.

**2.** In a large deep cast-iron skillet over medium-high heat, melt the lard or shortening and bring to 350° (hot but not smoking).

**3.** Beginning with the dark meat, drop the chicken, a few pieces at a time, into the plastic bag; close the bag and shake until the pieces are thoroughly coated. Remove pieces from bag, shaking off excess flour, and place into the hot fat. Repeat until all chicken pieces are coated and in the pan. (*Note: If you do not have a large enough pan, use two pans or cook the chicken in batches. If you fry in batches, preheat the oven to 150° to hold the cooked chicken. Do not hold chicken for more than 30 minutes or the chicken will dry out.*) Do not flour chicken until you are ready to fry it.

**4.** Reduce heat to medium; fry the chicken slowly 12 to 15 minutes or until the bottom side of each piece is a rich golden brown. Carefully turn the chicken pieces and continue cooking an additional 12 minutes or until each piece is golden brown on all sides and just cooked through. Remove from pan.

**5.** Pour off all but 2 tablespoons of the cooking fat. Put the skillet back over the heat and make the Cream Gravy.

## CREAM GRAVY

*2 tablespoons pan drippings left in the skillet along with the solid cooking residue*

*1 tablespoon all-purpose flour*

*2 cups milk or cream, room temperature*

*Salt and freshly ground black pepper*

**1.** In the same skillet in which you fried the chicken and left 2 tablespoons pan drippings, set to medium heat. Sprinkle flour over the fat and blend or whisk until smooth. Whisking or stirring constantly, slowly pour in milk or cream; continue stirring, scraping loose any browned bits that may be stuck to the skillet, until the gravy begins to boil. Season with salt and pepper to taste.

**2.** Reduce heat to low and simmer, stirring occasionally, 5 to 8 minutes or until gravy is thickened to the desired consistency and the flour has lost its raw, pasty taste. Remove from pan and serve hot.

Makes 4 to 6 servings.

# Texas Barbecued Brisket

**The brisket is so tender you don't need teeth to eat it.**

*— Texas saying*

In Texas, barbecue means beef, particularly brisket. Texans did not invent barbecue, they just perfected it. Hundreds of barbecue joints and smoke houses dot the urban landscape—every town has its own barbecue joint serving barbecued brisket.

Barbecue is more than just a meal, it's a social event, with people gathering around a fire to watch, smell, eat, and tell stories. The people of Texas are serious about their barbecue, and every person living in the state seems to hold a strong opinion about his or her favorite barbecue joint and is prepared to defend that preference at the drop of a hat. Pit bosses, the masters of the slow smoke cooking, debate the art of barbecuing for hours, bragging about the superiority of their own technique. In Texas, barbecue secrets are handed down from father to son.

During the 1800s, cattle drive bosses used lesser cuts to feed their hired hands. The toughest cut of beef was the brisket. Without refrigeration, meat had to be cooked and eaten quickly or preserved using a spicing or smoking process.

Central Texas is especially noted for the development of the art of barbecuing. The area is home to descendants of German immigrants who brought their skill of smoking meats to Texas. After the Civil War, refugees, both black and white, left the Deep South for a new start in Texas, bringing their recipes and cooking styles. After more than a hundred years of refinement, this combination of culinary talents has resulted in an abundance of world-class barbecues in Central Texas.

## Texas Barbecued Brisket

*1 (5- to 6-pound) beef brisket (with a thick layer of fat)*

*2 tablespoons ground paprika*

*2 tablespoons freshly ground black pepper*

*2 tablespoons coarse kosher salt*

*2 tablespoons sugar*

*Barbecue sauce*

1. Rinse the brisket under cold running water; pat dry with paper towels. In a small bowl, combine paprika, pepper, salt, and sugar; rub mixture onto all sides of the brisket. Wrap brisket in plastic wrap and marinate in the refrigerator for 4 to 8 hours or overnight.

2. Prepare the smoker according to manufacturer's instructions. Set temperature to high, then turn down when it is really smoking. Maintain a temperature of about 200° (no hotter).

3. Remove plastic wrap and place the brisket (with juices) in a pan or on aluminum foil, fat side up, on a rack in the smoker. Close the lid and cook for 4 to 5 hours, checking temperature and brushing meat juices from the foil or pan over the brisket every hour.

4. Remove brisket from the smoker and wrap in aluminum foil. Return the foil-wrapped brisket to the smoker and continue cooking for 2 to 3 hours or until well done and very tender or until thermometer registers 185°. Depending on the thickness of the brisket and the temperature maintained in the smoker, the cooking time may vary.

5. Remove from smoker and transfer to a cutting board; let stand 20 minutes before carving. To serve, trim the excess fat and slice thinly against the grain (watch the meat as you slice, because the grain changes directions). Transfer the sliced meat to a platter, pour the pan juices on top, and serve with your favorite barbecue sauce on the side.

*Note: If necessary, brisket can be smoked 1 day ahead. When done, cool 1 hour, wrap in aluminum foil, then refrigerate. When ready to use, rewarm brisket, still wrapped in aluminum foil, in a preheated 350° oven for 45 minutes.*

Makes 10 to 12 servings.

# Plate Lunch

The plate lunch is the one dish that combines the many ethnic cuisines of Hawaii. Sampling a plate lunch is one of the easiest ways to enjoy an authentic taste of Hawaii's cuisine and culture without the pretentiousness of the resorts that cater to tourists. Hawaiians cheerfully describe the plate lunch as "a heart attack on a plate."

The plate lunch is considered the centerpiece of local food, a hearty meal designed to appeal to working people from diverse ethnic backgrounds, available at lunch wagons and small eateries around the Hawaiian Islands. It evolved during the 1940s from the bento (a bucket of rice, meat, and pickled vegetables that Japanese plantation workers traditionally carried into the fields). Lunch wagons sprang up to serve the field workers who did not pack bentos. The plate lunch is a lot like the blue plate special of the 1950s lunch counter. In 1997, the Bishop Museum in Honolulu, Hawaii, sponsored an exhibit called "Bento to Mixed Plate," which featured information about the origins of the present-day plate lunch.

The plate lunch consists of two scoops of rice, one scoop of bland macaroni salad, and an entree. You can find plate lunches in sit-down restaurants that resemble coffee shops, at drive-ins, at fast-food chains, and at the favorite of most Hawaiians, the nomadic lunch wagon. The quality and quantity can vary with each location.

# Side Dishes

# Boston Baked Beans

The tradition of eating Boston baked beans, beans sweetened with molasses, gave Boston its famous nickname, "Bean Town." Until molasses arrived in Boston from the West Indies in the late seventeenth century, early settlers had to use what they called "Indian sweetening," which was maple syrup, to sweeten baked beans. Later they replaced maple syrup with molasses. There was, and still is, no official recipe for Boston baked beans as recipes varied from one family to another and restaurant to restaurant, with each "authentic" recipe a closely guarded secret.

When the first colonists arrived at Plymouth in 1620, local Indians were cultivating several types of beans that they baked in small holes in the ground lined with stones. Fires were started in the holes; beans were placed in covered pots, which were then placed in the holes. The holes were then covered with sod or flat stones to retain the heat, and the beans were slow cooked for hours. The colonists called the holes "bean holes." This was the first method of baking beans, and every colonial family had a bean hole until fireplaces with brick ovens became common.

In New England during the eighteenth century, the Puritan Sabbath, which lasted from sundown on Saturday until sundown on Sunday, was strict and stern. No work was allowed, except for tasks that could not be avoided, such as milking cows and serving food; however, no cooking was allowed. The bean pot was put to bake on a Saturday morning, or even on a Friday evening, at the side of the fireplace. Except for the addition of a little water now and then, the beans needed little tending. The beans were then eaten for Saturday night dinner and again for Sunday morning breakfast.

During the nineteenth century, housewives too busy with other chores were able to get baked beans from local bakers. The baker would come on Saturday morning to pick up the family bean pot and take it to a community oven, usually located in the cellar of a nearby tavern. The baker would then return the baked beans with some brown bread on Saturday evening.

## Boston Baked Beans

Many people believe that the rich brown goodness of Boston baked beans is a product of earthenware bean pots. Lacking one of these pots, you can use any deep earthenware casserole with a cover.

*2 cups dried pea beans or navy beans*

*2 teaspoons ground mustard*

*1 teaspoon salt*

*½ teaspoon black pepper*

*¼ cup firmly packed brown sugar*

*½ cup dark molasses*

*1 large onion, cut into eighths*

*¼ pound salt pork or bacon, cut into thick slices*

1. Rinse and drain beans. Place in a large soup pot, cover with cold water, and let sit overnight. Drain and rinse beans again.

2. In the same soup pot, add soaked beans and cover with fresh water; bring to a boil over medium heat. Reduce heat to low, cover, and simmer 30 minutes or until beans are just tender (do not boil or beans will burst). Remove from heat and drain, reserving bean liquid.

3. In a medium bowl, combine mustard, salt, pepper, brown sugar, molasses, and 3 cups of reserved bean liquid (adding hot water if necessary).

4. Preheat oven to 300°. Using a heavy oven-proof pot, 2-quart bean pot, or large casserole dish (with lids), place onion pieces on bottom of pot. Add beans; pour molasses mixture over top. Layer salt pork or bacon slices on top. Cover and bake 5 to 6 hours or until beans are tender, checking every 2 hours and adding hot water if liquid cooks down too much (keep the beans just barely covered with liquid). Remove the lid for the last 30 minutes of cooking.

Makes 6 servings.

# Ceviche

**Fish, to taste right, must swim three times—in water, in butter, and in wine in the stomach.**

*—Polish proverb*

The new "in food" for the beginning of the twenty-first century is actually an Old World dish from South America called ceviche. Although it has been one of South America's best-kept secrets for centuries, ceviche is becoming a popular seafood dish in the Northern Hemisphere, especially in New York. Ceviche bars or cevicherias are creating excitement and enticing people to vote with their mouth to make this the food for this millennium. This cuisine comes from the diverse cooking styles and tropical ingredients of the Caribbean, Latin America, and Central and South America.

Ceviche (also spelled seviche or cebiche) is seafood prepared using citrus juice instead of heat. It is actually a seafood salad, but can be eaten as a first course or main dish, depending on what is served with it. Ceviches are refreshing, invigorating, and very addictive—some restaurants even push the dish as an aphrodisiac.

Both Peru and Ecuador claim ownership; in fact, it is considered Peru's national dish. Diana Nuñez de Somlij, who is Peruvian and now lives in Ecuador, sent me the following information on the history of ceviche:

"The Incas cooked fish with a fruit called tumbo. They ate salted fish and marinated fish dishes. The Spanish contributed the Mediterranean custom of using lemons and onions. Ceviche's origin is Arabian, imported to Peru by Arab immigrants and reinvented by the Peruvians of the coastal areas."

## Ceviche

Leo Porter, manager of the Horseshoe Ranch in Fort Klamath, Oregon, gave this recipe to me. Leo spent several years in Peru and is a wonderful gourmet cook.

1 pound fresh fish fillet (red snapper, cod, halibut, flounder, bass, grouper, or salmon)*

1 pound raw small shrimp, peeled and deveined

3 tablespoons fresh lemon juice

½ cup fresh lime juice

3 tablespoons green onions (tops included), finely chopped

2 to 3 fresh tomatoes, finely chopped

¼ cup fresh cilantro leaves, finely chopped

¼ cup celery (use the tender inner stalks only), finely chopped

1 (6-ounce) can black olives, drained

1 cup prepared tomato salsa (mild to medium)

Freshly ground black pepper to taste

Celery salt to taste

1 (46-ounce) can tomato juice

Fresh cilantro sprigs

* Use only fresh seafood (not previously frozen), as texture is imperative to ceviche.

**1.** Run hands over top of fish fillets, pressing slightly to look for any remaining bones. Cut fish in ¾-inch strips, then cut into ½-inch pieces.

**2.** Using a gallon jug, add fish and shrimp; add lemon and lime juice to jug (juice should just cover seafood in jug). Cover with lid and shake. Marinate in refrigerator overnight or a minimum of 12 hours, shaking occasionally.

**3.** After seafood mixture has marinated and 1 hour before serving, add green onions, tomatoes, cilantro, celery, olives, salsa, pepper, celery salt, and tomato juice to jug. Shake, then refrigerate until ready to serve. To serve, place mixture (with juice) in individual serving bowls and garnish with cilantro sprigs.

*Note: Ceviche does not keep well. It becomes rubbery and can be described as overcooked when it sits for over 24 hours.*

Makes 6 to 8 servings.

# Chitterlings/Chitlins

et us consider what chitlins are—they are hog intestines or guts. Some people turn up their noses at the mention of chitlins; others leave the house while they are cooking, driven away by their odor. However, the volume sold for New Year's dinners, with Christmas and Thanksgiving not far behind, attests to chitlins popularity in the United States. They are a food that you either love or hate.

Chitterlings is the more formal name, but most people call them chitlins. Eating chitlins in the rural South is not as common as it once was. In colonial times, hogs were slaughtered in December, and hog maws or ears, pig feet, and neckbones were given to the slaves. Because of the West African tradition of cooking all edible parts of plants and animals, these foods helped the slaves survive in the United States.

Chitlins take a lot of time and effort to clean. They are partially cleaned when they are sold, but require additional hand cleaning before they are ready to eat. The secret to good and safe chitlins is in the cleaning, not in the cooking. They are available in supermarkets in African-American neighborhoods, especially during the holiday season. They can also be ordered from a butcher, but be prepared to buy 10 pounds of chitlins to get 5 pounds to cook.

Animal innards have long been treasured foods around the world. Scotland's national dish is haggis (sheep's stomach stuffed with the animal's minced heart, liver, and lungs). Throughout Europe, tripe (cow or ox stomach) is popular, and French chefs in upscale restaurants serve dishes based on cow's brains and kidneys.

In 1996, the town of Salley, South Carolina, inaugurated the annual Chitlin' Strut. The first festival attracted about a hundred people. Today, the festival draws about 70,000 people. It is estimated that more than 128,000 pounds of chitlins have been eaten during the festival's history.

## Chitlins

Most families who love to cook chitlins have their own recipe passed down from generation to generation. My friend, Andra Cook of Raleigh, North Carolina, says her mother, Martha McCollum, always fried the chitlins after they were simmered. Andra says, "If you can get past the smell, they have an interesting flavor. When my mother prepared them, the whole neighborhood smelled!"

*10-pound bucket fresh or frozen chitterlings*

*Cold water to cover*

*1 cup cider vinegar*

*5 bay leaves*

*2 large onions, coarsely chopped*

*2 large potatoes, peeled and coarsely chopped*

*1 green or red bell pepper, cored, seeded, and coarsely chopped*

*3 cloves garlic, minced*

*Salt and freshly ground black pepper to taste*

*Hot pepper sauce*

If chitterlings are frozen, thaw. Using a small soft brush, clean chitterlings thoroughly; rinse in several changes of water. Cut into 1½ to 2-inch pieces. Place the cleaned chitterlings into a large pot; cover with water and vinegar. Add bay leaves, onions, potatoes, green or red pepper, garlic, salt and pepper. Bring to a boil; turn heat to low and simmer for 2½ to 3 hours or until chitterlings are tender. Remove from heat, drain well. Serve with your favorite hot pepper sauce.

*Makes 6 servings.*

# Florida Lobster Salad

There are two types of lobster popular in the United States: Maine clawed lobsters and spiny nonclawed lobsters. Everyone knows about Maine lobsters, but few people, except the lucky ones living in southern Florida, experience the pleasure of eating the spiny lobster. Most old-timers and some restaurants call them crawfish (not to be confused with actual crawfish found in Louisiana, an unrelated species), but the state of Florida renamed them Florida lobster many years ago.

Spiny lobster are caught off the Keys and around the southern tip of the state from the waters of the Atlantic Ocean. Monroe County boasts the largest lobster population. Every year a frenzy known as "bug fever" catches when thousands of Florida divers, from the first of August until Labor Day, converge on the waters off the coast. The season runs until the end of March, but the frenzy is greatest through Labor Day.

The Florida lobster has skinny feelers (instead of claws) that are not worth eating. The tails of the Florida lobster can be boiled, steamed, grilled, deep-fried, or broiled. The meat is removed from the shell and used in many recipes. A favorite dish of southern Florida is the lobster or crawfish salad.

## Florida Lobster Salad

The recipe comes from Marilyn Essek Fausti of Edgewater, Florida. Marilyn tested and revised several recipes for lobster salad to come up with her favorite version. Since everyone loves a party, Marilyn invited several friends over to taste test the results. Everyone agreed that the following is the best. Marilyn says, "Everyone thought this was very refreshing and light-tasting. The Florida lobster meat is a little tougher and stringier than Maine lobster, and it definitely has a 'sea' taste. We are not complaining, because living in Florida, we have sunshine everyday and we do not have to pay state taxes."

½ cup heavy cream

1 tablespoon mayonnaise

1 teaspoon grated orange peel

2 tablespoons fresh orange juice

1 (11-ounce) can mandarin oranges, drained

1 mango, peeled, seeded, and cubed

2 cups diced flaked Florida lobster tail meat*

Mixed salad greens

* To cook, steam lobster tails 5 to 7 minutes or until meat is opaque in center (cut to test). If using frozen lobster tails, thaw first, then steam for 9 to 10 minutes (frozen lobster takes a little longer to cook).

In a medium bowl, beat heavy cream until soft peaks form. In a large bowl, combine mayonnaise, orange peel, and orange juice; fold in whipped cream. Fold in mandarin oranges, mango, and lobster. Cover and refrigerate 2 to 3 hours. Serve chilled on mixed salad greens.

Makes 6 to 8 servings.

# Corn on the Cob

**People have tried and they have tried, but sex is not better than sweet corn.**

—*Garrison Keillor, radio personality and storyteller*

In American regional cooking, corn is important in many recipes, such as corn chowder, creamed corn, succotash, and cornbread. But no preparation can come close to the timeless appeal of simple buttered corn on the cob. All over the Midwest and Great Plains, small towns celebrate the harvest with sweet corn festivals. Settlers adapted the Indian style of roasting corn with the husks removed, and to this day, street vendors around the world sell husked corn.

In Iowa, the heart of the Corn Belt, almost half of all cultivated land is devoted to corn, making it first in the nation for corn production. Corn is the largest crop in the United States, in terms of acres planted and the value of the crop produced. It is also the most widely distributed crop in the world.

In Native American usage, the word for corn means "our life," or "our mother," or "she who sustains us." It was the cultivation of corn that turned Native American tribes from nomadic to agrarian communities.

It was from the Native Americans that the first European settlers learned about corn. Native Americans had spent hundreds of years developing what we now know as corn from seed-bearing grass. Long before Christopher Columbus sailed from Spain in 1492, Native Americans were cultivating this grass in North, Central, and South America. Native American farmers in the Ohio River Valley had been growing corn for more than 1,700 years before the first white men crossed the Appalachian Mountains, and there is evidence that they used corn to brew beer before Europeans arrived in the Americas.

The Pawtuxet Indian tribe in Massachusetts was cultivating corn when the first settlers arrived, and corn was on the first Thanksgiving table in 1621. If it had not been for corn, the Pilgrims of Plymouth Colony might have starved to death during their first year in America. The Indians taught settlers how to grow corn, pound corn into meal, and how to cook with it. The words of Governor William Bradford, first governor of the Plymouth Colony, now inscribed on a brass plaque at Truto (Corn Hill) on Cape Cod, Massachusetts, reflect the settler's gratitude: "And sure it was God's good providence that we found this corne for we know not how else we should have done."

# How to Cook Fresh Corn—The Right Way

My grandmother, Mabel Amelia Myers, said to put a pot of water on the stove. While you wait for the water to come to a boil, pick your corn and husk it. Drop the corn into the boiling water, and when the water starts to boil again, remove the corn.

**In Water:** Choose a pot large enough to hold the amount of corn you wish to cook, with room for water to cover the corn. Cover pot and bring water to a boil on high heat. Add husked corn ears and continue to cook on high heat (covered or not) 3 or 4 minutes or until kernels are very hot.

**Tip:** If you're having a party, borrow this trick from open-air markets in Mexico. Vendors selling ears of corn for snacks keep them ready and waiting for several hours in tubs of lukewarm water. Instead of butter, ears are rubbed with lime wedges and sprinkled with salt. This nonfat alternative is very good.

**In the Husk—Grilled or Baked:** Corn cooked this way is steamed and tastes similar to boiled corn. It is handy to serve in the husk because you can season or butter the corn before it is cooked.

To prepare, pull husk back from each ear of corn, but leave attached at base of cob. Pull off and discard silk; trim off any insect damage, and rinse ears. If you want to butter the corn, pat ears dry and rub with soft butter. Pull husks back up around corn.

If you want the husk to stay snugly against the ear, pull off one or two of the outer husk layers, tear lengthwise into thin strips, and tie them around ear in several places. Just before cooking, immerse the ears in cool water for 10 to 20 minutes (this keeps husks from burning); Remove from water and drain. *(Note: For a sweeter corn, add a few cups of sugar to the water before soaking.)*

Grill the corn, turning frequently, for 15 to 20 minutes, until the husks are dry and the kernels are tender when pierced.

To bake, preheat the oven to 375°. Bake 20 to 25 minutes or until kernels are tender when pierced.

**To Grill:** Husk corn and discard silk; wrap each ear loosely with aluminum foil. Over gas or hot coals, place corn onto a hot grill over medium heat. Cover barbecue with lid, open any vents, and cook 15 to 20 minutes; turn occasionally.

**To Bake:** Preheat oven to 375°. Prepare corn as directed for grilling, but put ears in a single layer, separating them slightly, directly onto the oven rack or onto a baking pan. Bake 20 to 25 minutes or until corn is tender when pierced and very hot.

**To Microwave:** Perfect for cooking just one ear of corn. Husk corn and discard silk. Rinse and wrap each ear loosely in a paper towel. Cook on full power 1 to 2 minutes or until ears are very hot to touch.

# Cracked Crab & Crab Louis Salad

**Crab is probably the most American of all shellfish. It is eaten to some extent in England, where it is properly considered a great delicacy, but in France it is seldom served, and other countries it is never found in the abundance that we enjoy.**

*—James Beard (1903–1985), American chef and author, from his cookbook* James Beard's American Cookery

The Dungeness crab is unique to the West Coast of the United States and is considered one of its greatest treasures. Dungeness crab is to the West Coast what lobster is to New England. On much of the West Coast, it is a traditional Thanksgiving and Christmas treat.

Dungeness crab is also considered the symbol of the San Francisco fishing industry, with sidewalk vendors selling fresh-boiled crab during the winter months. The wharves there carry the scent of crabs boiling in large outdoor pots, to be sold in walk-away crab cocktails or taken home. In Chinatown, dozens of fish markets and restaurants keep crabs alive in saltwater tanks, ready to be steamed in the Cantonese style with ginger and scallions.

The best and most flavorful way to eat a Dungeness crab is in its plainest form, with absolutely nothing on it. It is hard to beat Dungeness crab, just plucked from the shell and eaten with good bread and white wine. This is West Coast eating at its best!

The second best way is in the famous salad Crab Louis (sometimes written Crab Louie). Credit for the origin of Crab Louis depends on whom you talk to and in which West Coast state you are. Some attribute this dish to the chef at Seattle's Olympic Club, while others say it was created in San Francisco by either the chef at Solari's restaurant or the chef at the St. Francis Hotel. Some historians suggest that the salad was named for King Louis XIV. King Louis was known for his enormous appetite. After his death, it is said that an autopsy revealed that his stomach was twice the size of that of ordinary men. In 1904, when the New York Metropolitan Opera Company played in Seattle, Enrico Caruso (1873–1921), Italian tenor and opera star, kept ordering the salad from the Palace Hotel Restaurant until none was left in the restaurant's kitchen.

The crab is named for the town on Washington's Olympic Peninsula where the first commercial harvesting began in the 1880s. The town in turn was named for a point on the English coast near the Strait of Dover. Dungeness crab can be found from southern California to the Aleutian Islands in Alaska. This large crab usually weighs from 1¾ to 4 pounds and is brown to purple in color. Law requires the crab to be at least 6¼ inches long to be harvested, and only males can be taken. Prime season is in the winter months.

*Dungeness crab and prepared salad.* Courtesy Oregon Dungeness Crab Commission.

# Cracked Dungeness Crab

**1.** Using ¼ cup of salt per quart of water, bring water to a boil in a large pot. One at a time, plunge the live crabs into the water. When all of the crabs have been put in the pot, cover, then let the water return to a boil; reduce heat to low and simmer 15 to 18 minutes, depending on the size of the crabs.

**2.** When cooked, remove crabs from boiling water to an ice water bath to chill; drain the crabs well, then clean them by removing the skirt (the triangular piece of shell under the crab), the upper shell, gills, and soft inner part. Break the legs and claws from the body. Cut the body into four pieces with a heavy knife. Pile on a preheated platter and serve at once with melted butter, or chill and serve on cracked ice with mayonnaise or your favorite cocktail sauce. Serve with nutcrackers and picks to help dig out every last piece of the savory crabmeat.

# Crab Louis Salad

This recipe is from Peggy Bucholz and her daughter-in-law, Laurie Bucholz. As a family, they go crabbing at Nehalem Bay, Oregon, several times a year, then, they confess, "pig out on Crab Louis." Peggy also always makes fresh French bread and serves a good-quality Chardonnay to enjoy with it.

*1½ pounds flaked Dungeness crabmeat (including crab legs)*

*4 whole lettuce leaves*

*Shredded fresh iceburg lettuce*

*3 hard-cooked eggs (2 finely chopped and 1 sliced)*

*2 tomatoes, quartered*

*Black olives*

*Avocados, sliced*

*Lemon wedges*

*Louis Dressing (recipe follows)*

Carefully check the crabmeat, removing all bits of shell and cartilage. On each individual plate, line salad plates with whole lettuce leaves. Add a mound of shredded lettuce, a mound of crabmeat, and top with big pieces from the legs. Around the crab, arrange a ring of finely chopped hard-cooked eggs. Top with a few slices of hard-cooked egg. Garnish with tomatoes, olives, avocado slices, and lemon wedges. Pass the Louis Dressing separately.

Makes 4 servings.

## LOUIS DRESSING

*1 cup mayonnaise*

*¼ cup heavy cream, whipped*

*¼ cup chili sauce*

*¼ cup chopped green pepper*

*2 tablespoons chopped green onions (tops included)*

*1 teaspoon fresh lemon juice*

*Salt and freshly ground black pepper to taste*

In a medium bowl, combine mayonnaise, cream, chili sauce, green pepper, green onions, and lemon juice. Season to taste with salt and pepper; chill thoroughly in the refrigerator before using.

Makes 1½ cups.

# Hoppin' John

**Eat poor that day, eat rich the rest of the year.
Rice for riches and peas for peace.**

*—Southern sayings on eating a dish of Hoppin' John on New Year's Day*

Hoppin' John is found in most states of the South, but it is mainly associated with the Carolinas. Gullah or Lowcountry cuisine reflects the cooking of the Carolinas, especially the Sea Islands (a cluster of islands stretching along the coasts of South Carolina and northern Georgia). Black-eyed peas, also called cow peas, are thought to have been introduced to America by African slaves who worked the rice plantations. Hoppin' John is a rich bean dish made of black-eyed peas simmered with spicy sausages, ham hocks or fat pork, rice, and tomato sauce.

This African-American dish is traditionally a high point of New Year's Day, when a shiny dime is often buried among the black-eyed peas before serving. Whoever gets the coin in his or her portion is assured good luck throughout the year. For maximum good luck in the new year, the first thing that should be eaten on New Year's Day is Hoppin' John. At the stroke of midnight on New Year's Eve, many southern families toast each other with Champagne and a bowl of Hoppin' John.

There are many tales that explain how Hoppin' John got its name:

- It was the custom for children to gather in the dining room as the dish was brought forth and hop around the table before sitting down to eat.

- A man named John came "a-hoppin" when his wife took the dish from the stove.

- An obscure South Carolina custom was inviting a guest to eat by saying, "Hop in, John."

- The dish goes back at least as far as 1841, when, according to tradition, it was hawked in the streets of Charleston, South Carolina, by a crippled black man who was known as Hoppin' John.

## Hoppin' John

*2 cups dried black-eyed peas*

*Cold water*

*1 pound lean slab bacon or 1 pound meaty ham hocks*

*1 large onion, chopped*

*¼ to ½ teaspoon crushed red pepper flakes*

*4 cups water or chicken broth*

*2 cups uncooked long-grain white rice*

*Salt and black pepper to taste*

1. Before preparing dried beans, sort through them thoroughly for tiny pebbles or other debris. Soak, rinse, and drain dried black-eyed peas. Place black-eyed peas in a large soup pot over medium-high heat and cover with cold water; bring to a boil. Remove from heat; cover and let stand 1 to 2 hours. Drain and rinse beans.

2. Using the same large soup pot over medium-high heat, add black-eyed peas, bacon or ham hock, onion, and red pepper. Add water or chicken broth; bring to a boil. Reduce heat to medium-low and cook for 1½ to 2 hours or until black-eyed peas are tender (do not boil or beans will burst). Remove bacon or ham hock and cut meat into bite-size pieces. Return meat to pot. Stir in rice, cover, and cook 20 to 25 minutes or until rice is tender and liquid is absorbed. Remove from heat and season to taste with salt and pepper.

*Makes 8 servings.*

# Greens

**But I have never tasted meat,**
**Nor cabbage, corn nor beans,**
**Nor fluid food on half as sweet**
**As that first mess of greens.**

—*James T. Cotton Noe (1869–1953),*
*American writer and poet, from* The Loom of Life, *1912*

Southerners love their greens. A time-honored tradition in southern kitchens, greens have held an important place on the table for well over a century, and there is no other vegetable that is quite so unique to the region. Greens are any sort of cabbage in which the green leaves do not form a compact head. They are mostly kale, collards, turnip, spinach, and mustard greens. In the South, a large quantity of greens to serve a family is commonly referred to as a "mess o' greens." The exact quantity that constitutes a "mess" varies with the size of the family.

The traditional way to cook greens is to boil or simmer slowly with a piece of salt pork or ham hock for a long time (this tempers their tough texture and smoothes out their bitter flavor) until they are very soft.

Typically, greens are served with freshly baked corn bread to dip into the pot-likker. Pot likker is the highly concentrated, vitamin-filled broth that results from the long boil of the greens. It is, in other words, the "liquor" left in the pot.

The cooking of greens came with the arrival of African slaves to the southern colonies and the need to satisfy their hunger and provide food for their families. The slaves on the plantations were given the leftover food from the plantation kitchens. Some of this food consisted of the tops of turnips and other greens. Ham hocks and pig's feet were also given to the slaves. Forced to create meals from these leftovers, slaves created the famous southern greens. One-pot meals also represent a traditional method of food preparation, which is linked directly back to West Africa. In spite of what some consider their unpleasant smell, reaction to the smell of cooking greens separates true southern eaters from wannabes.

According to folklore, collards served with black-eyed peas and hog jowl on New Year's Day promises a year of good luck and financial reward, hanging a fresh leaf over your door will ward off evil spirits, and a fresh leaf placed on the forehead promises to cure a headache.

## Collard Greens

This is a family recipe from Andra Cook of Raleigh, North Carolina. Andra says, "It is difficult to measure weight and size for each serving. My mother-in-law, Belle Cook, says she buys a grocery bag full and can serve four with that. Collard greens are available 8 months out of the year in the South. I don't include June through September because the greens are much better after they have a 'good hard frost.' That's not to say you can't get them in the other months (June-September), but the taste is much better after the frost."

*Collard greens (whole collard heads or leaves)*

*2 ham hocks*

*Water*

*Salt to taste*

*Toppings (suggestions follow)*

**1.** Wash greens thoroughly, approximately 3 or 4 times, to ensure they are clean and free of insects. Remove large stems. Place ham hocks in an extra-large pot with enough water to completely cover them. Add salt and cook ham hocks at least 30 minutes before adding collard greens. Add collards, big leaves first, let them start boiling, then add remainder of greens. Cook 45 minutes to 1 hour, stirring once about midway to ensure thorough cooking. Test for tenderness of stems at 45 minutes by piercing with a sharp knife. Cook additional time if necessary.

**2.** Remove from heat and drain in a colander, reserving the juice, or pot likker. Chop collards with a collard chopper or a knife, leaving no large leaves or pieces. Add some of the pot likker if the greens are too dry. Salt to taste. Serve hot or at room temperature with your choice of toppings.

### TOPPINGS
*Hot pepper vinegar, onions and vinegar (chopped onions and vinegar mixed together), salsa, small whole tomatoes*

# Grits

**Jimmy crack corn, an' I don't care
Jimmy crack corn, an' I don't care
Jimmy crack corn, an' I don't care
The master's gone away.**

—American folk song called "The Blue Tail Fly," by
Daniel Decatur Emmett (1815–1904), American musician
and songwriter, 1846.

To a southerner, eating grits is practically a religion, and breakfast without grits is unthinkable. Outside of the southern states, the reaction to grits is mixed. Grits are served as a side dish for breakfast or dinner and are traditionally eaten with butter and milk. Three-quarters of the grits sold in the United States are from a belt of coastal states stretching from Louisiana to the Carolinas, known as the "Grits Belt." A true grit lover would not consider instant or quick-cooking grits; only long-cooking stone-ground grits are worth eating.

Grits (or hominy) were one of the first truly American foods, as the Native Americans ate a mush made of softened corn or maize. In 1584, during their reconnaissance party of what is now Roanoke, North Carolina, Sir Walter Raleigh and his men met and dined with the local Indians. Having no language in common, the two groups quickly resorted to food and drink. One of Raleigh's men, Arthur Barlowe, recorded notes on the food of the Indians. He made a special note of corn, which he found "very white, faire, and well tasted." He also wrote about being served a boiled corn or hominy.

When the colonists came ashore in Jamestown, Virginia, in 1607, the Indians offered them bowls of this substance. The Indians called it *rockahominie*, which was later shortened to *hominy* by the colonists. The Indians taught the colonists how to thresh the hulls from dried yellow corn. Corn was a year-round staple and each tribe called it by a different name.

In 1976, South Carolina declared grits the official state food: "Whereas, throughout its history, the South has relished its grits, making them a symbol of its diet, its customs, its humor, and its hospitality, and whereas, every community in the State of South Carolina used to be the site of a grist mill and every local economy in the State used to be dependent on its products; and whereas, grits has been a part of the life of every South Carolinian of whatever race, background, gender, and income; and whereas, grits could very well play a vital role in the future of not only this State, but also the world, if, as *The Charleston News and Courier* proclaimed in 1952: 'An inexpensive, simple, and thoroughly digestible food, [grits] should be made popular throughout the world. Given enough of it, the inhabitants of planet Earth would have nothing to fight about. A man full of [grits] is a man of peace.'"

# Grits Pudding or Baked Cheese Grits

This recipe is from Anne Davis of Melborne, Florida. Anne serves this as a traditional holiday dish for her family. She says, "This recipe was given to me twenty years ago by a friend in Atlanta, Georgia. It could be used in place of Yorkshire pudding, if that appeals to you. When it's done, it is set, but still soft. If you have never liked grits, or never thought you would like them, I'll bet you anything you will love this dish."

*4 cups water*

*1½ teaspoons salt*

*1 cup quick-cooking grits (not instant)*

*½ cup yellow cornmeal (preferably stone ground)*

*3 tablespoons butter*

*1 teaspoon sugar*

*½ teaspoon red (cayenne) pepper*

*2 teaspoons baking powder*

*½ cup milk*

*4 eggs, lightly beaten*

*1½ cups shredded sharp Cheddar cheese, divided*

*½ cup thinly sliced green onions (including tops)*

1. In a large, heavy saucepan over high heat, bring water and salt to a boil; stir in grits and cornmeal; return to a boil. Reduce heat to low; cover and cook, stirring occasionally, for 5 to 6 minutes or until the mixture is very thick. Remove from heat and add butter, sugar, and cayenne pepper; stir until the butter is melted. Set aside.

2. Preheat oven to 325°. Butter a 2-quart baking dish. In a large bowl, dissolve baking powder in milk; add eggs and beat until mixture is well combined. Add grits mixture and blend thoroughly. Stir in 1¼ cups Cheddar cheese and green onions. Pour the mixture into prepared baking dish and bake for 1 hour. Sprinkle the pudding with the remaining ¼ cup Cheddar cheese and bake for an additional 15 to 20 minutes or until pudding is puffed and golden. Remove from oven and serve.

Makes 8 servings.

# Classic Grits and Cheese Casserole

True grit lovers will not consider instant or quick-cooking grits. They believe in only the regular, long-cooking or more expensive stone-ground grits, which take up to 30 minutes to cook. The eggs are the secret to light, fluffy grits that melt in your mouth. You may adjust or eliminate the hot sauce to suit your taste.

*5 cups water*

*1 teaspoon salt*

*1 cup stone-ground grits*

*½ cup butter or margarine, cut into pieces*

*2 cups shredded sharp Cheddar cheese*

*3 eggs, beaten*

*⅛ teaspoon Tabasco sauce, or to taste*

1. Heat oven to 350°. Butter a 1½-quart casserole dish.

2. In a large, heavy saucepan over medium-high heat, bring water to boil; add salt. Slowly stir in grits, stirring or whisking after each addition to prevent lumping. Return grits to a boil, then reduce heat to low. Cover and cook slowly for 25 minutes, stirring frequently to prevent sticking.

3. Remove from heat and stir in butter and Cheddar cheese; let cool to lukewarm. When cool, stir in eggs and Tabasco. Pour grits into prepared casserole dish. Bake in preheated oven for approximately 35 to 40 minutes, or until top is golden brown. Remove from heat and serve immediately.

Makes 8 servings.

# Perfect Baked Potato

**What I say is that, if a fellow really likes potatoes, he must be a pretty decent sort of fellow.**

—A. A. Milne (1882–1956), British author

Because Americans eat more potatoes than any other vegetable, most people consider the sight of a baked potato, split and topped with a pat of butter or a daub of sour cream, the ultimate food. A perfect baked potato is rubbed with oil and coarse salt, then baked—not microwaved or steamed in aluminum foil.

In the 1850s, most Americans considered potatoes to be food for animals rather than for humans. As late as the middle of the nineteenth century, the Farmer's Manual recommended that potatoes "be grown near the hog pens as a convenience towards feeding the hogs." In Book of Household Management (1861), Isabella Beeton wrote about the potato: "It is generally supposed that the water in which potatoes are boiled is injurious; and as instances are recorded where cattle having drunk it were seriously affected, it may be well to err on the safe side, and avoid its use for any alimentary purpose."

Although potatoes are grown throughout the United States, no state is more associated with the potato than Idaho. The first potatoes in Idaho were planted by a Presbyterian missionary, Henry Harmon Spalding. Spalding established a mission at Lapwai in 1836 to bring Christianity to the Nez Perce Indians. He wanted to demonstrate that they could provide food for themselves through agriculture rather than hunting and gathering.

It was not until the Russet Burbank potato was developed by horticulturist Luther Burbank in 1872 that the Idaho potato industry really took off. Burbank, while trying to improve the Irish potato, developed a hybrid that was more disease resistant. By the early 1900s, the Russet Burbank potato began appearing throughout Idaho.

## Perfect Baked Potato

The best potatoes for baking are Russets from Idaho or Washington. Select potatoes of uniform size and as smooth skinned as possible.

1. Preheat oven to 350°. Scrub potatoes under cold running water; pat dry, and pierce skin in several places with a fork (this allows steam to escape and speeds the cooking time). Lightly rub skin of each potato with olive oil and sprinkle lightly with coarse salt. Place on baking sheet, ½-inch apart, and bake approximately 1 to 1½ hours, depending on size. Potato will yield to pressure with thumb and forefinger when done.

2. Remove from oven and cut each open with sharp knife; squeeze ends. Serve immediately with your favorite condiments.

# Oregon Truffle

**At the time I write, the glory of the truffle has now reached its culmination. . . . In fine, the truffle is the very diamond of gastronomy. . . . The truffle is not an outright aphrodisiac, but it may in certain circumstances make women more affectionate and men more amiable.**

*—Jean Anthelme Brillat-Savarin (1755–1826), French author and gastronomist, from his book* The Physiology of Taste, *1825*

The mention of truffles brings up images of the expensive black and white truffles of France. But the truffles from Oregon are just as aromatic and less than one-tenth the price of their famous French counterparts. The Oregon truffles grow in the needles and topsoil around the Douglas fir tree. Instead of hunting them with dogs or pigs, as the French do, a rake is used. Most of the harvest takes place on tree farms.

What is it about truffles that make them so irresistible to gourmet cooks? Part of the reason is their scarcity. Truffles are buried in the earth like little black diamonds (so nicknamed by French gastronome Brillat-Savarin). It seems to be human nature to crave what is hard to come by. A truffle's flavor and aroma are so unique, that it is almost impossible to explain. Some describe their smell as musky, earthy, even sexy. Once you have smelled a truffle, you long to smell it again and again.

The French consider Oregon truffles as "non-truffle truffles" or "false truffles," but chefs across the United States consider them every bit as delicious and exotic as their European cousins and are using them in their culinary masterpieces. You will find Oregon truffles in the markets from November to March, but they're sporadic. In other words, buy them when you see them.

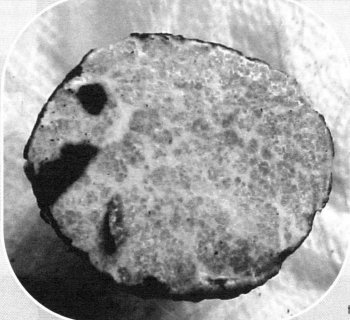

*An Oregon black truffle.* Daniel B. Wheeler photo, Portland, Oregon.

# Poke

**Lucky you live Hawai'i.**

—*favorite Hawaiian saying*

Poke (pronounced POH-kay) is served in most Hawaiian homes and restaurants as a side dish, and no gathering in Hawaii would be complete without a few bowls of poke. Poke is bite-size pieces of raw fish doused in seasonings. In Hawaiian, poke means "cut piece" or "small piece." Poke is actually the Hawaiian version of the elegant Japanese sashimi (a combining of the Hawaiian and Japanese taste for raw fish). The fish for poke is sometimes even lightly seared or fried. Poke is still evolving in the Hawaiian Islands. It was not until the 1970s that the recipes for poke started appearing in cookbooks. It is traditionally eaten with chopsticks or served in palm-size leaves of bok choy or romaine lettuce. In restaurants it is usually served on a bed of bean sprouts, chopped cabbage, or salad greens.

Mention regional foods to Hawaiians, and people think of poke. It is considered a local food or "local grind"—comfort food to the Hawaiians. Normally local food is not the cuisine that is served in upscale hotels and restaurants of Hawaii, but poke has crossed such boundaries. For centuries, Hawaiian fishermen cut their catch of raw fish into cubes and seasoned it with whatever ingredients they had. Modern versions make use of seasonings brought by the many different cultures of the Islands, such as soy sauce, onions, tomatoes, and chilies. Poke is so common in the Hawaiian culture, that you can stop at a local grocery store and choose from several freshly made varieties.

In September of each year, Sam Choy, one of Hawaii's most famous chefs, hosts an annual three-day poke festival. The contest draws over 2,000 entries from Western Canada, the Mainland United States, Hawaii, and the South Pacific. From these, seventy-eight entries are selected as finalists, with many wildly inventive variations of the basic poke. The public is invited to taste after the judging, and it does not take long for the poke to disappear amidst a murmur of mmmms and ahhhs.

# Ahi Tuna Poke

*2 pounds fresh or sashimi-grade ahi tuna steaks (or other firm
    white fish), cut into bite-size pieces\**

*½ cup soy sauce*

*¾ cup chopped green onions (tops included)*

*2 tablespoons sesame oil*

*1 tablespoon grated fresh ginger*

*1 to 2 chile peppers, cored, seeded, and finely minced*

*Coarse kosher salt to taste*

*1 tablespoon toasted sesame seeds\*\**

*1 tablespoon finely chopped toasted macadamia nuts\*\*\**

*Bok choy or romaine lettuce leaves*

\*    If you cannot buy freshly caught fish, purchase only fresh
    sashimi or sushi-grade fish. Sashimi-grade fish are con-
    sidered second only to live fish. Fish is graded on fat
    content, color, and freshness. The grades are listed as
    prime, choice, good, and so on, with sashimi grade as
    the prime grade.

\*\*   To toast sesame seeds: Place sesame seeds in a small
    dry saucepan over medium heat; stirring occasionally,
    toast 3 minutes or until golden brown (watch closely as
    seeds burn easily).

\*\*\*  To toast whole macadamia nuts: Spread whole nuts on a
    cookie sheet and toast in a preheated 300° oven for 5
    to 8 minutes or until lightly browned (watch closely, as
    nuts burn easily).

In a large bowl, combine tuna, soy sauce, green onions,
sesame oil, ginger, chile pepper, salt, sesame seeds, and
macadamia nuts; mix lightly. Cover and refrigerate at least 2
hours before serving. To serve, tear leaves into comfortable
holding sizes and spoon approximately 3 tablespoons of
poke onto each piece. Either eat with your fingers or use a
fork.

Makes 4 to 6 servings.

*Creative display of poke entries is part of the competition at the annual Sam Choy
Poke Festival. Courtesy Hapuna Beach Prince Hotel, Hawaii.*

# Rice Pilaf

A popular dish of the Carolinas is rice pilaf (also spelled pilau, purlow, and perloo). The word *pilau* comes from the Persian word *pilav* or *pilaw*. This technique for cooking rice originally came from the Middle East and was introduced to Africa by Arabs long before the African slave trade. Pilaf has been a popular dish in many southern states for three hundred years, particularly in South Carolina, where it is considered a signature dish. There are many variations from region to region and from cook to cook, with a variety of ingredients complementing the essential rice. The original recipes were made with the famous Carolina Gold Rice, but since Carolina Gold is very hard to obtain in today's market, it is generally now made with long-grain rice.

Most historians agree that the famous Carolina Gold Rice first arrived in Charleston (then known as Charles Towne), South Carolina, around 1685. It came by accident when a storm-battered ship sailing from Madagascar came into the Charles Towne harbor for repair. The captain of the ship, James Thurber, gave a bushel of rice as a gift to Dr. Henry Woodward, one of the original founding fathers of the Carolinas. Thus began a three-hundred-year history of Carolina Gold.

Original efforts to grow the rice failed until slaves, who had grown rice in Africa, showed the English how to grow it in wet areas. The plantation owners purchased slaves from various parts of Africa, but they preferred slaves from what they called the "Rice Coast" or "Windward Coast," the traditional rice-growing region of West Africa. Today, descendants of these slaves are known as Gullah in South Carolina and Geechee in northern Georgia. The cultivation process was labor intensive, and slaves performed most of the tasks. They came with their knowledge of how to cultivate rice and with their own traditions of cooking.

The rice flourished and was to become so important to South Carolina's economy that in the eighteenth century it was used for currency and was called "Carolina Gold." Hundreds of plantations, from Cape Fear River in North Carolina to northern Florida, grew Carolina Gold, with South Carolina's Lowcountry growing the most. The end of slavery was the end of rice growing in the South, as no labor pool was available to take the place of the slaves. Also, the ravages of hurricanes and competition from other crops moved rice cultivation westward to Louisiana and then to California.

## Rice Pilaf with Peas

*4 bacon slices*

*1 small onion, finely chopped*

*1 clove garlic, chopped*

*1 cup uncooked long-grain rice*

*1 (10-ounce) package frozen green peas*

*1 medium carrot, grated*

*2 cups liquid (chicken broth, water, wine, or combination)*

*1 teaspoon ground turmeric*

*2 teaspoons salt*

*¼ teaspoon black pepper*

*¼ cup slivered almonds*

*Sliced tomatoes for garnish*

1. In a large frying pan over medium heat, cook bacon until crisp. With slotted spoon, remove bacon to paper towels to drain; set aside. Dice bacon when cool. Pour off all but ¼ cup bacon drippings from the pan. Add onion and garlic to remaining bacon drippings and sauté 5 minutes or until soft, stirring occasionally.

2. Add rice, peas, carrots, liquid, turmeric, salt, and pepper; heat to boiling. Reduce heat to low; cover and simmer 20 minutes or until rice is tender. Remove from heat. To serve, toss rice mixture together with the reserved bacon and almonds until well mixed. Serve immediately on a warm plate; garnish with tomato slices.

Makes 4 to 6 servings.

# Shrimp and Grits

What has twenty legs, swims forward and backward, and glows in the dark? It's a shrimp, the most valuable seafood crop in South Carolina. In the Low Country of South Carolina and particularly Charleston, shrimp and grits has been considered a basic breakfast for coastal fishermen and families for decades during the shrimp season (May through December). Simply called "breakfast shrimp," the dish consisted of a pot of grits with shrimp cooked in a little bacon grease or butter. Before the 1930s, shrimp were primarily caught in bays and coastal inlets for use in home recipes and were referred to as "bugs." In fact, shrimp used to be sold door to door in Charleston by hawkers calling out "Swimpee, swimpee."

During the past decade, this dish has been dressed up and taken out on the town to the fanciest restaurants. Not just for breakfast anymore, it is also served for brunch, lunch, and dinner. Shrimp and grits is now served in various ways with other ingredients. One of the most popular versions in Charleston is creamy grits with shrimp.

## Creamy Grits with Shrimp

1 pound large raw shrimp, peeled and deveined*

1 cup heavy cream

2 cups water

1½ cups hot stock (shrimp, chicken, or vegetable)

¼ cup butter

Salt and black pepper to taste

1 cup stone-ground grits**

3 tablespoons fresh lemon juice

Salt and black pepper to taste

6 bacon slices

2 tablespoons finely chopped onion

1 clove garlic, minced

2 tablespoons finely chopped green or red bell pepper

* To add flavor, place the shells of the shrimp in a saucepan and cover with water. Simmer over low heat approximately 7 to 10 minutes. Remove from heat and strain the broth, discarding shells. Add shrimp broth to hot stock.

** If using quick-cooking grits (not instant), reduce cream to ½ cup and reduce stock to 1 cup.

1. In a large saucepan over medium-high heat, combine cream, water, and hot stock; bring to a gentle boil. Add butter, salt, and pepper. Slowly add grits, stirring constantly (so that the grits do not settle to the bottom and scorch), until all are added; reduce heat to medium-low. Cook for 20 minutes, stirring occasionally (be careful not to scorch mixture), or until the grits are tender. Grits should have absorbed all of the liquid and become soft and should have the same consistency as oatmeal (moist, not dry). If the grits become too thick, add warm stock or water to thin. Remove from heat.

2. Sprinkle shrimp with lemon juice, salt, and pepper; set aside. In a large frying pan over medium-high heat, cook bacon until brown but not crisp. Remove from heat and pat dry with paper towels; set aside. Coarsely chop bacon when cool. Reserve 4 tablespoons bacon grease in the frying pan. Add onion, garlic, and green or red bell pepper; sauté 10 minutes or until the onion is transparent. Add shrimp mixture and bacon; sauté 5 to 7 minutes or until shrimp are opaque in center (cut to test). Remove from heat. To serve, spoon hot grits onto individual serving plates and top with shrimp mixture.

Makes 4 servings.

# Swamp Cabbage/Hearts of Palm Salad

Bessie Gibbs, creator of the hearts of palm salad, was known to chastise customers who failed to clean their plate. She was famous for saying to customers, "After I worked so hard to cook you a nice dinner, I expect you to eat it. Now eat those vegetables!"

To be a true Floridian, you have to have eaten, at one time or another, hearts of palm or swamp cabbage. Hearts of palm come from the Sabal palmetto tree, also known as swamp cabbage or cabbage palm. The nickname swamp cabbage comes from the Seminole Indian dish of that name, which somewhat resembles cooked cabbage. It was long regarded as "poor people's" food and was popular during the Great Depression of the 1930s.

The hearts of palm resemble white asparagus and taste a lot like artichokes. They are available fresh in Florida where you can occasionally find them at local farmers' markets. Canned hearts of palm can be found in most supermarkets. In 1953, after years of controversy, the Florida legislature designated the Sabal palmetto the state tree. Although this tree grows wild, it is protected from indiscriminate cutting by its state tree designation. It was also adopted as the official state tree of South Carolina in 1939. These days, most palm hearts are grown, harvested, and canned as a cash crop throughout Central and South America, especially in Brazil and Costa Rica.

The central Florida town of Labelle hold an annual Swamp Cabbage Festival in February. Thousands of people come to hear music and dance, eat barbecue and hearts of palm, drink a little beer, and watch a huge Saturday-morning parade with floats decorated with Sabal palmetto fronds.

Cedar Key, a tiny island of the west coast of Florida, has made the hearts of palm salad famous. Gibby and Bessie Gibbs, who owned the Island Hotel and Restaurant from 1946 to 1973, created the salad. To this day, the salad is a regional treat and continues to be served at the Island Hotel. Other restaurants throughout Florida serve their own version of this famous salad. Because of the expense of preparing a salad of palm hearts, it is often called "millionaire's salad."

# Swamp Cabbage

This recipe comes from Margaret Davis of Merritt Island, Florida. Margaret has spent her life, eighty plus years, in Florida as, among other things, a wonderful country cook. She has stewed squirrel, roasted wild hog, baked every kind of fish, and prepared a thousand vegetables, including swamp cabbage. Margaret says, "The hardest part of preparing swamp cabbage is finding some to cook. Unless you know someone who's about to cut down a tree, you'll have to watch for signs along the old Florida highways offering it for sale or look for it in small town grocery stores."

*¼ pound fat back (white bacon), chopped fine*

*Swamp cabbage (hearts of palm), chopped or sliced\**

*½ cup water*

*Salt and freshly ground black pepper, to taste*

\*  This recipe is for swamp cabbage from one average palm, which provides about 2½ pounds.

In a large-heavy pot, fry bacon until crisp. Add swamp cabbage and water. Over medium-high heat, bring to a boil; reduce heat to low, cover, and simmer 15 to 20 minutes or until cabbage is tender. Remove from heat and season with salt and pepper. In a bowl, serve swamp cabbage hot with some of the broth.

Makes 6 to 8 servings.

# Hearts of Palm Salad

*2 (14-ounce) cans Hearts of Palm, drained and thinly sliced*

*2 cups chopped lettuce greens*

*Ice Cream Dressing (recipe follows)*

*1 medium pineapple, cubed*

*2 bananas, sliced*

*2 to 3 tablespoons chopped dates*

*Candied ginger for garnish*

In a salad bowl, combine sliced hearts of palm and lettuce greens; gently toss with Ice Cream Dressing. Place salad onto individual plates. Sprinkle pineapple, bananas, and dates over the top of each salad; garnish with candied ginger.

Makes 4 servings.

## ICE CREAM DRESSING

*½ cup softened vanilla ice cream*

*½ cup mayonnaise*

*1 tablespoon creamy peanut butter*

*1 drop of green food coloring (optional)*

In a blender or food processor, combine ice cream, mayonnaise, peanut butter, and food coloring; whirl 1 minute or until well blended. Store, covered, in the refrigerator. Serve at room temperature.

Makes 1 cup.

# Texas Caviar

Before the Civil War, black-eyed peas were used strictly as cattle feed. During the battle of Vicksburg, however, the town, which was under siege for more than forty days, had no supplies. According to legend, Yankee troops destroyed all the crops in the area but left the black-eyed peas because they considered them unfit to eat. To fend off starvation, the citizens of Vicksburg had to eat the humble peas. There are some people who believe that the South would have eventually won the war if a trainload of the peas that were being sent to the Confederate soldiers on the front lines had not been blown up. From that beginning, the ritual of eating black-eyed peas on New Year's Day continues as a gesture of humility. The folk belief is that those who eat black-eyed peas, a modest food, will prosper throughout the year.

Many people migrated to Texas from other parts of the South, and their traditions came with them. Texans have taken the New Year's Day tradition of eating black-eyed peas to a new height with their own Texas Caviar, a spicy relish made from pickling black-eyed peas. Texans gave the dish the tongue-in-cheek name of Texas Caviar, even though no fish eggs are involved. The first thing you must eat on New Year's Day is a dish made with black-eyed peas, and to most Texans it is Texas Caviar. Restaurants and clubs around Texas also serve this wonderful dish for their annual New Year's festivities.

The Texas town of Athens is considered the black-eyed pea capital of the world. During the late 1930s and early 1940s, several canning plants operated in town. For many years, the peas, labeled "Homefolks," were sold throughout the world. Even the famous department store chain Neiman Marcus carried pickled black-eyed peas. The canning plants closed in the early 1970s, but many of the area farmers and backyard gardeners still grow the peas. Athens now celebrates the black-eyed pea annually with a jamboree. The festival draws crowds from throughout Texas and surrounding states. Black-eyed peas are used to concoct a variety of dishes from cakes and pies to pizza and even wine.

## Texas Caviar

This is one of those wonderful recipes that you can add to or delete from, as you desire. If you don't have an ingredient or don't like one, just leave it out and substitute something else.

2 (16-ounce) cans black-eyed peas, drained and rinsed

¼ cup minced red bell pepper, cored and seeded

¼ cup minced green bell pepper, cored and seeded

2 cloves garlic, minced

1 bunch green onions (tops included), thinly sliced

1 jalapeño pepper, cored, seeded, and finely chopped

¼ cup chopped fresh cilantro or parsley leaves

2 large tomatoes, finely chopped

2 tablespoons red wine vinegar

1 tablespoon balsamic vinegar

⅓ cup extra-virgin olive oil

1½ teaspoons ground cumin

1 teaspoon salt

1 teaspoon freshly ground black pepper

1 tablespoon fresh oregano, basil, or thyme leaves, chopped

1. In a large bowl, combine black-eyed peas, red pepper, green pepper, garlic, green onion, and jalapeño pepper. Stir in cilantro or parsley and tomatoes.

2. In a blender or food processor, combine wine vinegar, balsamic vinegar, olive oil, cumin, salt, pepper, and oregano, basil, or thyme; whirl 1 minute or until well blended. Pour the vinegar mixture over the black-eyed peas mixture; stir to combine. Cover with plastic wrap and refrigerate at least 24 hours or up to 3 days (the longer it sits, the better it gets).

Serve with a slotted spoon to drain well. Serve with crackers or corn chips, or place on lettuce leaves on individual plates.

Makes 8 servings.

# Stone Crab Claws

Crack open a stone crab claw and discover one of Florida's ultimate crustaceans and one of the most popular shellfish. In season from October 15 through May 15, stone crab claws come in four sizes: medium, large, jumbo, and colossal. The latter not only looks impressive but commands the highest price.

Stone crabs are found along the coast from North Carolina to Texas, but the crab is more prolific in Florida waters. Its name comes from the rocklike, oval shape of the crab, of which only the claw meat is eaten. Fishermen simply twist off the claws and throw the crab back to grow new ones. This regeneration process can take from twelve months to two years, and during the life of a stone crab, the same appendage may be generated three or four times. Removing the claws in no way inhibits the crab's feeding capabilities, as the claws are used for defensive purposes only.

Stone crabs are usually cooked on the docks upon arrival in large vats of boiling water. Sometimes, they are cooked on the fishing boats. They are always sold cooked because freezing or icing raw stone crab claws causes the meat to stick to the shell.

The restaurant that started the stone crab craze and made stone crabs big business in South Florida is Joe's Restaurant in Miami. Every celebrity who comes to South Florida usually ends up at Joe's at least once during his or her stay. In 1921, a local researcher brought a burlap bag full of some strange-looking live stone crabs, and asked owner Joe Weiss to cook them. Not sure how to cook the crabs, Joe took a few and threw them in boiling water. After testing, they decided the crabs were better cold. The restaurant started serving them cracked with hash brown potatoes, cole slaw, and mayonnaise. To this day, this is the way stone crabs are served.

# Sandwiches

# Beef on Weck

Some people consider beef on weck—thinly sliced rare roast beef (piled as high as 6 inches) on a freshly baked kummelweck roll—the best roast beef sandwich in America. This sandwich is a staple of Buffalo, New York. Few, if any, restaurants outside the Buffalo area serve this sandwich or even know what it is.

This sandwich is sometimes called beef on wick, an alternative spelling usually used by older people and eastern suburbanites. The key to the sandwich is the German roll, called kummelweck, with chunks of salt and caraway seeds sprinkled on top. *Kummelweck* is simply shortened to weck. The sandwich is usually served with sinus-clearing horseradish (you can tell a native Buffalonian by the amount of horseradish he or she uses), a couple of huge kosher dill pickle slices on the side, and extra beef juice served straight from the roast. Wash it all down with a cold, locally brewed ale.

## Beef on Weck

1 (3- to 4-pound) beef roast (tenderloin, prime rib, or eye of round)

¼ cup olive oil

Salt and coarsely ground black pepper

Cornstarch Glaze (recipe follows)

8 kummelweck or kaiser rolls

2 tablespoons caraway seeds

2 tablespoons coarse kosher salt

Prepared horseradish

**1.** Preheat oven to 425°. Rub roast with olive oil, salt, and pepper. Place roast on a rack in a shallow baking pan, tucking the thin end under to make it as thick as the rest of the roast. Insert a meat thermometer into the thickest part of the roast. Bake, uncovered, 40 to 45 minutes or until thermometer registers 135°. Remove from oven and transfer to a cutting board; let stand 15 minute before carving. Reserve meat juice, and carve meat into very thin slices.

**2.** Reduce oven temperature to 350°. Brush the prepared Cornstarch Glaze on the top of each kummelweck or kaiser roll; sprinkle equal amounts of caraway seeds and coarse salt over the top. Place rolls on a baking sheet and heat in the oven for 3 minutes or until tops of the rolls get crusty and the caraway seeds and salt begin to stick. Remove from oven, and cut rolls in half.

**3.** To assemble sandwiches, divide sliced beef on the bottom half of each roll; spoon with reserved beef juice. Serve open-faced with horseradish on the side.

Makes 8 sandwiches.

## CORNSTARCH GLAZE

½ cup cold water

1 tablespoon cornstarch

In a small saucepan over medium-high heat, stir together water and cornstarch. Heat mixture to a gentle boil. Reduce heat to low, and stir until mixture thickens and is translucent. Remove from heat and cool.

# Bierocks/Runzas

These savory sandwiches are basically the same with just a few variations in the shape and size of the dough. Both are yeast doughs (bread pockets) with a filling of beef, cabbage or sauerkraut, onions, and seasonings. They come in different shapes—half-moons, rectangles, rounds, squares, triangles, and so on. The official Nebraska runza is always rectangular, and the bierocks of Kansas are buns.

If you travel in Nebraska, you will find eateries called runza—sometimes a place name, often the specialty of the house. In 1949, Sarah "Sally" Everett and her brother, Alex Brening, opened the first Runza Drive-Inn in Lincoln, Nebraska. The trade name and trademark of Runza Restaurants now belong to Donald R. Everett, Sarah's son.

Both the bierock and the runza have German-Russian roots going back to the eighteenth century. Recipes were passed down from one generation to the next, eventually finding their way to the Midwest, particularly Kansas and Nebraska. Originally bierocks were served to the field workers for lunch. Today bierocks are enjoyed any time and can be found at just about every church fund-raiser in the Kansas area.

## Bierocks/Runzas

1 loaf prepared white bread dough

2 tablespoons butter

2 cups thinly sliced green cabbage

1 small yellow onion, chopped

½ pound lean ground beef

½ teaspoon salt

⅛ teaspoon black pepper

1 tablespoon all-purpose flour

1 egg, beaten

¼ teaspoon caraway seeds

**1.** Thaw bread dough if frozen, or make the equivalent amount using your favorite bread recipe. Let dough rise.

**2.** In a large frying pan over medium-high heat, melt butter. Add cabbage and onion; stir until they are coated with butter. Cover the pan and cook 10 minutes or until vegetables are tender, stirring occasionally. Increase heat to high and add ground beef; cook, stirring frequently, until beef loses its pink color. Reduce heat to medium; stir in salt, pepper, and flour. Cook an additional 1 minute, stirring constantly. Remove from heat; set aside.

**3.** Lightly grease a baking sheet. On a lightly floured surface, cut bread dough into 4 to 6 equal pieces. With floured rolling pin, roll and stretch each piece into an oval about ⅛ inch thick. Spoon beef mixture onto center of each dough piece. Pull up the corners of the dough and pinch seams together to hold the mixture inside. Place seam side down on prepared baking sheet; set aside, cover, and allow to rise for 20 to 30 minutes. Preheat oven to 350°. Brush with beaten egg, and sprinkle with caraway seeds. Bake 25 minutes or until golden brown. Remove from oven and serve warm or at room temperature.

Makes 4 to 6 servings.

# Breakfast Tacos

**When a person is hungry, he only thinks about tortillas.**

*—Mexican-American saying*

Breakfast tacos or burritos are available at many restaurants across Texas and the Southwest. The breakfast taco is a fried tortilla that is rolled and stuffed with a mixture of seasoned meat, eggs, or cheese, and other ingredients such as onions and salsa. Much like sandwiches, these tacos can be as simple or complex as imagination allows. They are served for breakfast, lunch, or dinner, and they have gone mainstream to meet demands.

The tortilla, a thin, round bread made of corn or wheat flour, is the basis of many southwestern dishes. It is the plate and spoon at Mexican–American meals, used to layer and wrap other ingredients or to scoop up food.

Corn tortillas were made long before European settlers introduced wheat flour to the New World. They were a traditional food among southwestern Indian tribes, created as a way to preserve their harvested corn kernels from one season to the next. According to a Mayan legend, a peasant of ancient times invented tortillas for his hungry king.

Four tortillas are the foundation of Mexican border cooking and a relatively recent import. Their popularity was driven by the low cost of inferior grades of flour provided to border markets and by their ability to keep and ship well. Taqueria or taco trucks are found throughout the West and Southwest. There are two kinds of taco trucks: traveling trucks that cruise around neighborhoods and business areas, and non-cruising trucks parked permanently in lots.

## Breakfast Tacos

*6 flour or corn tortillas*

*2 tablespoons butter*

*1 small onion, chopped*

*1 clove garlic, minced*

*¼ teaspoon ground cumin*

*6 eggs, beaten*

*½ cup prepared salsa, divided*

*1½ cups shredded Cheddar cheese, divided*

1. Preheat oven to 350°. Wrap stacked tortillas in aluminum foil and heat in oven 15 minutes or until hot. To microwave, wrap a stack of tortillas lightly in paper towels and warm on high for 6 or 7 seconds per tortilla.

2. In a large frying pan over medium heat, melt butter. Add onion, garlic, and cumin; sauté until onion is soft. Pour in beaten eggs and ¼ cup salsa; scramble egg mixture until eggs are thickened and no visible liquid remains; remove from heat.

3. Remove tortillas from oven. Using tortillas, one at a time (keep tortillas covered as you work with them), spoon scrambled egg mixture into center of each tortilla; sprinkle with approximately 3 tablespoons of Cheddar cheese. Fold tortillas and serve with remaining salsa and Cheddar cheese.

Makes 6 servings.

# Buffalo Burgers

Today, the only place you will see buffalo roaming freely are on large ranches on the Plains and in Rocky Mountain regions. The buffalo is no longer considered an endangered species, and buffalo ranchers are raising them by the thousands. Buffalo burgers taste great, and many people feel that buffalo is the most flavorful meat they have every eaten. It has a sweeter and richer flavor than beef and is not gamey. Many consider this the meat of the new millennium.

The mighty American bison, or Plains buffalo, once roamed the plains. It is estimated that nearly sixty million head roamed at one time over a third of the entire landmass of North America. It was not unusual for a herd to comprise four million animals and graze an area covering some 1,000 square miles.

Over the vast prairies, the buffalo provided food, clothing, and shelter for the Plains Indians. In the late 1800s, many buffalo were massacred for their hides and in an effort to subdue the tribes who had come to depend on bison for meat. In 1866, General Philip Sheridan, who was in charge of the United States forces in the West, stated, "If you kill the buffalo, you kill the Indian." Without food, the tribes had no choice but to retreat to the reservations the U.S. government had set aside for them.

## Buffalo Burgers

*1 pound ground buffalo meat*

*Salt and black pepper to taste*

*4 hamburger buns, split in half*

Preheat barbecue grill. Divide ground buffalo meat into four patties, at least ½ inch thick. Place patties on hot grill (grill buffalo over a low charcoal heat, not in the flames). Cover barbecue with lid, open any vents, and cook 6 to 8 minutes; turn patties over and cook another 6 to 8 minutes. Season patties with salt and pepper. Lightly grill the inside of the buns. Remove patties and buns from grill; place patties on buns and serve with your favorite condiments.

*Note: The leanest grades of ground buffalo may require a little more moisture. Place a small amount of butter on the top of each patty while cooking.*

Makes 4 servings.

## Did You Know?

The explorers Meriwether Lewis and William Clark wrote about the many buffalo herds they observed during their 1804–1806 expedition across western America. When encountering one herd at the White River (in today's South Dakota) in 1806, they wrote "The moving multitude . . . darken the whole plains."

# Cornish Pasties

**The devil is afraid to come to Cornwall, for fear of being baked into a pasty.**

*—old Cornish saying*

The Cornish people who migrated to Michigan's Upper Peninsula (between Lakes Michigan and Superior) in the mid-nineteenth century to work in the copper mines brought the interesting and delicious pasty with them. Imagine a miner, overwhelmed by hunger and fatigue, opening his dinner pail to the aroma of a still warm pasty filled with beef and vegetables. The miners would reheat the pasty on a shovel held over the candles worn on their hats. The copper mines of Butte, Montana, also lured a large number of Cornish miners to the area. Pasties remain a local favorite there as well.

The pasty (pronounced PAS-tee) is now a favorite of other national groups and there is an unspoken rivalry as to who makes the best. Some cooks use a suet-lard crust, while others a regular pie crust. What goes with a pasty is the good old American tradition of ketchup and a dill pickle.

The Michigan legislature declared May 24 as Michigan Pasty Day. Today pasty stores dot the landscape of the Upper Peninsula, much like hamburger stands in the rest of the country. You can even order a homemade pasty on the Internet. There is a saying that all pasty lovers agree on: "A pasty is properly made when the juice runs off your elbow as you eat it."

A pasty is like a pot pie—an individual pie filled with meats and vegetables. Some were even made with a dual mixture, savory at one end and sweet at the other. In the case of the dual mixture, the housewife would distinguish one end from the other by marking the meat end with an X. Before the introduction of lunch pails, pasties were wrapped in a crib bag, an all-purpose cotton mesh pouch, used to keep the freshly baked pasty warm and crisp.

The identifying feature of the pasty is the pastry itself and its crimping (the solid ridge of pastry, hand crimped along the top). The miners of Cornwall, England, would hold the pasties by these crusts, then throw the crusts away after they had eaten the body of the pasties. The crusts weren't wasted though; the miners were firm believers in knockers (ghosts or mischievous little people of the mines), who would cause all manner of misfortune unless they were placated with a small amount of food. The miners left their pasty crusts behind for the knockers, who could prove to be a source of good luck if they were fed.

# Cornish Pasties

This pasty recipe comes from Kim Miller of Newberg, Oregon. A native of Traverse City, Michigan, Kim says that she does not know which family member this recipe originally came from, but that it has been passed down and shared by three generations of women in her family since the late 1930s.

*Pasty Crust (recipe follows)*

*1 beef bouillon cube*

*½ cup hot water*

*5½ cups diced potatoes*

*2 medium carrots, shredded*

*1 medium onion, finely diced*

*½ cup finely diced rutabaga\**

*1 pound lean ground beef*

*½ pound lean ground pork*

*1 teaspoon black pepper*

*1½ teaspoons salt*

*Tomato ketchup*

\*  Turnips may be substituted.

**1.** Make Pasty Crust. Preheat oven to 425°.

**2.** In a large bowl, dissolve beef bouillon cube in hot water. Add potatoes, carrots, onion, rutabaga, ground beef, ground pork, pepper, and salt; gently stir until well mixed. Place 1½ cups of filling in the center of each rolled dough rectangle; bring short (6-inch) sides together and seal by crimping edges together. Make 3 or 4 small slits in the top of the pasty to allow steam to escape during cooking.

**3.** Place pasties onto a large ungreased baking sheet. Bake 45 to 55 minutes or until golden brown; remove from oven.

**4.** Can be served warm, but real Michiganites eat their pasties cold with tomato ketchup. They make a great sack lunch and freeze well.

Makes 6 pasties.

## PASTY CRUST

*4½ cups all-purpose flour*

*1 teaspoon salt*

*1 cup solid vegetable shortening or lard*

*1¼ cups chilled water*

In a large bowl, sift together flour and salt. With a pastry blender or two knives, cut vegetable shortening into flour mixture until particles are the size of small peas. Sprinkle in water, a little at a time, tossing with fork until all flour is moistened and pastry dough almost cleans side of bowl. Form dough into a ball and cut dough into 6 sections. On a lightly floured surface with a floured rolling pin, roll out each section into 6 x 8-inch rectangles. Fill and bake as directed in recipe.

# Cuban Sandwich

Tasty, toasted Cuban sandwiches are Miami's favorite snack. These treats can be found in most Miami restaurants, but the best places to buy them are from street corner-snack bars, called loncherias. The sandwiches have a submarine-style layering of ham, roast pork, cheese, and pickle between a sliced length of Cuban bread. The key to a great, versus a good, Cuban Sandwich lies in the grilling. A great Cuban sandwich is grilled in a sandwich press (called a plancha) until the ham, pork, and pickles have warmed in their own steam. (Cuban restaurants use a sandwich press, but you can substitute a waffle iron.) These sandwiches use no mayonnaise, lettuce, onions, bell peppers, or tomatoes; however, butter and mustard are optional. Cuban sandwiches are sold hot (pressed) or cold (room temperature).

In Miami, the community known as Little Havana hosts a large Cuban population that fled to the United States after the 1959 Cuban revolution. The community keeps alive the rich culinary traditions of Cuba and has altered the eating style of South Florida. People who have not tried Cuban food sometimes think it is similar to Mexican cuisine. But Cuban food is not hot. It does not rely on chili pepper and cheese, but uses spices that are unique and without "heat." It is more like Spanish cooking than Mexican cooking.

## Cuban Sandwich

*1 loaf Cuban bread**

*Prepared yellow mustard*

*½ pound baked ham, thinly sliced*

*½ pound roast pork, thinly sliced*

*8 thin dill pickle slices*

*½ pound Swiss cheese, thinly sliced*

\* Italian or French bread may be substituted.

Slice the bread horizontally to open. Spread a thin layer of mustard on top and bottom halves of bread. Arrange ham, pork, pickle slices, and Swiss cheese evenly over the bread. Cover the sandwiches with the top halves of the bread. Cut into 4 sandwiches.

**Sandwich Press:** Grill sandwiches in a hot buttered sandwich press until flat, bread is browned, and cheese has melted. Remove from heat; cut each sandwich in half and serve immediately.

**Waffle Iron:** Turn over metal plates to the flat surface. Place sandwich in hot buttered waffle iron, close cover, and grill for 3 minutes on each side.

**Griddle:** Place sandwich on a hot griddle, and position a heavy iron skillet or bacon press on top of the sandwich. Flatten the sandwich to about ¼ of its original size. Grill the sandwich for 2 to 3 minutes on each side.

Makes 4 servings.

*Cuban sandwich served with beans and rice on the side.*
©1986–2001 Great American Stock.

**I'll Have What They're Having**

# Fish Tacos

The people of San Diego, California, have been hooked on fish tacos since 1983. In fact, fish tacos are the fast-food signature dish of San Diego: They're cheap to buy and fast to make.

Fish tacos were created by Ralph Rubio, who first tasted them while on spring break in Baja, Mexico. According to the story he tells, there was one Baja vendor he especially liked, a man named Carlos, who ran a hole-in-the-wall taco stand with a 10-foot counter and a few stools. Carlos fried fish to order and put it on a warm tortilla. Customers added their own condiments. Rubio tried to persuade Carlos to move to San Diego, but Carlos was happy where he was and would not budge. He did agree, however, to share his recipe, which Rubio scrawled on a piece of paper pulled from his wallet. Several years later, Rubio opened his own restaurant in San Diego, called Rubio's—Home of the Fish Taco. Today, fish tacos are legendary and are sold throughout San Diego and the Southwest.

## Grilled Fish Tacos

Recipe from Brad Bolton of San Diego, California.

*1 pound fresh, mild white fish fillets (snapper, halibut, mahi, swordfish, sea bass, tuna)*

*⅓ cup fresh lime juice*

*3 tablespoons tequila (optional)*

*12 small corn tortillas*

*Salt and freshly ground black pepper*

*Juice of 1 lime*

*1 cup shredded cabbage (green, purple, or combination)*

*1 bunch fresh cilantro leaves, chopped*

*1 jalapeno chile pepper, cored, seeded, and finely chopped (optional)*

*Prepared salsa*

**1.** Place fish fillets in a large glass bowl or resealable plastic bag; pour ⅓ cup lime juice and tequila over the fish; turn to coat. Marinate in the refrigerator for 1 hour, turning occasionally.

**2.** Preheat barbecue grill. Preheat oven to 350°. Wrap stacked tortillas in aluminum foil and heat in oven 15 minutes or until hot. To microwave, wrap a stack of tortillas lightly in paper towels and warm on high for 6 or 7 seconds per tortilla.

**3.** Remove marinated fish from the refrigerator and pat dry with paper towels. Season both sides of the fish with salt and pepper. Brush grill liberally with olive oil or spray with vegetable spray. Place prepared fish on the grill, turning once, and cook 8 to 10 minutes or until the fish is slightly opaque at thickest part (cut to test). Remove from grill and transfer onto a cutting board. With two forks, shred or flake the fish.

**4.** To serve, place some of the flaked fish in the center of each tortilla. Sprinkle a generous amount of lime juice over the fish; add cabbage, cilantro, chile pepper, and salsa to taste.

Makes 12 fish tacos.

# French Dip Sandwich

Connoisseurs of French dip sandwiches would not think of going anywhere else for one than "Philippe the Original" in Los Angeles. Although the French dip sandwich is not French, the inventor, Philippe Mathieu, was. In 1918, Philippe owned the L. A. delicatessen and sandwich shop called Philippe the Original (still open for business). According to the story at the restaurant, Philippe was preparing a sandwich for a police officer one day and accidentally dropped the sliced French roll into the drippings of a roasting pan. The customer liked the sandwich and came back the next day with some friends to order the sandwich "dipped" in the meat pan. The French dip was born.

The French dip is a beef sandwich on a long, white French roll that is dipped into pan juices. American menus often describe the pan juice as "au jus." *Au jus* is French for "with broth" or "with juice."

## French Dip Sandwich

*1 (4-pound) beef rib eye, sirloin, or tenderloin roast*

*½ cup coarsely ground pepper*

*Dipping Sauce (recipe follows)*

*8 French rolls*

*Butter*

1. Preheat oven to 425°. Place beef roast onto a rack in a shallow baking pan; firmly press pepper onto roast. Bake, uncovered, 30 to 45 minutes or until thermometer in the thickest part of roast registers 135°. Remove from oven and transfer onto a cutting board; let stand 15 minutes before carving; slice beef thinly. Reserve juice and pour into a medium saucepan. Prepare Dipping Sauce.

2. For each sandwich: Cut French rolls in half. Toast and butter each French roll. Layer about ½ pound of sliced beef on bottom slice of each French roll; place remaining tops of rolls on top of the beef. Slice sandwiches in half and serve on individual plates with a small bowl (¼ cup) of hot Dipping Sauce.

Makes 8 sandwiches.

### DIPPING SAUCE

*Drippings from cooking pan*

*1 (10.5-ounce) can beef broth*

*½ cup water*

*Salt and pepper to taste*

In a medium saucepan, add beef drippings, beef broth, water, salt and pepper; bring just to a boil. Turn off heat, cover, and let sit 10 minutes before serving.

# Hoagies

The hoagie was originally created in Philadelphia, Pennsylvania, where it has been declared the "Official Sandwich." In other parts of the United States, it's known as a sub, hero, bomber, po' boy, grinder, torpedo, or rocket. Hoagies are built-to-order sandwiches filled with fresh meats and cheeses, as well as lettuce, tomatoes, and onions, topped off with a dash of oregano-vinegar dressing on an Italian roll. A true Italian hoagie is made with Italian ham, prosciutto, salami, and provolone cheese, along with the works.

There are a number of different stories as to how the hoagie got its name, but no matter what version is right (historians cannot seem to agree), all maintain that it started in Philly.

The most widely accepted story centers on an area of Philadelphia known as Hog Island, which was home to a shipyard during World War I. The Italian immigrants working there would bring giant sandwiches made with cold cuts, spices, oil, lettuce, tomatoes, onions, and peppers for their lunches. These workers were nicknamed "Hoggies." Over the years, the name was attached to the sandwich as well, but with a different spelling.

Another variation of this story says that workers at Hog Island did bring this type of sandwich, but it was never called a hoagie. The story goes that one day an Irish worker, who everyday carried an American cheese sandwich, looked enviously at his coworker's lunch and said: "If your wife will make me one of those things, I'll buy it from you." The Italian worker went home and said to his wife, "Tomorrow, make two sandwiches—one for me and one for Hogan," which was his coworker's name. So everyone started calling the sandwich Hogans, which eventually got shortened to hoagie.

A third story says that during the Great Depression, out-of-work Philadelphian Al DePalma went to Hog Island near the naval shipyards in South Philly to find work. When he saw the shipyard workers on lunch break wolfing down their giant sandwiches, his first thought was "Those fellas look like a bunch of hogs." Instead of applying for a job at the shipyard, DePalma opened a luncheonette that served big cold cut sandwiches, listed on the menu as "hoggies" (so named for the hogs he saw during that lunch hour). During the late 1930s, DePalma joined forces with Buccolli's Bakery and developed the perfect hoagie roll (an 8-inch roll that became the standard for the modern-day hoagie). By World War II, Al DePalma turned the back room of his restaurant into a hoagie factory to supply sandwiches round the clock to workers at the shipyard, DePalma became known as "The King of Hoggies." At some point after World War II, the "hoggie" became the "hoagie." It is said that because his customers kept calling them hoagies, he changed the name.

## Italian Hoagie

*2 teaspoons red wine vinegar*

*2 teaspoons dried oregano*

*1 tablespoon extra-virgin olive oil*

*4 hoagie or French rolls, cut in halves*

*Mayonnaise*

*¼ pound prosciutto or baked ham, thinly sliced*

*¼ pound bologna slices*

*¼ pound salami, thinly sliced*

*¼ pound provolone or fontina cheese, thinly sliced*

*1 large tomato, thinly sliced*

*1 small onion, thinly sliced*

*½ green bell pepper, cored, seeded, and thinly sliced*

*12 dill pickle slices*

*4 romaine lettuce leaves, shredded*

1. In a small bowl, add red wine vinegar and oregano; slowly whisk in olive oil until emulsified; set aside.

2. From the center of each half roll, remove some of the bread. Spread each half of roll with mayonnaise. Place the meats and then the cheese in layers on top of the mayonnaise on four of the halves. Top with tomatoes, onions, green bell peppers, dill pickles, and the lettuce. Drizzle with the prepared vinegar dressing. Top each with the other half of roll. Serve immediately.

*Makes 4 sandwiches.*

# Horseshoe Sandwich

Springfield, Illinois, has a favorite sandwich. Called the Horseshoe, this sandwich will make your arteries cringe and your taste buds rejoice. The secret to this sandwich is in the sauce, and area restaurants and chefs seem to have their own secret cheese sauce recipe.

The sandwich starts with two or three slices of thick toasted bread. On top of that you have two traditional choices: a thick fried ham steak or two large hamburger patties. A generous amount of cheese sauce is poured over the top of the meat, then hot french fries top and encircle each sandwich.

It is generally accepted that the sandwich was created in 1928 by the chefs at the Leland Hotel in Springfield. The shape of the ham prompted the name, with the fries representing the horseshoe nails and the heated steak platter as the anvil. A Pony Shoe is half a Horseshoe (usually one slice of toast).

## Horseshoe Sandwich

*Frozen french fries*

*Cheese Beer Sauce (recipe follows)*

*8 slices toasted white bread*

*Sliced baked ham or 8 cooked hamburger patties*

*Dash of ground paprika*

**1.** Prepare frozen french fries according to package directions. Prepare Cheese Beer Sauce.

**2.** To assemble sandwich: Place 2 slices of toasted bread side by side on individual serving platters; top with either ham slices or cooked beef patties, cover with Cheese Beer Sauce, and mound a large amount of french fries on top and along the sides. To garnish, sprinkle with paprika. Serve immediately.

Makes 4 servings.

### CHEESE BEER SAUCE

*2 egg yolks*

*½ cup beer*

*2 tablespoons butter*

*3 cups shredded sharp Cheddar cheese*

*1 teaspoon Worcestershire sauce*

*¼ teaspoon dry mustard*

*½ teaspoon salt*

*½ teaspoon freshly ground black pepper*

*½ teaspoon red (cayenne) pepper*

In a small bowl, combine egg yolks and beer until mixed; set aside. In the top of a double boiler over hot water, melt butter and Cheddar cheese. Add Worcestershire sauce, dry mustard, salt, pepper, and cayenne pepper; stir until well mixed. Add egg mixture, a little at a time, stirring constantly. Cook and stir until mixture thickens and begins to bubble around the edges. Remove from heat and keep warm until sandwiches are assembled.

# Limburger Sandwich

You can tell you are approaching Monroe, Wisconsin, when cheese factories and dairy cows begin to appear all over the countryside. Just veer off the highways onto Wisconsin's back roads to discover the dozens of small, quality cheese producers. One cheese in particular stands alone in Monroe. That is Limburger, undoubtedly one of the stinkiest cheeses in the world. Limburger actually smells worse than it tastes. For many people though, the aroma is both the beginning and the end of the acquaintance. This cheese gets more pungent with age, but despite its aroma, Limburger cheese has legions of fans.

The people of Wisconsin have such affection for strong-smelling Limburger that their state is probably the only place in America where you can go into a tavern and order a Limburger on rye bread with raw onions and brown mustard. The sandwich is usually served on freezer paper and is traditionally washed down with a locally brewed beer. Some places even give you a breath mint.

Although Limburger originated in Belgium, most Limburger today comes from Germany. Cheese-making began in Wisconsin around 1840, when immigrants with cheese-making skills began arriving in the area. A group of Swiss immigrants settled in Green County, around Monroe, and began producing the same cheese they had enjoyed in their homeland. In 1867, Rudolph Benkerts, Green County's first cheese maker, began making Limburger in his home cellar. By 1880, Limburger was being made at twenty-five cheese factories in Green County, and by 1930, there were more than a hundred companies producing it. Today, only one company in the United States still makes it, the Chalet Cheese Co-op of Monroe, Wisconsin.

*Limburger cheese gives the pungent sandwich its punch.* ©2001 Wisconsin Milk Marketing Board, Inc.

## Limburger Sandwich

My father, Kenneth Stewart, loved Limburger sandwiches. As a young girl, whenever Dad would eat one of his strong-smelling sandwiches, my brothers and I would cover our noses and make funny noises as he shooed us off.

*2 slices rye bread (dark, light, or pumpernickel)*

*Prepared brown mustard*

*Limburger cheese, sliced*

*Thick slices of sweet onion*

To assemble sandwich, spread mustard on rye bread slices; layer with Limburger cheese and sweet onion slices. Serve with your favorite beer.

Makes 1 sandwich.

# Hot Brown

**Lunchtime favorite was always the Hot Brown. Maybe two hundred people would be eating lunch, and 190 of them would be eating Hot Brown sandwiches.**

—*Fred Caldwell, head waiter of the Brown Hotel*

Chef Fred K. Schmidt at the Brown Hotel (later renamed Camberley Brown Hotel) in Louisville, Kentucky, invented the Hot Brown sandwich in 1926. Wealthy Louisville businessman J. Graham Brown (1881–1969), built the hotel as a tribute to his brother. In the 1920s, the Brown Hotel drew more than 1,200 guests each evening for its dinner dance. The band would play until late. When the band took a break, people would retire to the restaurant for a bite to eat. Bored with the traditional ham and eggs, Chef Schmidt delighted his guests by creating the Hot Brown.

The following story, about the creation of the Hot Brown sandwich, by Rudy Suck, hotel manager during the 1920s, was given to me by the Camberley Brown Hotel:

The Hot Brown was developed three or four years after the hotel opened when the supper dance business was falling off. The band would play from 10:00 P.M. until 1:00 A.M. When they took a break, around midnight, people would order food. It was usually ham and eggs.

We decided we needed something new. The chef, Fred K. Schmidt, said, "I have an idea for an open-faced turkey sandwich with Mornay sauce over it." At that time turkeys were only used at Thanksgiving and Christmas, and they had just started selling them year-round.

I said, "That sounds a little flat." The chef said, "I'm going to put it under the broiler." The maître d' said, "It should have a little color, too." So Schmidt said, "We'll put two strips of bacon on top of it." I said, "How about some pimiento." That's how the Hot Brown came to be.

Today the Hot Brown sandwich is still a Louisville favorite and still the signature dish of the Camberley Brown Hotel. A visit to Louisville is not complete without tasting this wonderful sandwich.

*The Hot Brown sandwich served alongside a display of the Brown Hotel's history.*
Courtesy the Brown Hotel, Louisville, Kentucky.

# Original Hot Brown

This is the recipe presently used at the Camberley Brown Hotel in Louisville, Kentucky.

6 tablespoons butter

6 tablespoons all-purpose flour

3 cups milk

½ cup freshly grated Parmesan cheese

1 egg, room temperature and beaten

Salt and black pepper to taste

½ cup prepared whipped cream

8 slices toasted white bread, crust trimmed off

1 pound cooked turkey breast, thinly sliced

Grated Parmesan cheese for topping

1 (2-ounce) jar diced pimientos, drained

8 bacon slices, fried crisp

**1.** In a large saucepan over medium heat, melt butter. Gradually add flour, stirring constantly, until smooth and free from lumps. Gradually stir in milk until sauce comes to a gentle boil, stirring constantly; remove from heat. Add Parmesan cheese and stir until melted and well blended.

**2.** In a small bowl, beat egg. Gradually add 1 cup of hot sauce, ⅓ cup at a time, to the egg, stirring constantly. Gradually add egg mixture to remaining sauce, stirring constantly until well blended; add salt and pepper to taste. Fold in whipped cream.

**3.** For each Hot Brown sandwich, place two slices of toasted bread on a metal (or flameproof) dish. Cover the toast with a liberal amount of turkey. Pour a generous amount of sauce over the turkey. Sprinkle with additional Parmesan cheese. Place entire dish under a broiler until the sauce is speckled brown and bubbly. Remove from broiler, sprinkle with diced pimientos, cross two pieces of bacon over the top, and serve immediately.

Makes 4 servings of two open-faced sandwiches each.

# Boiled Lobster/Lobster Roll

Lobster is the definitive king of Maine seafood. New Englanders love their lobsters, especially boiled or steamed whole, or made into a lobster roll. Order lobster boiled or steamed at a restaurant and you will get a plastic bib, a nutcracker (for the claws), a pick (for the legs), drawn butter (for dipping), and a bowl (for the rest). If you order a stuffed lobster, you are immediately tagged as a tourist. A trip along the Maine coast is considered incomplete until you've stopped at a local roadside stand or restaurant for a boiled lobster or a lobster roll. Lobster rolls, which are basically lobster salad on a hot dog bun, can range from the almost virginal "hot lobster roll" that contains nothing more than chunks of warm lobster meat stuffed into a hot dog roll to the contemporary creations with jalapeño peppers.

Lobsters used to be so plentiful that Native Americans used them to fertilize their fields and to bait their hooks for fishing. During the seventeenth and eighteenth centuries, lobsters were considered "poverty food." To feed anyone lobster was considered demeaning. Seasonal dock workers insisted on a contract that they would be fed only a minimum amount of lobster meat, preferring beef and pork. Lobster was so commonly used as a food for servants and prisoners that Massachusetts passed a law forbidding its use as prison food more than twice a week, as a daily lobster dinner was considered cruel and unusual punishment.

In the nineteenth century, lobsters gained their status as a luxury food item, mostly as a result of their popularity with the wealthy. Since that time, lobsters have become big business and perhaps are the most recognized symbol of New England fishing.

According to regional legend, John D. Rockefeller, Sr. (1834–1937), American industrialist and philanthropist, rescued the lobster in 1910. The legend is that a bowl of lobster stew, meant for the servants' table, was accidentally sent upstairs, where it was rapturously received. From then on, it was given a permanent place on Rockefeller's menu. During the 1900s in New York, what was good enough for John D. was good enough for the rest of society.

*All the fixings needed for a traditional lobster dinner. Nathanael Greene photo.*

# Boiled Lobsters

Nothing tastes quite like a lobster, and nothing is as succulent when properly prepared. Usually, the simpler the preparation, the better. Serve with corn on the cob and barbecue baked beans.

**1.** Using ¼ cup salt per quart of water, bring water to a boil in a large pot. One at a time, plunge the live lobsters head first into boiling water. *(Note: Hold them behind the heads and pincers, taking care not to be pinched.)* When all of the lobsters have been put in the pot, cover the pot. Let the water return to a boil, then reduce heat to low and simmer 10 to 15 minutes for a small-sized lobster (1 to 1¼ pounds), 15 to 20 minutes for a medium-sized lobster (1½ pounds), or 20 minutes for a large-sized lobster (2 pounds). Lobsters are cooked when they turn reddish or bright red.

**2.** When cooked, remove lobsters from pot and allow to cool just long enough to be handled. Separate the head from the tail. Cut lobster tail down the center (from the shoulder down toward the tail) with cutlery shears, removing black vein from down the back, small sack in the back of the head, and spongy lungs. Crack the claws with a claw cracker (nut crackers also work). *(Note: Don't forget to provide a scrap bowl when serving.)* Serve with lots of melted butter.

# Lobster Rolls

*2 cups flaked lobster meat*

*2 tablespoons mayonnaise*

*¼ cup celery, finely chopped*

*Salt and black pepper to taste*

*4 hot dog buns*

*Melted butter*

*Dill pickles*

*Potato chips*

**1.** In a large bowl, blend lobster meat and mayonnaise. Add celery, salt and pepper; mix gently to combine. Place in the refrigerator until ready to use.

**2.** Lightly spread hot dog buns with melted butter. In a large frying pan over medium-low heat, cook for 2 minutes or until golden brown; turn and toast the other side. Remove from heat and fill buns with lobster mixture. Serve with dill pickles and potato chips.

Makes 4 servings.

---

### Did You Know?

Alice B. Toklas (1877–1967), American writer and cook, liked to keep several live lobsters in the bath tub of the Paris home she shared with Gertrude Stein. Her logic was simple: "In addition to having a supply of lobsters on hand, it prevented [Ernest] Hemingway from jumping into the bathtub when he was drunk."

# Muffuletta

**Do not make a stingy sandwich. Pile the cold-cuts high, customers should see salami coming through the rye.**

*—Allan Sherman (1924–1973), American musical humorist*

A New Orleans muffuletta is made with a round loaf of Italian bread with a unique, eye-catching olive salad. It is considered as much a signature sandwich as the po' boy (see page 156). In New Orleans, it is pronounced either "muff-uh-LOT-uh" or "moo-foo-LET-ta," with a nickname of simply "muff."

It is the olive salad that gives the sandwich its special flavor. Imagine a sandwich that is almost as wide as a Frisbee and so high that it is hard to bite into. A true muffuletta must always be served at room temperature, never toasted or heated.

Muffulettas can be found all over New Orleans, from delis to pool halls and corner grocery stores. The Central Grocery on Decatur Street claims to have invented this sandwich in 1906. They started making sandwiches for the men who worked at the nearby wharves and produce stalls of the French Market. The sign over the covered sidewalk proudly proclaims, HOME OF THE ORIGINAL MUFFULETTA. Central Grocery's biggest competitor, Progress Grocery, is just two doors away. The Progress Grocery started in 1924 as an offshoot of Central Grocery. Their sign proclaims the FINEST MUFFULETTA. To this day, tourists and locals line up at both stores out into the street, waiting for their sandwiches. Muffulettas are more than just sandwiches, they're a tourist attraction, especially during Mardi Gras.

## Muffuletta

*1 round loaf Muffuletta Bread (recipe follows) (10-inch diameter)\**

*Olive Salad (recipe follows)*

*Extra-virgin olive oil or marinade from Olive Salad*

*2 ounces salami, thinly sliced*

*2 ounces prosciutto or baked ham, thinly sliced*

*2 ounces Provolone cheese, thinly sliced*

\*Italian bread may be substituted.

**1.** Make Muffuletta Bread and Olive Salad.

**2.** Cut bread in half crosswise, and scoop out about half of the soft dough from top and bottom pieces (this is to provide more room for the sandwich ingredients). Brush the inside bottom of loaf with olive oil or marinade from the Olive Salad. Layer salami, prosciutto, and Provolone cheese on the bottom piece. Top with as much Olive Salad as will fit without spilling out. Add top of loaf and press down gently. Slice in quarters and serve.

Makes 1 to 4 servings.

## MUFFULETTA BREAD

*1 cup lukewarm water (110° to 115°)*

*1 tablespoon sugar*

*1½ teaspoons salt*

*2 tablespoons extra-virgin olive oil*

*3 cups bread flour or all-purpose flour*

*3 teaspoons instant active dry yeast*

*Yellow cornmeal*

*Sesame seeds*

*Olive oil*

**1.** Using a mixer with dough hook, place water, sugar, salt, olive oil, flour, and yeast in a bowl. Beat until smooth. If using a bread machine, add the same ingredients, select dough setting, and press Start. When dough cycle has finished, remove dough from pan and turn out onto a lightly oiled surface. Form dough into an oval, cover with plastic wrap, and let rest for 10 minutes.

**2.** After resting, turn dough bottom side up and press to flatten. Form dough into a 1-inch-high circle and place on a baking sheet dusted with cornmeal. Press sesame seeds into surface of dough and brush with olive oil. Cover with plastic wrap and let rise in a warm place 30 to 50 minutes or until doubled in size.

**3.** Preheat oven to 425°. After rising, bake loaf for 10 minutes. Reduce heat to 375° and bake 15 minutes or until loaf sounds hollow when tapped. A good check is to use an instant thermometer to test bread. The temperature should be about 200°. Remove from oven and cool completely on a wire rack before slicing.

Makes 1 loaf.

## OLIVE SALAD

*⅔ cup pitted and coarsely chopped green olives*

*⅔ cup pitted and coarsely chopped kalamata olives*

*1 (2-ounce) jar diced pimiento*

*3 cloves garlic, minced*

*1 anchovy fillet, mashed*

*1 tablespoon capers, drained and rinsed*

*½ cup finely chopped fresh parsley leaves*

*1 teaspoon finely chopped fresh oregano leaves*

*½ teaspoon freshly ground pepper*

*½ cup extra-virgin olive oil*

In a medium bowl, combine all the ingredients, then allow the flavors to mingle for at least 1 hour prior to serving. Store, covered, in the refrigerator until ready to use.

# Navajo Fry Bread & Indian Tacos

As with many cultures around the world, Native Americans have an all-purpose flat bread that is a staple of their cuisine. Fry bread is considered a food of intertribal unity and is made at all Indian powwows. The dough is a variation of that used for flour tortillas, consisting of wheat flour, shortening, salt, and water, leavened with baking powder or yeast. Navajo Fry Bread is a tradition in Arizona and New Mexico, and fry bread with honey butter is a specialty in New Mexico.

Although considered a "traditional food," Navajo fry bread actually evolved in the mid-nineteenth century. Beginning in 1860, approximately eight thousand Navajos spent four years imprisoned at Fort Sumner, New Mexico, and were given little more than white flour and lard to eat. American scout Kit Carson and his troops drove the Navajo people from their lands by destroying their means of survival. They killed sheep, goats, and horses; poisoned wells; burned orchards and crops; and destroyed shelters and anything else that was of value to the Navajo. Carson and his troops then rounded up thousands of starving Navajo and sent them on the "Long Walk" to Fort Sumner at Bosque Redondo, New Mexico, one of the saddest events in United States history. The U.S. government provided those on the reservation with wheat flour as part of a commodities program. Because of this, lard and wheat flour became the main ingredients in the making of Navajo fry bread. The Navajo women had to make the best of what was often considered poor-quality rations in reservation camps and the varying availability of government-issued commodities. They thus created fry bread.

Indian fry bread is the foundation of a popular dish called Indian tacos. Originally known as Navajo tacos, they have been adopted by other tribes. The Navajo taco was voted the State Dish of Arizona in a 1995 poll conducted by the Arizona Republic newspaper.

Every weekend, from April through October, thousands of Native Americans throughout the United States and Canada pack up their cars and head to powwows. Indian tacos are the universal modern powwow food. They are also popular attractions at many fairs, festivals, and outdoor summer shows held in the Southwest. People will line up to wait their turn to buy some freshly made tacos.

Indian tacos are a combination of beans or ground beef, chopped lettuce, sliced tomato, shredded Cheddar cheese, and optional green chile atop plate-sized rounds of crispy Navajo or Indian fry bread. No plates or silverware are needed, as you just fill the fry bread with your desired fillings, roll it up, and eat.

# Navajo Fry Bread

*2 cups all-purpose flour*

*2 teaspoons baking powder*

*¼ cup instant nonfat dry milk*

*¼ teaspoon salt*

*Warm water*

*Vegetable oil*

*Honey or powdered sugar*

**1.** In a large bowl, combine flour, baking powder, dry milk, and salt. Slowly add enough warm water to form a workable dough (start by adding 1 cup of water, then more if needed); knead until smooth but still slightly sticky. Cover the bowl with plastic wrap and let the dough rest at room temperature for 30 minutes or up to 2 hours. After resting, divide dough into 4 equal pieces. On a lightly floured surface, roll each piece into a small ball and pat into a flat circle about 8 inches in diameter and ¼ inch thick (it will puff up a lot); cut a steam vent in the middle of each circle of dough.

**2.** In a large, deep frying pan, heat 1 to 2 inches of vegetable oil (enough oil to float the dough) to 375°. Fry the dough pieces, one at a time and turning once, for 2 minutes on each side or until golden brown (the bread will puff slightly and become crisp and brown). Remove from hot oil and drain on paper towels. Keep warm until ready to serve. Use for Indian Tacos (recipe follows); or serve with honey or powdered sugar.

Makes 4 Navajo fry breads.

# Indian Tacos

*1 pound lean ground meat (beef, lamb, venison, or pork)*

*1 cup diced onion*

*4 cooked Navajo Fry Breads*

*1 head iceberg lettuce, shredded*

*3 tomatoes, diced*

*2 cups shredded sharp Cheddar cheese*

*1 (3-ounce) can diced green chiles, drained*

*Sour cream (optional)*

**1.** In a large frying pan over medium-high heat, brown ground meat and onions until cooked; remove from heat.

**2.** Place Fry Bread, cupped side up, on separate plates. Layer ground meat, lettuce, tomatoes, Cheddar cheese, and green chiles onto top of each Fry Bread. Top with sour cream, if desired, and either roll up or serve open-faced with a fork.

Makes 4 servings.

# Philadelphia Cheese Steak

A cheese steak sandwich is not really a steak at all—it's a sandwich made with chipped steak (steak that has been frozen and sliced really thin) and cooked on a grill top. Locals think in terms of steak sandwiches with or without cheese. Without cheese, the sandwich is referred to as a "steak." With cheese, it's a "cheese steak" or "cheesesteak." Cheese Whiz is the topping of choice for serious steak connoisseurs. However, you can also use provolone cheese.

The Philadelphia cheese steak is truly one of the most delightful and beloved foods available in Philadelphia, Pennsylvania. It is said by most Philadelphians that if a restaurant offers something called a "Philly Cheese Steak," then it's not authentic. According to locals, you simply cannot make an authentic Philadelphia Cheese Steak sandwich without an authentic Philadelphia roll. The rolls must be long and thin, not fluffy or soft, but also not too hard. Of course, they also say that if you are more than one hour from South Philly, you cannot make an authentic sandwich.

During the 1930s, in the Italian immigrant section of South Philly, Pat Olivieri sold hot dogs and sandwiches. Business was not doing well, so he decided to make lunch for himself. He had a slab of steak that he could not cook on the hot dog grill. So he sliced it thin, then put it on the grill, added some onions for taste, and put it onto a roll. Pat never got a bite because a cab driver drove by, smelled the sandwich, and asked "how much?" Pat didn't know what to charge, so he said a nickel. After paying for and enjoying the sandwich, the cab driver supposedly said, "Hey . . . forget about those hot dogs, you should sell these." Thus the Philadelphia steak sandwich was born. It was not until twenty years later that a longtime employee, Joe Lorenzo, who was tired of the usual sandwich, added cheese to the meat filling.

## Philadelphia Cheese Steak

2 tablespoons vegetable oil

2 medium onions, sliced as thin as possible and rings separated

½ cup sliced mushrooms

12 ounces chipped steak (thin sliced eye of round, rib eye, or sirloin tip roast)*

Salt and coarsely ground black pepper

Cheese Whiz or provolone cheese slices

1 Italian, French, or hoagie roll

Dill pickle spears

*Freeze steak before slicing. Slice it paper thin.

1. In a large frying pan over high heat, add olive oil and heat so that a drop of water will sizzle when you drop it in the oil; lower heat to medium. Add onions and mushrooms; stir and cook until mushrooms darken and onions start to look transparent. Add steak slices and cook for 3 minutes or until meat lightly browns. Add salt and pepper to taste. Heap cooked meat mixture in a long pile across pan. Lay cheese slices over meat until melted. If using Cheese Whiz, melt in a double boiler or in the microwave.

2. Slice bread lengthwise. Using a spatula, scoop meat mixture and cheese and lay on bread with cheese on top. If using melted Cheese Whiz, ladle it on top. Slice sandwich into 2 or 4 pieces, and serve with a dill pickle spear.

Makes 2 servings.

# Soft-Shelled Crab Sandwich

In the Chesapeake Bay area, the fried soft-shelled crab sandwich is considered a true delicacy. Soft-shelled crabs are renowned all over the world, but savored in Maryland as a delicious local tradition. Around the first full moon of May, crabs start to molt (the process of shedding their old shell to grow a new one). Before the new shells form, the crabs are harvested. Because they are available only in the spring and early summer, devotees of this specialty seek out restaurants that serve them.

To the uninitiated, a sandwich with pointy legs hanging from it looks like something you would be more inclined to squish than to swallow. But once you try it, you are certain to be a convert.

The blue crab is the only type that is commercially harvested for soft shells. When shedding occurs, the crab expands by one-third. Finding these crabs when they are large enough to eat (5 to 7 inches) and just about to molt takes skill. They are kept in special tanks in crab shantys and watched constantly as they complete the shedding process. Once molted, the soft-shell crab should be quickly removed from the saltwater before it repeats the cycle, as it will continue to harden within a few hours. Once the crab is cleaned or dressed, the entire crab is edible.

## Soft-Shelled Crab Sandwich

*4 large soft-shelled crabs, dressed\**

*½ cup all-purpose flour*

*Salt and freshly ground black pepper*

*3 tablespoons butter*

*2 tablespoons vegetable oil*

*4 slices white bread or round rolls (such as kaiser rolls)*

*Tartar sauce*

*Lettuce*

\*  To dress a soft-shell crab, first cut crab across in an upward angle so that the eye sockets and scaly section of the lower mouth are removed. Then lift each side of the shell and remove gills. Turn crab over and cut off the bottom apron.

**1.** In a shallow bowl or plate, mix flour with salt and pepper. Dredge crabs in seasoned flour, shaking off any excess.

**2.** In a large frying pan over medium-high heat, add butter and vegetable oil; heat until hot. Fry the seasoned crabs 2 to 3 minutes per side or until brown and crisp. Remove from pan and drain on paper towels. Spread tartar sauce on one side of each of the 4 pieces of bread or rolls. Use 1 crab and a couple of leaves of lettuce per sandwich. Serve with additional tartar sauce.

Makes 4 servings.

# Po' Boy Sandwich

**I have always believed that New Orleans jazz can be exported; it's the oyster loaves that won't travel.**

*—Calvin Trillin, American journalist and author, from his book Alice Let's Eat, 1978*

Po' boy sandwich, considered a New Orleans institution, is the generic name for the standard New Orleans sandwich made with French bread. Never say "poor boy"—that's a give-away that you're a tourist. The sandwich can be filled with fried oysters, shrimp, fish, soft-shelled crabs, crawfish, roast beef and gravy, roast pork, meatballs, smoked sausage—just about anything. It's served either "dressed," with a full range of condiments (usually mayonnaise, lettuce, and tomatoes), or "undressed," (plain with just butter). This sandwich is purely American in its variety of sauces and condiments, but uniquely New Orleans, especially made with local oysters and crisp French bread.

According to some accounts, it was created by Madame Begue, owner of a coffee stall in New Orleans' Old French Market, in 1895. She took a long, thin loaf of French bread, slit it in half lengthwise, buttered it generously, sliced it in thirds or fourths (not cutting through the bottom crust), and put a different filling into each section. The name is said to derive from the pleas of hungry youths who begged, "Please give a sandwich to a po' boy."

It is also said that the sandwich was invented in 1919 by two brothers, Clovis and Benjamin Marin, at their restaurant in the French Market. This sandwich extravaganza began during a local transit workers' strike. The two brothers took pity on those "poor boys," or union members, and began offering sandwiches made from leftovers to any workers who came to their restaurant's back door at the end of the day. For five cents, a striker could buy a sandwich filled with gravy and trimmings (end pieces from beef roasts) or gravy and sliced potatoes.

Soon the sandwich, which quickly became known as the po' boy, was being filled with seafood such as fried oysters and shrimp. Shellfish were abundant and cheap in the 1900s, and at lunch or snack time, a po' boy filled with oysters was easier to eat and digest than one filled with roast beef.

## Oyster Po' Boy Sandwich

*1 cup yellow cornmeal*

*1 cup all-purpose flour*

*Red (cayenne) pepper to taste*

*Salt and black pepper to taste*

*24 shucked oysters, drained*

*Vegetable oil for deep-frying*

*2 loaves French bread (approximately 8 inches long)*

*1 cup mayonnaise or tartar sauce*

*2 cups shredded iceberg lettuce*

*12 tomato slices*

*12 dill pickle slices*

*Hot pepper sauce*

**1.** In a heavy-duty plastic bag, combine cornmeal, flour, cayenne pepper, salt, and pepper. Working in batches of 6, coat oysters with cornmeal mixture, knocking off excess. In a heavy pan, heat 1½ inches of vegetable oil to 375°. Fry oysters in batches of 6, turning occasionally, 1½ to 2 minutes or until golden and just cooked through (when done, oysters will curl and firm slightly). Transfer oysters, using a slotted spoon, to paper towels to drain.

**2.** Halve bread loaves lengthwise, then cut each loaf in half to make 8 pieces. Pull out some of the bread in the interior of each piece of bread. Spread the inside of each piece of bread with 2 tablespoons mayonnaise or tartar sauce.

**3.** To make sandwiches, top each bottom half of bread with ½ cup lettuce, 6 oysters, 3 tomato slices, and 3 dill pickle slices; sprinkle with hot pepper sauce to taste. Top each with remaining bread, pressing together gently.

Makes 4 servings.

# Slugburgers

Eating slugburgers is a matter of preference, not of practicality. You either love 'em or hate 'em. In fact, some people actually crave 'em. Don't worry, slugburgers are not made from terrestrial gastropods, commonly called slugs. These burgers get their name from the slang term for a nickel used during the 1930s and 1940s. For many years, slugburgers sold for a nickel each.

During the Great Depression and World War II, beef was scarce, and rationing resulted in some pretty weird recipes. To make ground beef go further, fillers such as cereal, potatoes, flour, cornmeal, soybeans, and onions were added. Today, the beef mixture for the slugburger is made into small patties, which are fried once in hot grease, then frozen until needed. They are then fried once again when the slugburger is ordered. Because they are small, about the size of a cookie, people order two or three dozen at a time. They are traditionally served topped with mustard, dill pickles, and onions on a small-sized hamburger bun.

Corinth, Mississippi, seems to be the birthplace of these hamburgers. In Corinth, slugburgers are still very popular, with an annual Slugburger Festival held every year. Young women compete for the title of Miss Slugburger. In Corinth, if you go into a restaurant and order a hamburger, a slugburger is what you will get. To actually get a traditional hamburger, you must specify a "beef burger."

# Spiedie

If you find folks who know of spiedies, they are most likely originally from Binghamton in Broome County, New York, or they know someone who is. Broome County is in New York's Southern Tier, southeast of the Finger Lakes and just north of Pennsylvania. People who live in the area eat spiedies at restaurants or from street vendors, buy them from supermarkets, and make their own at backyard cookouts. They even hold an annual Spiedie Cook-Off. Spiedies have been completely integrated into the food culture of the region, and natives who have moved

*A traditional spiedie sandwich.*
Courtesy Lupo's Spiedies and the Spiedie Fest Balloon Rally, Binghamton, New York.

away from the area have been known to have commercial spiedie sauce shipped, by the case, to their new homes.

The name comes from the Italian *spiedo*, meaning "kitchen cooking spit." Spiedies (pronounced SPEE-dees) are not shish kebabs despite similarities. Originally made with just lamb, they are now made with any meat. Spiedies were a peasant food, a favorite with foreign-born workers on the railroad and at the local shoe factory. They originated with Binghamton's Italian immigrant population in the 1920s. Spiedies normally consist of chunks of lamb, pork, chicken, beef, or venison that have been marinated for days in a tart sauce, then grilled on metal skewers, usually over charcoal or gas. The traditional way of serving the meat is between sliced Italian bread with extra sauce poured on top. The spiedie, skewer and all, is inserted in sliced Italian bread. The bread is used as a sort of mitt wrapped around the meat. Pull out the skewer and you have a wonderful, delicious hot sandwich.

The distinctive smell of the meat cooking makes spiedies hard to forget. This wonderful smell and unique taste are primarily due to the marinade. Marinade secrets are passed down through families, and everyone argues the merits of commercial brands.

## Spiedie

*2 pounds meat (chicken, lamb, pork, or beef)* *

*1 cup extra-virgin olive oil*

*¼ cup lemon juice*

*¾ cup red wine vinegar*

*2 tablespoons sugar*

*4 cloves garlic, minced*

*1 bay leaf*

*¼ teaspoon red (cayenne) pepper*

*1½ teaspoons dried thyme*

*1½ teaspoons dried basil*

*1½ teaspoons dried oregano*

*½ teaspoon salt*

*½ teaspoon coarsely ground black pepper*

*1 loaf Italian or French bread, thickly sliced*

Metal skewers

* Use boneless and skinless chicken breasts, pork tenderloin, top round steak, or leg of lamb.

1. Cut meat into 1½-inch bite-sized cubes. In a large bowl, combine olive oil, lemon juice, vinegar, and sugar. Add garlic, bay leaf, red pepper, thyme, basil, oregano, salt, and pepper; stir until well blended.

2. Place prepared meat in a large resealable plastic bag set into a shallow dish. Pour marinade mixture over meat and close bag. Marinate in the refrigerator for at least 24 hours and up to 3 days; turn bag occasionally to distribute marinade. Remove meat from refrigerator and let stand in marinade at room temperature for 1 hour; drain, reserving marinade.

3. Preheat barbecue grill. Thread 4 to 5 cubes of meat onto each metal skewer. Place onto hot grill and cook 8 to 10 minutes or until done to your preference, basting with reserved marinade. Remove from grill and serve immediately. To serve, fold the bread over the contents of the skewer and pull the skewer out, leaving the meat sandwiched within the bread. Eat and enjoy.

Makes 6 servings.

# Walleye Sandwich

**Do not tell fish stories where the people know you; but particularly, don't tell them where they know the fish.**

—Mark Twain, American writer

They call it a fever and it strikes the strongest of fishermen every spring from April through July during spawning season in the Great Lakes region. The cure is simple—go walleye fishing! When the walleye spawning ritual is complete, these battered and exhausted fish move to the deepest part of the lake to rest for four to ten days. After the rest period, the walleyes are extremely hungry, and that's when they move back to their spawning areas and the early spring action is at its best. As the water temperature rises and the spawn ends, in mid-July and August, the fish start moving into deeper and colder waters.

Walleye's delicate meat is white and flaky and no matter how it is prepared, it is delicious. One of the locals' favorite ways to eat walleye is in a sandwich. A day of fishing would not be complete without a traditional shore lunch featuring freshly caught walleye from the icy waters. Thin fillets are breaded and either deep-fried, grilled, or pan-fried, and served in a fresh French loaf or on a hamburger bun with lettuce, tomato, and tartar sauce. The walleye sandwich is also a favorite at the many fishing lodges, pubs, and restaurants in the Great Lakes region.

The walleye, a member of the perch family, is the most sought-after eating fish in Minnesota, Wisconsin, and Michigan. The walleye takes its name from its unusual marblelike eye, which appears transparent in certain light. Because of the eye structure, walleyes are extremely light sensitive. Their large eyes help them easily find their prey. Anglers enjoy walleye year-round. During the day, these fish often rest on the bottom of the lake or hover in the shade of submerged objects or in the shadows of deep water. They emerge at dusk to feed over shallow weed beds or rocky shoals. In mid-summer, they often remain near the bottom, even at night. The best fishing times are early evening, early morning, and just after midnight

## Walleye Sandwich

4 (4- to 6-ounce) skinless, boneless walleye fillets

¼ cup liquid (water, milk, cream, white wine, or beer) of your choice

1 egg

½ cup all-purpose flour

½ cup saltine cracker crumbs or dry bread crumbs

1½ teaspoons baking powder

1 teaspoon salt

1 teaspoon freshly ground black pepper

2 teaspoons ground paprika

Vegetable oil

4 hamburger buns

Lettuce leaves

Sliced tomatoes

Tartar sauce

1. Rinse fillets and pat dry with paper towels; cut into sizes appropriate for sandwiches. In a flat dish, beat the liquid of your choice and egg until well blended. In another flat dish, combine flour, cracker or bread crumbs, baking powder, salt, pepper, and paprika until smooth.

2. Dip fillets into the egg mixture, then into the breading mixture (pat breading onto the fillets with your fingers), shaking off excess. Place the breaded fillets in a single layer on a platter or pan; refrigerate for 30 minutes (this will allow the breading to set).

3. Preheat oven to 150°. In a large frying pan, heat ½ inch of vegetable oil to 365°. Add the breaded fillets and fry 3 to 5 minutes on each side, turning once, or until fish flakes easily with a fork and is golden brown. Remove from hot oil and drain on paper towels. Keep warm, uncovered, in the oven.

4. Serve on hamburger buns with lettuce leaves, sliced tomatoes, and tartar sauce.

Makes 4 sandwiches.

# Desserts

Cookies & Candies
Cakes
Pies
Puddings

# Apple Candy

**Love is a fruit in season at all times, and within reach of every hand.**

—*Mother Teresa (1910–1997), Roman Catholic nun and humanitarian*

Aplets are a delicious Northwest candy that is made with gelatin, walnuts, and apples. Developed by two Armenian men, Armen Tertsagian and Mark Balaban, who bought an apple farm (called Liberty Orchards) in the small town of Cashmere in eastern Washington, Aplet candies are considered a Northwest delicacy.

Times were tough in 1918 for most orchardists, and Tertsagian and Balaban searched for new ways to make use of their surplus fruit. Apple dehydration seemed a logical first move, and coinciding with America's involvement in World War I, the orchard owners began providing apples for U.S. soldiers. After the war, they remembered the popular eastern candy they had loved as children called rahat locum or Turkish delight. After much research and development on their kitchen stove, they perfected a delicious apple and walnut recipe that they called Aplets. In 1963, at the Seattle World's Fair, they introduced hundreds of thousands of people from outside the Northwest to this candy.

Captain Aemilius Simmons, who planted seeds at Fort Vancouver in Washington, introduced apples to the Pacific Northwest in 1825. Previously, Captain Simmons attended a farewell banquet in his honor in London. At this party, a young lady slipped some apple seeds into his pocket and bade him plant them in the wilderness. Some time after his arrival at Fort Vancouver, he handed the seeds over to Dr. John McLoughlin, chief agent of the Hudson's Bay Company. Dr. McLoughlin, delighted by the gift, gave the seeds to his gardener to plant. His first tree produced only one apple, but the seeds of that single fruit bore future generations of hardier stock. The state of Washington is now the top producer of apples in the United States.

Hood River, Oregon, is also known for its abundant apple orchards. In 1908, Sydney Babson traveled around the state seeking "just the right spot" to start his apple orchard. He carefully tended his tiny apple seedlings as he traveled with only a small tent and his pack. He believed that when his eyes beheld just the right location for his orchard, he would receive "a sign from God." Emerging from his tent one morning, he looked toward the beauty of Mount Hood. Babson took this as the sign he was looking for and began to plant his orchards. Today, the Hood River Valley is one of the major growers of apples.

## Northwest Apple Candy

Here is my version of this favorite Northwest candy.

*1 cup grated (Red or Golden) Delicious apples*

*2 cups sugar*

*2 tablespoons unflavored gelatin*

*5 tablespoons cold water*

*⅛ teaspoon rose culinary essence\**

*1 cup finely chopped walnuts*

*Powdered sugar*

\* Culinary essence can be found in Asian or Indian grocery and spice stores. If you are unable to find culinary essence, substitute 1 tablespoon lemon juice.

**1.** Grease an 8-inch-square pan. In a large saucepan over medium heat, combine apples and sugar. Bring to a boil; boil 1 minute, stirring constantly. Turn heat to low and simmer another 30 minutes, stirring constantly. Remove from heat.

**2.** In a small bowl, combine gelatin and water; add to apple and sugar mixture, stirring constantly until dissolved. Add culinary essence and walnuts; stir until well blended. Pour into prepared pan; cool at least 2 hours but preferably overnight. With an oiled knife, cut into 1-inch squares, then roll in powdered sugar. Store, covered, in refrigerator.

Makes 64 candy squares.

**I'll Have What They're Having**

# Goo Goo Clusters

Goo Goo Clusters are a southern favorite and the first candy bar to combine milk chocolate, caramel, marshmallows, and peanuts. The Standard Candy Company in Nashville, Tennessee, has made them since 1912. Brian Hillman, director of marketing at the company, sent me the following history of Goo Goo Clusters:

In 1912, Howard Campbell, a Tennessee candy maker and owner/founder of Standard Candy Company, developed "America's First Combination Candy Bar." He was the very first confectioner to make a candy bar with multiple ingredients. He made Goo Goo Clusters by combining peanuts, caramel, marshmallow, and milk chocolate together into a delicious round cluster. They were originally sold unwrapped in big glass candy jars.

Soon after Campbell developed his new candy, word spread quickly about this tasty treat. People didn't know how to ask for or what to call this candy. Campbell was extremely excited that his newest concoction was the talk of the town, but even he was baffled as to what to call it. One day, he was discussing his dilemma with a fellow passenger, while riding a streetcar to work. The lady passenger, a school teacher, remarked that the candy bar is "so good, people will ask for it from birth." Thinking about what the woman said, he recalled the first sounds his newborn son made; "Goo Goo!" Goo Goo Clusters were officially a hit.

To promote the new candy bars, Campbell advertised them as "A Nourishing Lunch for a nickel!" Obviously, times have certainly changed from the 1920s and 1930s. Parents today wouldn't be too happy with their youngsters if they ate candy bars for lunch. But during the depression, Goo Goo Clusters were a great value for the many folks who did not have much money.

# Hawaiian Mochi

**For every new food you try, you add seventy-two days to your life.**

—*Japanese saying*

Hawaiians are crazy about mochi, a traditional Japanese chewy confection made from sweet brown rice flour. When visiting Hawaii, look past the poi and mai tai drinks and you'll find delicious local foods that include the beautiful pastel mochi. In Hawaii, mochi confections are filled with peanut butter, pumpkin, strawberries, mango, and whatever else sounds good to the maker.

Every Hawaiian cookbook seems to be full of new versions of mochi incorporating the many diverse cultures of the Islands. When mochi is used in the title (like butter mochi) it means that some form of the sweet rice flour is a key ingredient. A favorite and easy-to-make homemade mochi is a butter mochi cake that contains coconut milk and is served like brownies. In recent years, mochi ice cream has become popular. Mochi ice cream consists of two golf ball sized mounds of flavored ice cream encased in mochi. Unlike a bowl of ice cream, no spoon is needed since the mochi keeps the ice cream frozen so you can eat it with your fingers.

People of Asian descent have been living in Hawaii for many generations, immigrating to work in sugar plantation fields beginning in the 1880s. (By 1924, so many Japanese had come to the Islands that they constituted more than 40 percent of the population.) One of the many ritual foods Japanese–Americans eat, the Hawaiian mochi symbolizes long life and wealth. Traditionally, mochi is made by pounding the steamed glutinous rice in a large wooden mortar. Most people now purchase these candies ready-made at specialty stores and supermarkets. New cooking appliances and products have enabled mochi makers to cut the time needed to make this confection. A microwave mochi-maker can cut the traditional process from two hours to fifteen minutes.

## Hawaiian Butter Mochi

*3 cups (1 pound) mochiko (sweet rice flour)*

*2½ cups sugar*

*1 tablespoon baking powder*

*2 (12-ounce) cans coconut milk\**

*5 eggs*

*½ cup butter, melted*

*1 teaspoon vanilla extract*

*\* 1 (12-ounce) can evaporated milk may be substituted for 1 (12-ounce) can of coconut milk.*

Preheat oven to 350°. Butter a 13 x 9-inch baking pan. In a large bowl, combine sweet rice flour, sugar, and baking powder. In another large bowl, combine coconut milk, eggs, butter, and vanilla extract; add to flour mixture and combine until smooth. Pour mixture into prepared pan. Bake for 1 to 1½ hours or until a toothpick inserted in the middle comes out clean. Remove from oven and cool on a wire rack before cutting. Cut into brownie-sized squares to serve. *(Note: Store cooled mochi bars in a loose-lidded container for 2 to 3 days in warm weather and up to 5 days in cool weather.)*

Makes 24 pieces.

# Texas Pecan Pralines

**I want no monument of stone or marble, but plant at my head a pecan tree and at my feet an old-fashioned walnut. And when these trees shall bear, let the pecans and walnuts be given out among the plain people of Texas so they may plant them and make Texas a land of trees.**

*—James Hogg (1852–1906), former governor of Texas*

One of the favorite sweets of the South, particularly Texas, is pecan pralines. Pecan pralines were introduced to Texas by the French Louisianans and were originally considered a digestive aid to be taken at the end of a sumptuous dinner. The name is derived from a French diplomat, Marechal du Praslin (1598–1675), whose butler is said to have advised a similar confection prepared with almonds and white sugar as an antidote to overeating.

In its American adaptation, almonds were exchanged for pecans and the white sugar for brown. The making of pecan pralines by Mexican-Americans provided a major source of income, especially during the Great Depression of the 1930s. The gathering of pecans and the making of candy required a lot of labor, but no more capital than a cooking pot and some sugar. Once, nearly every Mexican restaurant in Texas served the old-fashioned pecan praline.

Texas and northern Mexico are the original home of the native pecan tree, and Texas leads the nation in the production of pecans. Texas adopted the pecan as its state tree in 1919.

Long before the first European settlers arrived in the Texas area, pecans were an important part of many Southwest Native American tribes' diets. Archaeological evidence indicates that pecans have been used for at least 8,000 years. Some tribes in the Southwest concentrated in the river valleys in the fall to harvest pecans. They depended on the pecan as their major food resource for about four months of the year.

Cabeza de Vaca (1490–1556), a Spanish explorer, was probably the first European to set foot in what is today the American Southwest. In his report to the Spanish authorities, he commented that he had been saved from starvation during the murderous winter of 1532 by pecans. The Spanish colonists and Franciscan missionaries were the first settlers in northern Mexico to cultivate the pecan in the early 1700s.

Most early Texas settlers considered pecans fit only for hog food, and it wasn't until around 1882 that a San Antonio baker, Gustave Duerfer, began including pecans in his cakes and cookies. His baked goods proved to be popular with customers. Duerfer began to ship the nuts to eastern states and created a market for shelled pecans. San Antonio became a pecan center for the next half century.

## Texas Pecan Pralines

*2 cups sugar*

*2 cups firmly packed light or dark brown sugar\**

*1 cup evaporated milk*

*2 cups pecan halves*

\* The type of brown sugar used will determine the color of the pralines.

**1.** In a large saucepan over medium heat, combine sugar, brown sugar, and milk; cook, stirring constantly until candy thermometer reaches 236° or when a small amount of sugar mixture dropped into very cold water separates into hard but not brittle threads. Immediately remove thermometer and remove sugar mixture from heat; set saucepan in a large pan of cold water to cool.

**2.** When sugar mixture has almost cooled, beat with a spoon 1 minute or until it begins to lose its gloss. Immediately stir in pecans and drop by tablespoonfuls onto buttered wax paper. Work quickly before mixture sets. If it thickens up, just place pan back on low heat to re-soften. When the pralines cool and become firm, wrap individually in aluminum foil or plastic wrap and store in covered container.

Makes 36 small or 20 large pralines.

# Sugar on Snow/Leather Aprons

**Grandma stood by the brass kettle and with the big wooden spoon she poured hot syrup on each plate of snow. It cooled into soft candy, and as fast as it cooled they ate it. They could eat all they wanted, for maple sugar never hurt anybody.**

—Laura Ingalls Wilder (1867–1957), American writer, from her book Little House in the Big Woods, 1932

From the first of March to the middle of April, as winter turns into spring, you will hear farmers saying, "Guess the sap will run today." After gathering the sap and boiling it down, there will be a "sugarin' off" with a large feast. The main dish, however, is sugar on snow, also called leather aprons—maple syrup cooked just enough to set in little pools on hard-packed snow, then popped into the mouth. The syrup forms a thick, waxlike confection that is chewy and ice cold. Visitors to sugar houses during the sugar season are often treated to this flavorful taffy-like treat.

Maple sugar was important to the early colonists, as it was something that could be made on their own farms or in nearby "sugar woods" at the end of a cold winter before spring planting. Most sugaring was done in outdoor camps that were set up in groves of maple trees.

Most likely Native Americans discovered the sweetness of the maple tree by eating "sapsicles," the icicles of frozen maple sap that form from the end of a broken twig. As the ice forms, some of the water evaporates, leaving a sweet treat hanging from the tree.

Native Americans also were the first to discover that sap from maple trees could be processed into maple sugar and syrup. Although there are no authenticated accounts, there are several interesting legends. According to one popular legend, a tribal chief supposedly hurled his tomahawk (probably in disgust) at a tree. The tree happened to be a maple, and sap began to flow. The clear liquid that dropped from the wound was collected in a container that happened to be on the ground below. His wife, believing the liquid to be water, used it to cook venison. Following cooking, both the meat and the sweet liquid that remained were found to be delicious. The process was repeated, and the rest is now history.

## Sugar on Snow

It is traditional to serve this treat with plain doughnuts and sour pickles, which provide a contrast to the sweetness of the maple. The snow is not eaten; it merely serves to cool the maple syrup.

*Clean snow*

*1 quart genuine maple syrup*

*12 plain raised doughnuts*

*12 dill pickles*

*Hot brewed coffee or prepared hot chocolate*

1. Use only freshly fallen snow. Go to a clean bank and brush off the top layer of snow. Using a spatula, gather and pack clean snow in pans. The pans of snow may be prepared ahead of time by placing them into a freezer. If the weather is cold, the pans can be packed into a cardboard box and kept outdoors, covered, until needed.

2. In a heavy saucepan over medium heat, boil maple syrup slowly until candy thermometer reaches 234°or until a small amount of syrup dropped into very cold water forms a ball that does not hold its shape when pressed. Immediately remove thermometer and remove syrup from heat. Using a tablespoon, drop hot syrup onto the snow, allowing it to form into patterns. Serve immediately, still in the pan, giving each person a fork to wind pieces up off the snow (it can be wound around the fork like spaghetti). Serve with doughnuts, dill pickles, and hot coffee or hot chocolate.

Makes 12 to 16 servings.

# Moon Pie

Moon Pie is definitely a treat to moooooon over! A Moon Pie is a chocolate-covered, marshmallow-filled double- or triple-layered cookie, about the size of a small saucer. If you like S'mores, you'll love Moon Pie. Generations of southerners have enjoyed this treat since the early 1900s—definitely a regional favorite.

In Mobile, Alabama, during Mobile's Mardi Gras celebration, participants actually throw Moon Pies from the floats in the parade. They began the practice of "throws" in the 1800s in the form of sweet bonbons and practical jokes. During the 1970s, Moon Pies were first thrown as an alternative to boxes of Cracker Jacks. Participants also throw similar, but smaller pies, called Mardi Gras pies.

The Chattanooga Bakery in Chattanooga, Tennessee, created Moon Pies in 1917. The bakery, a subsidiary of the Mountain City Flour Mill, was established simply to make use of excess flour from the parent company's mill. The bakery never documented the exact history of how the Moon Pie was invented, but one historian, Ronald Dickson of Charlotte, North Carolina, believes he found the "missing link." In his book, *The Great American Moon Pie Handbook,* he writes of a telephone call he received from Earl Mitchell, Jr., identifying his deceased father, Earl Mitchell, Sr., as the person responsible for the invention of the Moon Pie. Mr. Mitchell's story goes like this:

Early in the 1900s, Mr. Mitchell was visiting a company store that catered to coal miners. He asked them what they might enjoy as a snack. The miners said they wanted something for their lunch pails. It had to be solid and filling. "About how big?" Mr. Mitchell asked. About that time the moon was rising, so a miner held out his big hands, framing the moon and said, "About that big." So, with that in mind, Mr. Mitchell headed back to the bakery with an idea. Upon his return, he noticed some of the workers dipping graham cookies into marshmallow and laying them on the windowsill to harden. So they added marshmallows, another cookie, and a generous coating of chocolate and sent them back for the workers to try. In fact, they sent Moon Pie samples around with their other salespeople too. The response they got back was so enormous that the Moon Pie became a regular item for the bakery. By the late 1950s, the Moon Pie had grown so much in popularity, that the bakery started producing only Moon Pies.

# Boston Cream Pie

When is a pie not a pie? When it's a cake called Boston cream pie. A Boston cream pie is really two sponge cakes held together by a layer of rich custard and topped with a shiny chocolate glaze. Cooks in New England and Pennsylvania Dutch regions were known for their cakes and pies, and the dividing line between them was very thin. This cake was probably called a pie because in the mid-nineteenth century, pie tins were more common than cake pans. The first versions might have been baked in pie tins. The Boston cream pie seems to be a modified version of the Washington pie, a two-layer cake filled with jam and dusted with powdered sugar. The Washington pie was originally baked in special Washington pie plates, also called jelly-cake tins.

The Parker House Hotel (now the Omni Parker House), claims to have served Boston cream pie since their opening in 1856. French chef Sanzian, who was hired for the opening of the hotel, is credited with creating Boston cream pie. This cake was originally served at the hotel with the names Chocolate Cream Pie or Parker House Chocolate Cream Pie.

The Boston cream pie was proclaimed the official Massachusetts State Dessert on December 12, 1996. A civics class from Norton High School sponsored the bill.

## Boston Cream Pie

*2 cups cake flour*

*2 teaspoons baking powder*

*¼ teaspoon salt*

*½ cup butter or solid vegetable shortening, room temperature*

*1 cup sugar*

*3 eggs, well beaten*

*1 teaspoon vanilla extract*

*¼ teaspoon almond extract (optional)*

*¾ cup milk*

*Custard Cream Filling (recipe follows)*

*Chocolate Frosting (recipe follows)*

*Powdered sugar*

**1.** Preheat oven to 375°. Grease and flour two 8-inch round cake pans; line bottoms with rounds of wax or parchment paper.

**2.** In a medium bowl, sift together the cake flour, baking powder, and salt; set aside. In a large bowl, mix together butter or vegetable shortening, and sugar until light and fluffy. Add the eggs, one at a time, beating well after each addition; add vanilla extract and almond extract. Add the flour mixture alternately with milk, mixing only enough to blend thoroughly (do not overmix).

**3.** Divide the batter between the prepared cake pans. Bake 25 to 30 minutes or until a toothpick inserted into the center of the cake comes out clean. Remove from oven, place on a wire rack, and let cool in pans. Remove from cake pans when cool.

**4.** To assemble cake: Spread the cooled Custard Cream Filling over one of the cake layers. Place second cake layer over the filling and spread the Chocolate Frosting over the top of the cake. Dust top with powdered sugar. Store cake in the refrigerator.

Makes 12 servings.

## CUSTARD CREAM FILLING

*1 cup milk*

*3 egg yolks*

*½ cup sugar*

*¼ cup all-purpose flour*

*1 tablespoon butter*

*1 teaspoon vanilla extract*

In a small saucepan, heat milk to the boiling point; remove from heat. In the top of a double boiler over boiling water, beat egg yolks until smooth. Gradually add sugar and continue beating until pale yellow. Add flour and beat until combined. Pour the hot milk into the egg mixture in a steady stream, beating constantly. Cook over boiling water, stirring constantly, until thickened. Cook an additional 2 minutes, stirring constantly, and then remove from the heat. Stir in butter and vanilla extract; set aside and let cool.

## CHOCOLATE FROSTING

*1 (1-ounce) square unsweetened chocolate*

*2 tablespoons butter*

*½ cup powdered sugar*

*½ teaspoon vanilla extract*

*Hot water*

In the top of a double boiler over boiling water, melt the chocolate and butter; remove from heat. Add the powdered sugar and combine to make a thick paste. Add vanilla extract and enough hot water (a tablespoon at a time) until it reaches frosting consistency.

# Gooey Butter Cake

**Too much of a good thing can be wonderful.**

—*Mae West (1893–1980), American actress and writer*

To get your sugar shock, you must try St. Louis's Gooey Butter Cake. This ultra-sweet treat is a St. Louis tradition and available in local bakeries all around the city of St. Louis (in fact, St. Louis is said to have more than five hundred bakeries). The cake consists of a dry, flat base covered with a "goo" mixture. It is sticky and chewy and very delicious. The local people of St. Louis are wild about this cake.

The Gooey Butter Cake originated in the 1930s. According to legend, a German baker added the wrong proportions of ingredients in the coffeecake batter he was making. It turned into a gooey, pudding-like filling.

## Gooey Butter Cake

Most people prefer using the packaged cake mix when making this cake at home. It is very easy to make and so delicious.

*1 (18-ounce) package yellow cake mix*

*1 large egg*

*½ cup butter, melted*

*1 (8-ounce) package cream cheese, room temperature*

*2 eggs*

*1 teaspoon vanilla extract*

*4 cups powdered sugar*

*Powdered sugar for dusting top*

**1.** Preheat oven to 350°. Lightly grease a 13 x 9-inch baking dish.

**2.** In a large mixing bowl, combine yellow cake mix, egg, and butter. Press mixture onto bottom of prepared baking dish; set aside.

**3.** In a medium bowl, beat cream cheese until creamy; add eggs and vanilla extract. Blend in powdered sugar until well mixed. Pour into the crust-lined baking pan. Bake 30 to 40 minutes or until cake is nearly firm when you shake it (you want the center to be a little gooey, so do not overcook). Let cake cool in pan on wire rack. When cool, remove to a serving plate and sprinkle with powdered sugar. (Note: If making ahead of time, refrigerate in an airtight container up to one day.)

Makes 9 servings.

# Huguenot Torte

This is Charleston, South Carolina's most famous dessert—almost all restaurants in the area serve this wonderfully delicious apple and nut torte. It is generally thought that this modern dessert was adapted from the classic Ozark Pudding (which is more of a cake than a pudding) that originated in northwest Arkansas and southwest Missouri. The Ozark pudding probably developed from the Pennsylvania Dutch Apple Pudding Cake.

The Ozark Pudding was a favorite of the Huguenot community of Charleston and was made in homes and taverns. Forty-five Huguenots, Protestant French immigrants, arrived in the new province of Carolina on April 30, 1680, from London. King Charles II had subsidized the voyage so that Huguenot people might establish on British territory the crops and industries that had long been French monopolies. The group included grape-growers, wine makers, brick makers, weavers, businessmen, and at least one goldsmith. They also arrived with orders that the settlement be renamed "Charles Town."

This pudding was given the name Huguenot Torte to reflect the Huguenot's love of this dessert and their heritage. The name stuck in Charleston, and it continues to be called that to this day, even though the dessert is neither a torte nor is it of Huguenot origin.

## Huguenot Torte

2 eggs

¾ cup sugar

2 teaspoons vanilla extract

1 teaspoon fresh lemon juice

¼ cup all-purpose flour

½ teaspoon freshly grated nutmeg

2 teaspoons baking soda

¼ teaspoon salt

1½ cups toasted, chopped pecans, divided*

1 cup peeled and chopped tart apples

Prepared whipped cream

* To toast pecans: Spread shelled, whole pecans in a shallow pan and toast in a 275° oven 20 to 30 minutes.

Preheat oven to 325°. Butter a 13 x 9-inch baking dish. In a large bowl, beat eggs until very frothy and lemon colored. Add sugar, vanilla extract, lemon juice, flour, nutmeg, soda, and salt; stir until well combined. Fold in 1 cup pecans and apples. Pour batter into the prepared dish. Bake 30 to 35 minutes or until the top is brown and crusty; remove from oven. Serve warm or at room temperature. To serve, scoop up into serving bowls (keeping crusty part on top) and garnish with whipped cream and ¼ cup chopped pecans.

Makes 8 servings.

# Guava Chiffon Cake

The Guava Chiffon Cake can be called a "fusion" dessert that combines the classic California Chiffon Cake with the Hawaiian Island's favorite fruit of guava. This cake is a favorite in the Hawaiian Islands, and there are many lively debates held as to which baker on which Island makes the best cake. It is such a popular cake with the bakeries that customers often have to call ahead to reserve one.

A Hawaiian, Herbert Matsuba, who owns the Dee Lite Bakery, first created this cake in the early 1960s. He created the cake with the idea of incorporating Hawaiian flavors into a baked item, as he wanted a new cake that would set his new bakery apart from all the others in Hawaii. He started with a basic chiffon cake and added the guava (the guava fruit is well known in Hawaii and available in juices, jams, and as a flavoring for cakes and cookies). The popularity of the Guava Chiffon Cake soon spread by word of mouth and became a local favorite.

Harry Baker, a baker at the Los Angeles Brown Derby restaurant, invented the original chiffon cake in 1927. As word spread of his wonderful airy cake, he was continually asked for the recipe. But for two decades he carefully guarded his secret recipe, making his special cake only for the reigning royalty of the silver screen. In 1947, General Mills bought the recipe and the secret ingredient, vegetable oil, was revealed. *Better Homes and Gardens* magazine advertised the cake as "the first really new cake in 100 years." They introduced the cake in the May 1948 issue, and it became a nationwide sensation during the late 1940s and 1950s. Chiffon cakes, like angel food cakes, are baked in ungreased pans so that the batter will cling to the sides as it rises during baking.

## Guava Chiffon Cake

As the bakeries of Hawaii guard their personal recipes of this delicious cake, I had to try to recreate it. After several attempts, I feel this cake can compete with the popular Guava Chiffon Cake of Hawaii. I admit that this cake takes a little extra work to make, but it is well worth the time and effort.

*2¼ cups cake flour*

*1¼ cups sugar, divided*

*1 tablespoon baking powder*

*1 teaspoon salt*

*½ cup vegetable oil*

*1 cup frozen guava juice concentrate, thawed and undiluted*

*5 egg yolks, slightly beaten*

*2 to 3 drops red food coloring (optional)*

*8 egg whites, room temperature*

*½ teaspoon cream of tartar*

*Guava Topping (recipe follows)*

*Guava Frosting (recipe follows)*

**1.** Preheat oven to 325° and position rack in center of oven. Cover wire cooling racks with plastic wrap. In an extra-large bowl, sift cake flour, ¾ cup sugar, baking powder, and salt. Add vegetable oil, guava juice, egg yolks, and food coloring; beat, with an electric mixer at medium speed, 1 to 2 minutes or just until smooth; set aside.

**2.** In a large bowl, beat egg whites and cream of tartar until soft peaks form; add ½ cup sugar, 1 tablespoon at a time, beating until stiff peaks form. Using a rubber spatula, gently fold ⅓ of prepared cake mixture into egg mixture until barely mixed; gently fold in remaining cake mixture just until incorporated.

**3.** Pour batter into two 9-inch round, ungreased cake pans; smooth top with a rubber spatula. Bake 35 to 40 minutes or until a toothpick inserted in the center comes out clean (to prevent falling, do not open the oven door until near the end of the minimum baking time). Remove from oven and immediately invert on prepared wire racks to cool completely (cool with pan in place). When cool, gently remove from pan. Place cakes in refrigerator until well chilled.

**4.** When well chilled, remove from refrigerator. Place one cake layer onto a cake plate and spread top with ½ of lukewarm Guava Topping; top with remaining cake layer. To keep cake from sliding to one side, insert a long wooden skewer into the middle and all the way to the bottom. Spread Guava Frosting on sides and top of cake; spread remaining Guava Topping on top of cake. Store cake in the refrigerator until serving time.

Makes 16 servings.

## GUAVA TOPPING

*1 tablespoon cornstarch*

*2 tablespoons water*

*1¼ cups frozen guava juice concentrate, thawed and undiluted*

In a small bowl, combine cornstarch and water until cornstarch is dissolved. In a small saucepan over medium-high heat, bring guava juice concentrate just to a boil; reduce heat to low. Add cornstarch mixture and stir until mixture thickens to a sauce-like consistency. Remove from heat and let cool to lukewarm before spreading on the cake.

## GUAVA FROSTING

*1½ cups heavy cream*

*⅓ cup powdered sugar*

*½ cup frozen guava juice concentrate, thawed and undiluted*

In a large bowl, beat cream until soft peaks form. Gradually add sugar, beating until stiff peaks form. Fold in guava juice concentrate: blend well. Store in refrigerator until ready to spread on the cake.

# King Cake

**A house is beautiful not because of its walls, but because of its cakes.**

*—old Russian proverb*

Hundreds of thousands of King Cakes are eaten during Mardi Gras each year in New Orleans, Louisiana. In fact, a Mardi Gras party would not be authentic without the traditional King Cake as the center of the party.

The cake is made with a rich Danish dough, baked, and covered with a sugar topping in Mardi Gras colors; purple representing justice, green representing faith, and gold representing power. The cakes are easy to make, and in New Orleans every bakery seems to have its own version for sale. The cakes are prepared for the period between the Twelfth Night and Ash Wednesday. Many are shipped throughout the United States for those displaced New Orleanians longing for a taste of Mardi Gras.

The Mardi Gras or Carnival season officially begins on January 6th, or the Twelfth Night. Originally objects such as coins, beans, pecans, and peas were hidden inside of King Cakes. Wealthy Louisiana plantation owners in the late 1800s would sometimes put a precious stone or jewel in their King Cakes. In the mid-1900s, a small plastic baby became the symbol of this Holy Day and was placed inside of each King Cake. The New Orleans tradition is that each person takes a piece of cake hoping to find the plastic baby inside. The recipient of the plastic baby is "crowned" King or Queen for the day and that person is obligated to host the following year's party and supply the King Cake.

The King Cake tradition came to New Orleans with the French settlers around 1870, continuing a custom dating back to twelfth century France. Similar cakes were used then to celebrate the coming of the three wise men calling it the feast of Epiphany, Twelfth Night, or King's Day.

## New Orleans King Cake

*½ cup lukewarm water (110° to 115°)*

*½ cup lukewarm milk (110° to 115°)*

*½ cup sugar*

*2 teaspoons salt*

*1 teaspoon ground nutmeg*

*1 teaspoon grated lemon peel*

*5 egg yolks, room temperature*

*½ cup butter, room temperature*

*4¾ cups bread flour or all-purpose flour*

*3 teaspoons instant active dry yeast*

*1 teaspoon ground cinnamon*

*1 egg, slightly beaten with 1 tablespoon milk*

*1 tiny (1-inch) plastic doll (optional)*

*Lemon Frosting (recipe follows)*

*Colored Sugars (recipe follows)*

1. Using a mixer with a dough hook, place water, milk, sugar, salt, nutmeg, lemon peel, egg yolks, butter, flour, and yeast in the bowl. If using a bread machine, add same ingredients, select dough setting and press start. Check the dough (don't be afraid to open the lid). It should form a nice elastic ball. If you think the dough is too moist, add additional flour (a tablespoon at a time). The same is true if the dough is looking dry and gnarly. Add warm water (a tablespoon at a time). When dough cycle has finished, remove dough from pan and cover with plastic wrap; place in a draft-free place to rise for approximately 1 hour or until the dough doubles in volume.

2. Lightly coat a large baking sheet with butter or vegetable spray; set aside. Place dough on a lightly floured surface. Using your fist, punch dough down with a heavy blow. Sprinkle cinnamon over the top, pat and shape dough into a long "snake" or cylinder. Twist dough to form an oval and place onto the buttered baking sheet. Pinch the ends together to form a circle. Cover dough with a towel and let sit for 45 minutes or until the dough doubles in volume.

**3.** Preheat oven to 375°. Brush top and sides of cake with egg and milk mixture. Bake on middle rack of oven for 35 to 40 minutes or until golden brown. (A good check is to use an instant thermometer to test your bread. The temperature should be between 200° and 210°.) Remove from oven and place on wire rack to cool. Once the cake is cool, insert a small plastic baby doll into a seam of the cake before frosting. *(Note: Be sure to warn your guests of what to expect as you don't want anyone choking.)* Spread Lemon Frosting over the top of cooled cake. Immediately sprinkle on Colored Sugars, alternating between the three colors (a large stripe of each color).

Makes 8 to 10 servings.

## LEMON FROSTING

*¾ cups powdered sugar*

*¼ cup fresh lemon juice*

In a small bowl, combine powdered sugar and lemon juice until smooth (add water if mixture is too thick or additional powdered sugar if too thin).

## COLORED SUGARS

*Green, purple, and yellow coloring paste*

*¾ cup sugar*

In a small bowl, place a dot of paste and 2 tablespoons sugar; mix together until well mixed. Repeat process for other two colors; set aside.

*King Cakes are created in varied shapes and flavors. From braided King Cake (top left) to the traditional New Orleans King Cake (far right), they are all something to celebrate.*

# Lady Baltimore Cake

The classic Lady Baltimore Cake is a cherished and historic dessert in Charleston, South Carolina. It remains a Southern specialty today with many recipe variations. A favorite wedding cake, this mountainous cake is a white cake topped with a boiled or "Seven Minute Frosting." What makes the cake so distinctive is the combination of chopped nuts and dried or candied fruits in its frosting.

## Did You Know?

The Lady Baltimore Cake was a great favorite with Woodrow Wilson, twenty-eighth president of the United States. It is said that Mrs. Wilson liked to hide "treasures" for her husband to discover among the layers of the cake.

In 1906, Owen Wister, a popular novelist, picked Charleston, South Carolina, as the setting of his new romance novel. He modeled the central character, Lady Baltimore, after one of the city's former belles, Alicia Rhett Mayberry. In the novel, Lady Baltimore created a cake also called "Lady Baltimore." In his novel, Wister wrote:

> "I should like a slice, if you please, of Lady Baltimore," I said with extreme formality. I returned to the table and she brought me the cake, and I had my first felicitous meeting with Lady Baltimore. Oh, my goodness! Did you ever taste it? It's all soft, and it's in layers, and it has nuts— but I can't write any more about it; my mouth waters too much. Delighted surprise caused me once more to speak aloud, and with my mouth full, "But, dear me, this is delicious!"

Wister's description of the cake sent readers of his novel scrambling to find the recipe, which had not been created yet. According to historians, Florence and Nina Ottelengui, who managed Charleston's Lady Baltimore Tea Room for a quarter of a century, developed the cake toward the end of the nineteenth century from a version of the common "Queen" cake of that period. They are said to have annually baked and shipped a cake to Owen Wister. At Christmastime, they shipped hundreds of white boxes carrying tall, round, fragile gift cakes to all parts of the country.

# Lady Baltimore Cake

3 cups cake flour

3 teaspoons baking powder

½ teaspoon salt

½ cup butter, room temperature

1½ cups sugar

1¼ cups milk, room temperature

1 teaspoon vanilla extract

4 egg whites, room temperature.

Lady Baltimore Frosting (recipe follows)

6 dried figs, finely chopped

½ cup raisins

1 cup chopped walnuts or pecans

Candied cherries, chopped

1. Preheat oven to 375°. Grease and flour three 8-inch round cake pans. In a large bowl, sift flour once, measure, add baking powder and salt; sift together three additional times.

2. In another large bowl, cream butter and sugar together until light and fluffy. Add flour mixture, alternately with milk, a small amount at a time, beating after each addition until smooth. Beat in vanilla extract. In another large bowl, beat egg whites at high speed until stiff peaks form; fold into batter.

3. Pour batter into prepared cake pans, dividing equally. Bake 25 to 35 minutes or until cake pulls away from sides of pan and a toothpick inserted in center comes out dry. Remove from oven and cool on wire racks 10 minutes; remove from pans and continue to cool on racks.

4. Prepare Lady Baltimore Frosting. In a medium bowl, combine figs, raisins, nuts, and some of the prepared frosting to make a fruit filling that will spread easily. Spread fruit and nut filling between cake layers. Spread remaining Lady Baltimore Frosting on top and sides of cake. While frosting is still soft, sprinkle top of cake with chopped cherries.

Makes 8 to 10 servings.

## LADY BALTIMORE FROSTING

1½ cups sugar

5 tablespoons water

1½ teaspoons light corn syrup

2 egg whites, room temperature

1 teaspoon vanilla extract

1. In a double boiler over boiling water, combine sugar, water, and corn syrup; beat until thoroughly mixed; bring mixture to a boil. Using a candy thermometer, boil approximately 7 minutes, stirring constantly, until candy thermometer reaches 240° (firm ball) or when a small amount of sugar syrup dropped into very cold water forms a ball that holds its shape but is pliable. Remove from heat.

2. In a large bowl using a mixer, beat egg whites until stiff peaks form. Pour hot syrup in fine stream over egg whites, beating constantly until well blended; add vanilla and continue beating 10 to 15 minutes or until frosting is cool and of the right consistency to spread.

# Robert E. Lee Cake

One of the most famous Southern cakes of all times is the Robert E. Lee Cake. For some people in the South, Robert E. Lee (1807–1870) is an almost god-like figure. For others, he is a paradox. In 1861, he was made commander-in-chief of the Virginia forces during the Civil War. Following the war, Lee was almost tried as a traitor, but was only left with his civil rights suspended. In 1890, the General Assembly of Virginia passed a law to designate Robert E. Lee's birthday (January 19th) as a public holiday. The holiday has been changed to "Lee-Jackson-King Day" in modern times, but most Virginians still observe Robert E. Lee Day by partying and making this famous cake.

Making a Robert E. Lee Cake is definitely a labor of love because it is not simple to do. There are many recipes and many versions in old southern cookbooks. (This cake was extremely popular in the nineteenth century.) No two authorities seem to agree on the egg content of the cake (ranging from eight to ten eggs). The icing also varies with each recipe. Some use grated orange or lemon rind in the frosting and others use pure lemon filling with the white frosting.

## Robert E. Lee Cake

2 cups sifted all-purpose flour

½ teaspoon cream of tartar

1 ½ teaspoons baking powder

8 eggs, separated and room temperature

2 cups sugar

1 tablespoon grated lemon peel

¼ cup fresh lemon juice

Lemon Filling (recipe follows)

Lemon-Orange Frosting (recipe follows)

1. Preheat oven to 350°. Grease and flour two 9-inch cake pans. In a medium bowl, sift together flour, cream of tartar, and baking powder; set aside.

2. In a large bowl, beat egg yolks until very thick and creamy. Gradually add sugar, a few tablespoons at a time, and continue beating until mixture is smooth and pale yellow. Stir in lemon peel and lemon juice; gently fold in the flour mixture until well incorporated.

3. In another large bowl, beat egg whites until stiff peaks form. Fold ⅓ of the beaten egg whites into the egg batter, then fold in remaining egg whites until no streaks remain. Spoon batter into prepared cake pans. Bake 20 to 25 minutes or until cake begins to pull away from sides of pan. Remove from oven and let cool 10 minutes in the pan. Loosen edges with a knife and turn out onto cake racks while you prepare the Lemon Filling and Lemon-Orange Frosting.

4. When cake is cool, cut each layer horizontally in half to make 4 layers. Spread Lemon Filling between layers of cooled cake. To keep cake from sliding to one side, insert a long wooden skewer into the middle and all the way to the bottom. Spread Lemon-Orange Frosting on sides and top of cake. Store cake in the refrigerator until serving time.

Makes 8 to 10 servings.

## LEMON FILLING

*3 tablespoons grated lemon peel*

*½ cup fresh lemon juice*

*1½ cups sugar*

*6 tablespoons butter*

*3 eggs, lightly beaten*

In a medium saucepan over medium-high heat, combine lemon peel, lemon juice, and sugar. Bring just to a boil; reduce heat to medium-low and simmer 5 minutes. Add butter and stir until it has melted. Remove from heat and let mixture cool to room temperature. When cool, beat eggs into lemon-sugar mixture until well blended. Return to heat and cook, stirring constantly, 10 to 15 minutes or until mixture thickens and coats spoon. Cool in refrigerator until ready to use.

## LEMON-ORANGE FROSTING

*¼ cup butter, room temperature*

*1 tablespoon grated lemon peel*

*3 to 4 tablespoons grated orange peel*

*2 tablespoons fresh lemon juice*

*6 cups sifted powdered sugar*

*¼ cup fresh orange juice*

In a medium bowl, beat butter until it has the appearance of thick cream. Beat in lemon peel, orange peel, and lemon juice. Stir in powdered sugar and orange juice, a little at a time; continue beating until mixture is very smooth (stir in enough orange juice to make a spreadable frosting).

# Whoopie Pies

Whoopie pies are considered a New England phenomenon and a Pennsylvania Amish tradition. They're one of Maine's best known and most loved comfort foods. Mainers will even claim that they were weaned on whoopie pies. In Maine, these treats are more like a cake than a pie or a cookie, as they are very generously sized (about hamburger size). They're so huge that you'll want to share one with a friend. A big glass of milk is almost mandatory when eating a Whoopie Pie.

A whoopie pie is like a sandwich, but made with two soft cookies with a fluffy white filling. Traditional whoopie pies are made with vegetable shortening, not butter. The original and most commonly made whoopie pie is chocolate. But cooks like to experiment, and today pumpkin whoopie pies are a favorite seasonal variation.

The recipe for whoopie pies has its origins with the Amish, and in Lancaster County, Pennsylvania, it is not uncommon to find roadside farm stands offering these desserts. Amish cooking is about old recipes that have fed farm families for generations, with no trendy or cross-cultural fusions or mixtures. These cakelike whoopie pies were considered a special treat because they were originally made from leftover batter. According to Amish legend, when children would find these treats in their lunch bags, they would shout "Whoopie!"

The question of how the Amish dessert got to be so popular in New England probably is addressed in a 1930s cookbook called *Yummy Book* by the Durkee-Mower Company, the manufacturer of Marshmallow Fluff. In this New England cookbook, a recipe for Amish Whoopie Pie was featured using Marshmallow Fluff in the filling. Marshmallow Fluff was invented in the early 1900s by Archibald Query. He would make it in his kitchen, then sell it door to door. During World War I, shortages of ingredients forced him to close down. In 1920, he sold his rights and the recipe to H. Allen Durkee and Fred L. Mower. They later formed the Durkee Mower Company and began the manufacture of Marshmallow Fluff.

# Whoopie Pies

*½ cup solid vegetable shortening*

*1 cup firmly packed brown sugar*

*1 egg*

*¼ cup cocoa*

*2 cups all-purpose flour*

*1 teaspoon baking powder*

*1 teaspoon baking soda*

*1 teaspoon salt*

*1 teaspoon vanilla extract*

*1 cup milk*

*Whoopie Pie Filling (recipe follows)*

1. Preheat oven to 350°. Lightly grease baking sheets. In a large bowl, cream together shortening, sugar, and egg. In another bowl, combine cocoa, flour, baking powder, baking soda, and salt. In a small bowl, stir the vanilla extract into the milk. Add the dry ingredients to the shortening mixture, alternating with the milk mixture; beating until smooth. Drop batter by the ¼ cup (to make 18 cakes) onto prepared baking sheets. With the back of a spoon, spread batter into 4-inch circles, leaving approximately 2 inches between each cake. Bake 15 minutes or until they are firm to the touch. Remove from oven and let cool completely on a wire rack.

2. Make Whoopie Pie Filling. When the cakes are completely cool, spread the flat side (bottom) of one chocolate cake with a generous amount of filling. Top with another cake, pressing down gently to distribute the filling evenly. Repeat with all cookies to make 9 pies. Wrap whoopie pies individually in plastic wrap, or place them in a single layer on a platter (do not stack them, as they tend to stick).

3. To freeze, wrap each whoopie pie in plastic wrap. Loosely pack them in a plastic freezer container and cover. To serve, defrost the wrapped whoopie pies in the refrigerator.

*Makes 9 large whoopie pies.*

## WHOOPIE PIE FILLING

*1 cup solid vegetable shortening\**

*1½ cups powdered sugar*

*2 cups Marshmallow Fluff\*\**

*1½ teaspoons vanilla extract*

\*  Butter may be substituted for all or part of the vegetable shortening, although traditional Whoopie Pies are made with vegetable shortening only.

\*  Marshmallow Crème may be substituted.

In a medium bowl, beat together shortening, sugar, and Marshmallow Fluff; stir in vanilla extract until well blended.

# Avocado Pie

Did you know that California grows 95 percent of the world's avocados, and that Californians are the world's largest consumers of avocados? Avocados have a following in cultures worldwide, but Californians put them into everything from ice cream to sushi. San Diego County calls itself the Avocado Capital of the world. One of the most unusual and absolutely delightful dishes made with avocados is the Avocado Pie. Look into the family recipe books of most native Californians, and you will probably find an avocado pie recipe. There are many versions in making the pie, and they all taste wonderful!

The most popular California avocado is the Haas, which weighs about half a pound and has a pebbly black skin when ripe. Haas avocados are unique because they are the only avocado variety that is produced year-round. According to the Avocado Commission, the original Haas tree was really a mistake—a lucky chance seedling. In the late 1920s, Rudolph Haas purchased seedling trees for the purpose of developing two acres of budded trees of the Lyon variety. There was one particular tree that attracted the attention of his children, as they preferred the fruit from this tree. Since the quality was high and the tree bore well, Haas patented it in 1935 and began propagating this new variety.

The Fuerte, also from California, can weigh up to a pound and has a more pronounced pear shape and a smooth, dark-green skin. In 1911, Carl Schmidt was sent to Mexico to search for avocados of outstanding quality and to locate the trees from which they came. Only one of the trees he brought back survived the great freeze of 1913 in California. This surviving tree was given the name Fuerte, Spanish for "vigorous." The Fuerte tree created California's avocado industry.

The avocado is a tropical fruit native to Central America. It was introduced to Europe by returning Spanish explorers in the sixteenth century. In California, the first successful introduction of avocado trees was planted by Judge R. B. Ord of Santa Barbara, who secured the trees from Mexico in 1871.

The Aztecs used the avocado as a sex stimulant and the Aztec name for avocado was *ahuacatl,* meaning "testicle." Americans called it the alligator pear because they could not pronounce the Spanish word for avocado *aguacate.* European sailors called it "midshipman's butter" because they liked to spread it on hardtack biscuits.

*Ripe California avocados. Courtesy California Avocado Commission.*

**I'll Have What They're Having**

# Avocado Pie

Leo Porter, manager of the Horseshoe Ranch in Fort Klamath, Oregon, gave this wonderful dessert recipe to me. Leo grew up on an avocado farm in California. This is his version of the recipe for avocado pie that was created by his aunt in the 1970s, and is now the signature dish of the Horseshoe Ranch.

*Graham Cracker Crust (recipe follows)*

*¼ cup fresh lime juice*

*¼ cup fresh lemon juice*

*1 envelope unflavored gelatin*

*3 medium-size very ripe Haas avocados, skinned and pitted\**

*1 (14-ounce) can sweetened condensed milk*

*½ cup heavy cream*

*½ cup sour cream*

\* An avocado is ripe if it yields to gentle pressure.

**1.** Prepare Graham Cracker Crust. In a small bowl, combine lime juice, lemon juice, and unflavored gelatin; let stand 4 to 5 minutes or until softened.

**2.** In a large bowl or the food processor, combine gelatin mixture, avocados, and sweetened condensed milk. Pour mixture into prepared Graham Cracker Crust. Refrigerate at least 2 hours or until the filling is firm. In a small bowl, whip heavy cream and sour cream together until stiff peaks form. Serve pie topped with prepared whipped cream mixture.

Makes 8 servings.

## GRAHAM CRACKER CRUST

*¼ cup plus 2 tablespoons butter*

*1⅔ cups graham cracker crumbs*

*⅓ cup firmly packed brown sugar*

*1 teaspoon ground cinnamon*

*¼ cup walnuts, pecans, or hazelnuts*

Preheat oven to 350°. In a small saucepan over medium heat or the microwave, melt butter. In a food processor or blender, combine butter, graham crackers, brown sugar, cinnamon, and nuts; process until mixture is fine. Firmly press crumb mixture evenly over bottom and sides of a 9-inch pie plate. Bake 10 minutes. Remove from oven and refrigerate until well chilled.

# Key Lime Pie

Key limes are the pink flamingos of Florida food, and they are a celebrated part of local color. Key West, Florida, is famous for its fabulous key lime pie, one of America's best-loved regional dishes. Every restaurant in the Florida Keys, and especially in the city of Key West, serves this wonderful pie. There seems to be a key lime pie for every palate, with numerous versions made throughout the region. Recipes show up on postcards, place mats, lime juice bottles, and in guidebooks. Key lime pie was voted the dessert of record for the Keys by the Key West town council. People come from all over to taste this pie.

Aficionados of key lime pies argue endlessly about the proper way to make one. Graham-cracker or pastry crust? Meringue on top or whipped cream, or neither? Cooked or uncooked filling? The one thing that they do agree on is that under no circumstances should you ever add green food coloring. The filling of authentic key lime pie is a light yellow.

It was not until the 1930s that the first recipes were written down. Until then everyone just knew how to make the pie. No fresh milk, no refrigeration, and no ice was available in the Keys until the arrival of tank trucks with the opening of the Overseas Highway in 1930. Because of this lack of milk, local cooks had to rely on canned sweetened condensed milk, which was invented in 1856 by Gail Borden. Key lime may be the star ingredient of the key lime pie, but it is the sweetened condensed milk that makes it so smooth and delicious.

As to who made the first key lime pie, no one really knows for sure. There are a few legends and theories. One story insists that William Currie, a wealthy owner of a ship's chandlery had a cook that was simply known as Aunt Sally. It was Aunt Sally who invented the pie in the late 1800s. Some of the guidebooks say that the pie was created in the kitchen of the Milton Currie Mansion in Old Town in the early 1900s. There is even a theory that the pie was created on board a sponger's ship, where no one wanted to bake, so a sailor came up with this easy pie.

The key lime tree, which is native to Malaysia, probably first arrived in the Florida Keys in the 1500s with the Spanish. Key limes look like confused lemons, as they are smaller than a golf ball with yellow-green skin that is sometimes splotched with brown. They are also known as Mexican or West Indian limes. When a hurricane in 1926 wiped out the key lime plantations in South Florida, growers replanted with Persian limes, which are easier to pick and to transport. Today the key lime is almost a phantom and any remaining trees are only found in back yards and their fruit never leave the Florida Keys. Key limes are also grown for commercial use in the Miami area.

## Classic Key Lime Pie

This recipe comes from *What's Cooking America*, by Linda Stradley and Andra Cook.

1 (9-inch) prepared Graham Cracker pie crust (see recipe page 183 or purchase ready-made from the grocery)

1 (14-ounce) can sweetened condensed milk

Grated peel from 1 key lime (optional)

¼ cup fresh or bottled key lime juice*

2 eggs, separated

1 egg, room temperature

4 tablespoons sugar

*   Bottled key lime juice can be found in most supermarkets.

1. Refrigerate graham cracker crust until well chilled. Preheat oven to 350°. In a medium bowl, combine condensed milk, key lime peel, and key lime juice. Add 2 egg yolks and egg; stir until well blended. Pour into chilled Graham Cracker crust.

2. In a medium bowl, make a meringue by beating 2 egg whites until stiff peaks form; gradually fold in sugar. Spread meringue over key lime mixture, being careful to spread to edge of pastry to prevent shrinkage during baking. Bake 20 minutes or until meringue is golden brown. Remove from oven and cool completely on a wire rack. Refrigerate before serving.

Makes 6 to 8 servings.

# Sugar Cream Pie

**Promises and pie crust are made to be broken.**

*—Jonathan Swift*

Sugar cream pie, or Hoosier sugar cream pie, Indiana cream pie, sugar pie, or finger pie, is simply a pie shell spread with layers of creamed butter and maple or brown sugar with a sprinkling of flour, then filled with vanilla-flavored cream and baked. It was known as finger pie because the filling was stirred with a finger during the baking process to prevent breaking the bottom crust. People used to skim the thick yellow cream from the top of chilled fresh milk to make this delectable dessert.

The recipe originated in Indiana with the Shaker community in the 1850s as a great pie recipe to use when the apple bins were empty. The Shakers believed in eating hearty and healthy food. They definitely must have had a sweet tooth, though, judging by the sugar cream pie. Today, you can find this delicious pie on the menus of small-town restaurants throughout Indiana.

## Sugar Cream Pie

*Pastry for 9-inch one-crust pie (recipe follows)*

*½ cup all-purpose flour*

*2 tablespoons butter, room temperature*

*1 cup firmly packed brown sugar*

*⅛ teaspoon salt*

*1 cup heavy cream*

*1 cup milk*

*1 teaspoon vanilla extract*

*Ground nutmeg*

**1.** Prepare pie pastry. Preheat oven to 350°.

**2.** In a food processor or blender, whirl the flour, butter, brown sugar, and salt until combined. Add cream and whirl until well combined; pour into prepared unbaked pie shell. In a measuring cup, combine the milk and vanilla extract; pour over the top of the pie, but do not stir. Sprinkle generously with nutmeg. Cover crust edges with aluminum foil to prevent excessive browning.

**3.** Bake 60 to 75 minutes, shaking pie every 15 to 20 minutes during baking (the center of the pie will be bubbly and still a little wiggly but will become more firm as it cools). *Note: This will seem too long of a baking time, but it does require long baking to set properly. The top of the pie will be a deep golden brown.* Remove from oven and cool completely on a wire rack before cutting and serving.

Makes 8 servings.

## 9-INCH ONE-CRUST PIE PASTRY

*⅓ cup plus 1 tablespoon solid vegetable shortening*

*1 cup all-purpose flour*

*½ teaspoon salt*

*2 to 3 tablespoons chilled water*

**1.** In a large bowl with a pastry blender or two knives, cut shortening into flour and salt until particles are the size of small peas. Sprinkle in water, 1 tablespoon at a time, tossing with fork until all flour is moistened and pastry dough almost cleans side of bowl (1 to 2 teaspoons additional water can be added if necessary).

**2.** On a lightly floured surface, form pastry into a ball; shape into a flattened round. Using a floured rolling pin, roll pastry 2 inches larger than an inverted pie plate. Fold pastry into quarter folds and ease into plate, pressing firmly against bottom and side.

**3.** Trim overhanging edge of pastry 1 inch from rim of pie plate. Fold and roll pastry under, even with pie plate; flute. Fill and bake as directed in recipe.

# Chess Pie

**An old-timer is someone who remembers when a pie was set on the windowsill to cool, not to thaw.**

*—author unknown*

Chess pies are a favorite southern specialty that originated in the eighteenth century to utilize the most readily available ingredients—the eggs and butter that were plentiful and the molasses arriving in southern ports catering to the West Indies rum-molasses trade. As refined sugar became available, brown sugar and white sugar began to replace the molasses. These pies have a simple filling of eggs, sugar, butter, and a small amount of flour. Some recipes include cornmeal, and others are made with vinegar. Flavorings, such as vanilla, lemon juice, and chocolate are added to vary the basic recipe.

The origin of the name is uncertain, but there are plenty of guesses and a bit of folklore surrounding the name. One explanation suggests that the word is *chest*, pronounced with a drawl and used to describe these pies baked with so much sugar they could be stored in a pie chest rather than refrigerated. In the South, a common piece of furniture was the pie chest or pie safe.

Another story claims a plantation cook was asked what she was baking that smelled so good. "Jes' pie" was her answer. Some people theorize that since the English lemon curd pie filling is very close to lemon chess pie, the word *chess* is an Americanization of the word *cheese*, referring to curd pie.

## Lemon Chess Pie

Jeanne Ewert of Atlanta, Georgia, sent this recipe to me. Jeanne says, "Until I moved to Atlanta five years ago, I had never tasted Chess Pie. This is now my favorite pie. The following recipe was a gift from a former student of mine at Georgia Tech. The indispensable ingredients are cornmeal and buttermilk."

Pastry for 9-inch one-crust pie (recipe follows)

4 eggs

1½ cups sugar

⅛ teaspoon salt

4 tablespoons buttermilk

2 tablespoons yellow cornmeal

½ cup butter, melted

1 tablespoon lemon peel

3 tablespoons fresh lemon juice

⅛ teaspoon ground nutmeg

Whipped cream

1. Prepare Pie Pastry. Preheat oven to 350°. In a large bowl, beat eggs lightly with a wire whisk; add sugar, stirring until well mixed. Stir in the salt, buttermilk, cornmeal, and butter until smooth. Add lemon peel, lemon juice, and nutmeg.

2. Pour the custard mixture into the partially baked pie shell. Place pie in oven and immediately reduce oven temperature to 325° and bake 45 to 50 minutes or until a toothpick inserted between the center and outer edge comes out clean (do not overbake as the pie will continue to cook after it has been removed from oven). The top of the pie will be a light golden brown. Remove from oven and cool completely on a wire rack before cutting and serving. Serve at room temperature with a dollop of whipped cream.

Makes 8 servings.

# 9-INCH ONE-CRUST PIE PASTRY

⅓ cup plus 1 tablespoon solid vegetable shortening

1 cup all-purpose flour

½ teaspoon salt

2 to 3 tablespoons chilled water

**1.** Preheat oven to 450°. In a large bowl with a pastry blender or two knives, cut shortening into flour and salt until particles are the size of small peas. Sprinkle in water, 1 tablespoon at a time, tossing with fork until all flour is moistened and pastry dough almost cleans side of bowl (1 to 2 teaspoons additional water can be added if necessary).

**2.** On a lightly floured surface, form pastry into a ball; shape into a flattened round. Using a floured rolling pin, roll pastry 2 inches larger than an inverted pie plate. Fold pastry into quarter folds and ease into plate, pressing firmly against bottom and side.

**3.** Trim overhanging edge of pastry 1 inch from rim of pie plate. Fold and roll pastry under, even with pie plate; flute. Prick bottom and sides thoroughly with a fork. Partially bake 5 minutes; remove from oven and let cool. Fill and bake as directed in recipe.

*Lemon juice and lemon peel add extra flavoring to this southern specialty.*

# Huckleberry Pie

**If you would know the flavor of huckleberries, as the cowboy or the partridge. It is a vulgar error to suppose that you have tasted huckleberries who never plucked them.**

**Peaches are unquestionably a very beautiful and palatable fruit, but the gathering of them for the market is not nearly so interesting to the imaginations of men as the gathering of huckleberries for your own use.**

—Henry David Thoreau (1817–1862),
  American essayist, poet, and philosopher

Whoever invented huckleberry pie was a great person. There is absolutely nothing else that tastes quite like a huckleberry pie. It is the ultimate comfort food, especially after you have been picking huckleberries all day. Huckleberries are not cultivated commercially so you have to find them in the wild. The flavor is hard to describe as they have a unique sweet-tart flavor all their own. When you taste fresh huckleberries or eat a delicious huckleberry pie, you will know what I mean. They are definitely the gourmet berry of the West—very special and very difficult to find or even purchase.

A wide range of animals eats huckleberries. Bears often travel great distances to find them, as the berries are one of their major late summer and fall foods. If you do go huckleberry picking, be aware that you may be in some bear's favorite patch.

Berries with the name huckleberry can be found throughout the Rocky Mountains and the Pacific Northwest, but the berry that grows in the high mountains of Montana, called *Vaccinium globulare* are the favorite berry of the people of Montana. The huckleberry has achieved something of a cult following in Montana and some communities even have huckleberry festivals every year.

Huckleberries have been a staple of life for Northwest and Rocky Mountain Native American tribes for thousands of years.

There are special areas in western Montana that are notorious for huckleberries and have the reputation for producing more berries than any other area. During the 1930s and 1940s, the picking was so great that much of western Montana's population converged on this area and set up huckleberry camps. The Native Americans on one side of the road with as many as five hundred tipi lodges, and on the other side of the road would be the encampments of other Montanans. The camps might last a few days, a week, or as much as two months, depending on the crop and the inclinations of the family. It was said the big huckleberry camps had a boomtown atmosphere, much like the gold mining towns of the West. Those years produced boxcar-loads of huckleberries.

## Huckleberry Pie

*Pastry for 9-inch two-crust pie (recipe follows)*

*1 cup sugar*

*¼ cup firmly packed brown sugar*

*1 teaspoon ground cinnamon*

*4 tablespoons quick-cooking tapioca*

*6 cups fresh huckleberries, washed and drained\**

*1 tablespoon fresh lemon juice*

*2 tablespoons butter, cut into small pieces*

*1 tablespoon sugar*

\*  If using frozen huckleberries, thaw first and then drain before using. Blueberries may be substituted for huckleberries.

1. Prepare Pie Pastry. Preheat oven to 425°.

2. In a large bowl, combine sugar, brown sugar, cinnamon, and tapioca (making sure brown sugar is well crumbled). Gently fold in the huckleberries and lemon juice; let mixture sit for 15 minutes.

3. Using a floured rolling pin, roll pastry 2 inches larger than an inverted pie plate. Fold pastry into quarter folds and ease into plate, pressing firmly against bottom and side. Spoon huckleberry mixture into pastry-lined plate; trim overhanging edge of pastry ½ inch from rim of plate.

4. Roll other round of pastry. Fold into quarters. Place over filling and unfold. Trim overhanging edge of pastry 1 inch from rim of plate. Fold and roll top edge under lower edge, pressing on rim to seal; flute. Cut slits so steam can escape. Sprinkle 1 tablespoon sugar onto top of pie crust. Cover edge of crust with aluminum foil to prevent excessive browning.

5. Bake for 35 to 40 minutes or until crust is golden brown and juice begins to bubble through slits in crust. Remove aluminum foil during last 15 minutes of baking. Remove from oven and cool on a wire rack before cutting and servings. Serve warm or at room temperature.

Makes 8 to 10 servings.

## 9-INCH TWO-CRUST PIE PASTRY

⅔ cup plus 2 tablespoons solid vegetable shortening

2 cups all-purpose flour

1 teaspoon salt

5 to 6 tablespoons chilled water

1. In a large bowl with a pastry blender or two knives, cut shortening into flour and salt until particles are the size of small peas. Sprinkle in water, 1 tablespoon at a time, tossing with fork until all flour is moistened and pastry dough almost cleans side of bowl (1 to 2 teaspoons additional water can be added if necessary).

2. On a lightly floured surface, form pastry into a ball; shape into a flattened round. Divide pastry into halves and shape into two rounds. Wrap the pastry rounds in wax paper or plastic wrap and refrigerate 30 minutes before rolling out.

*Huckleberry pie is a favorite way to use the hard-to-acquire berries famous in the Northern Rockies. Carol Rublein, Northern Exposure photograph.*

# Macadamia Nut Pie

One of Hawaii's most amazing treasures is the macadamia nut. Often the first thing travelers to Hawaii notice is the huge displays of macadamia nut products such as dry roasted nuts, chocolate-covered nuts, and macadamia nut brittle. Hawaii is also known for its macadamia nut pie. This plantation-style pie gives a traditional southern pecan pie an exotic Island flavor.

The macadamia nut tree originated in the rain forests of Australia where, for thousands of years, the harvested nut was a staple and a prized delicacy of the Aborigine people. The nuts were usually eaten raw, but some tribes extracted the oil to be used in decorating the face and body. The nuts were frequently collected as items for sale or barter. Individual Aborigine tribes had different names for the nut. In the Pine River area, they called it *burrawang,* in New South Wales, *boomera,* and in Queensland, *kindal kindal.*

Baron Ferdinand von Mueller, director of the botanical gardens in Melbourne, and Walter Hill, director of the botanical gardens in Brisbane, formally "discovered" the tree in 1857. They named the tree for John Macadam Esq. M. D. (1827–1865), president of the Victoria Philosophical Society, since he was reportedly the first person to find the nuts edible.

Hawaii was the site of the world's first commercial macadamia plantation. In the early 1880s, William Herbert Purvis obtained seeds for the trees and planted them on Hawaii. Ernest Shelton Van Tassel gets credit for pioneering the macadamia nut as a cash crop in 1921. Crippled by polio, Van Tassel left his home in Massachusetts and traveled to Hawaii in hopes of regaining his health. Having tasted some home-roasted macadamia nuts (often served in Hawaiian homes), he decided to plant an orchard. His first orchard died, but he went on to plant more and to develop Van's Macadamia Nuts. By the late 1940s, the macadamia nut industry was well established in Hawaii. In the late 1950s and early 1960s, the nuts became more widely popular due to increased tourism to the Hawaiian Islands.

## Did You Know?

It takes three hundred pounds per square inch to break the shell of a macadamia nut. Old-timers are said to have cracked the nuts by driving their cars over them.

# Macadamia Nut Pie

*Pastry for 9-inch one-crust pie (recipe follows)*

*⅓ cup butter, room temperature*

*¾ cup firmly packed brown sugar*

*3 eggs*

*1 cup light corn syrup*

*1 cup coarsely chopped toasted macadamia nuts\**

*1 teaspoon rum or vanilla extract*

*Macadamia nut halves to garnish*

\*  To toast whole macadamia nuts: Spread whole nuts on a baking sheet and toast them in a preheated 300° oven for 5 to 8 minutes or until lightly browned (watch them closely as they burn easily).

**1.** Prepare Pie Pastry. Preheat oven to 375°.

**2.** In a large bowl, cream butter until light and fluffy; gradually add brown sugar. Beat in eggs, one at a time, beating well after each addition. Add corn syrup, macadamia nuts, and rum or vanilla extract; stir until well blended. Pour into the partially baked pie shell. Sprinkle the nut halves onto the top of the pie.

**3.** Bake 40 to 50 minutes or until the pie center has a slight jiggle to it when shaken. Remove from oven and cool completely on a wire rack before cutting and serving.

Makes 8 to 10 servings.

## 9-INCH ONE-CRUST PIE PASTRY

*½ cup butter or butter-flavored solid shortening, room temperature*

*1¼ cups all-purpose flour*

*½ cup toasted finely chopped macadamia nuts*

*½ teaspoon salt*

*4 to 5 tablespoons chilled water*

**1.** Preheat oven to 425°. In a large bowl with a pastry blender or two knives, cut shortening into flour, macadamia nuts, and salt until particles are the size of small peas. Sprinkle in water, 1 tablespoon at a time, tossing with fork until all flour is moistened and pastry dough almost cleans side of bowl (1 to 2 teaspoons additional water can be added if necessary).

**2.** On a lightly floured surface, form pastry into a ball; shape into a flattened round. Wrap the pastry round in wax paper or plastic wrap and refrigerate 20 to 30 minutes before rolling.

**3.** Place dough on a sheet of floured wax paper. Using a floured rolling pin, roll pastry 2 inches larger than an inverted pie plate. Fold pastry into quarter folds and ease into plate, pressing firmly against bottom and side. Trim overhanging edge of pastry 1 inch from rim of pie plate. Fold and roll pastry under, even with pie plate; flute. Prick bottom and sides thoroughly with a fork. Partially bake 5 minutes; remove from oven and let cool. Fill and bake as directed in recipe.

# Scuppernong Grape Pie

The land (North Carolina) . . . is so full of grapes, as the very beating and surge of the Sea over-flowed them. . . . I think in all the world the like abundance is not to be found; and my selfe having seene those parts of Europe that most abound. . . .

—*Sir Walter Raleigh (1554–1618), English explorer and adventurer*

Scuppernong grape pie has its place in the hearts of the South. These pies have been made by North Carolina housewives for centuries. Homemade pies have been a favorite dessert of Southerners for generations. Old-timers remember picking buckets of Scuppernong grapes so that their mothers could turn them into pies. When ripe, Scuppernong grapes make wonderful jams, jellies, pies, juice, and wines. In the early days, Scuppernong grape arbors were commonplace on family farms and homesteads.

The Scuppernong is a variety of the Muscadine grape and has a tough skin. Rather than being black or purplish as other grapes, it is bronzy green in color and has a plumlike flavor. The grape can grow as large as a plum and grows in clusters of four or more. To eat a Scuppernong grape, hold the grape with the stem scar up, put the grape with the stem scar facing upward in your mouth, and squeeze or bite the grape. The pulp and juice will burst through the skin into your mouth. Most people prefer not to chew the skin since it is bitter, but some people simply swallow them whole.

The nation's first cultivated wine grape, the Scuppernong, is native to the state of North Carolina. The first record of these grapes occurs in the logbook of Giovanni de Verrazano, Florentine explorer, who in 1524 discovered them in the Cape Fear River Valley. He wrote that he saw "Many vines growing naturally there that without doubt would yield excellent wines." The colonists learned about these unusual grapes from the Algonquin Indians who preserved them as dried fruit. Soon the grapes were being used in making jams, jellies, brandies, and wines. Sir Walter Raleigh's colony discovered the famed Scuppernong "mother vine" on Roanoke Island in Virginia and introduced it elsewhere. It is said that the mother vine still exists and is growing on Roanoke Island.

Originally the grape was simply called "the big white grape" by early settlers. The Scuppernong grape is named after a town that is named after a river that is named after an area that is named after a tree. The word *Scuppernong* comes from an Algonquin Indian name of *ascopo* for the sweet bay tree and *Asupernung* meaning place of the Ascopo.

# Scuppernong Pie

*Pastry for 9-inch one-crust pie (recipe follows)*

*2 cups Scuppernong grapes\**

*¼ cup butter*

*1 cup sugar*

*1 teaspoon vanilla extract*

*2 egg yolks*

*2 tablespoons all-purpose flour*

*Meringue Topping (recipe follows)*

\*  Concord grapes may be substituted.

**1.** Prepare pie pastry. Preheat oven to 325°.

**2.** In a colander over a bowl, place whole grapes. Squeeze or mash grapes, separating pulp and hulls from the juice. Put remaining pulp and hull mixture through a sieve to remove seeds; discard seeds.

**3.** In a large saucepan over low heat, cook the pulp and hull mixture with the juice 45 to 60 minutes or until the skins become tender. Stir in butter, sugar, vanilla extract, egg yolks, and flour; cook until mixture thickens and coats spoon. Remove from heat and pour into baked pie shell.

**4.** Prepare Meringue Topping. Spread Meringue Topping over pie filling, being careful to spread to edge of pastry to prevent meringue from shrinking during baking. Bake 20 minutes or until meringue is golden brown. Remove from oven and cool completely on a wire rack before cutting and serving.

Makes 8 servings.

## 9-INCH ONE-CRUST PIE PASTRY

*⅓ cup plus 1 tablespoon solid vegetable shortening*

*1 cup all-purpose flour*

*½ teaspoon salt*

*2 to 3 tablespoons chilled water*

**1.** Preheat oven to 475°. In a large bowl with a pastry blender or two knives, cut shortening into flour and salt until particles are the size of small peas. Sprinkle in water, 1 tablespoon at a time, tossing with fork until all flour is moistened and pastry dough almost cleans side of bowl (1 to 2 teaspoons additional water may be added if necessary).

**2.** On a lightly floured surface, form pastry into a ball; shape into a flattened round. Using a floured rolling pin, roll pastry 2 inches larger than an inverted pie plate. Fold pastry into quarter folds and ease into plate, pressing firmly against bottom and side. Trim overhanging edge of pastry 1 inch from rim of pie plate. Fold and roll pastry under, even with pie plate; flute edges. Prick bottom and sides thoroughly with a fork. Bake 8 to 10 minutes or until light brown; remove from oven and let cool. Fill and bake as directed in recipe.

## MERINGUE TOPPING

*3 egg whites, room temperature*

*½ teaspoon vanilla extract*

*6 tablespoons sugar*

In a large bowl, beat egg whites and vanilla extract until frothy. Add sugar, 1 tablespoon at a time, beating until stiff peaks form.

# Shoofly Pie

**Better a burst stomach than wasted food.
A plump wife and a big barn never did any man
harm.**

—*old Pennsylvania Dutch sayings*

*Clemens Family Market of Greater Philadelphia ships its famous
shoofly pies to consumers throughout the country.
Courtesy Clemens Family Market, www.clemensmarkets.com.*

Visit the Lancaster area of Pennsylvania and indulge in a Pennsylvania Dutch original, the shoofly pie. First-time visitors to the area always comment on this pie and its strange name. Most of the area restaurants and bakeries sell this favorite pie. Today, most recipes are generally the same with the biggest debate being whether to use a flaky or a mealy crust for the pie dough. The bottom of the pie can be thick or barely visible and is referred to as either a "wet bottom" or a "dry bottom." Everyone agrees that shoofly pie is best when slightly warmed and with whipped cream on top.

Pennsylvania Dutch cooking is indigenous to those areas of southwestern Pennsylvania that were settled by the Mennonites and Amish. William Penn (1644–1718), founder of Pennsylvania, was seeking colonists for the Pennsylvania area. Because of Penn's appeal, many decided to immigrate to America to seek freedom to worship as they pleased. The first settlers attracted by Penn arrived in Pennsylvania in 1683.

These settlers were addicted to pies of all types and they ate them at any time of day. The most famous of their pies is the shoofly pie, which is basically a molasses crumb cake within a pie shell. As the very earliest settlers came to North America by boat, they brought with them the staples of their diet—long-lasting nonperishables that would survive a long boat trip.

These staples were flour, brown sugar, molasses, lard, salt, and spices. Arriving in the new land during late fall, they had to live pretty much on what they had brought with them until the next growing season. The women, being masters of the art of "making do," concocted a pie from the limited selection that could be found in the larder. This resourcefulness led to the creation of shoofly pie.

The origin of the name shoofly pie has been debated for years and will probably never ultimately be solved. The most logical explanation is related to the fact that during the early years of our country, all baking was done in big outdoor ovens. The fact that pools of sweet, sticky molasses sometimes formed on the surface of the pie while it was cooling, invariably attracting flies, shows how such a pie could come to be called shoofly pie.

# Wet-Bottom Shoofly Pie

*Pastry for 9-inch pie one-crust pie (recipe follows)*

*3 tablespoons solid vegetable shortening or butter, room temperature*

*1½ cups all-purpose flour*

*⅔ cup firmly packed brown sugar*

*¼ teaspoon salt*

*1 teaspoon baking soda*

*1 cup hot water*

*1 cup dark molasses\**

*1 egg*

\* Can substitute ½ cup dark molasses and ½ cup light or dark corn syrup.

**1.** Prepare pie pastry. Preheat oven to 400°.

**2.** In a large bowl, using a pastry blender or two knives, cut shortening or butter into flour, brown sugar, and salt until mixture is crumbly and particles are the size of small peas; set aside.

**3.** In a large bowl, add baking soda and hot water; stir until baking soda is dissolved. Add molasses (or molasses and corn syrup combination) and egg; beat until blended. Pour into prepared unbaked pie shell, filling half full (you may not use all the filling—if you overfill the shell, it will overflow during baking). Gently sprinkle prepared crumb mixture evenly over top of the pie (crumbs will both partly sink and partly float). Bake 10 minutes and then reduce oven to 350°. Bake an additional 35 to 40 minutes or until knife inserted in center comes out clean. Remove from oven and cool on a wire rack before serving. This pie is best served at room temperature.

Makes 8 servings.

## 9-INCH ONE-CRUST PIE PASTRY

*⅓ cup plus 1 tablespoon solid vegetable shortening*

*1 cup all-purpose flour*

*½ teaspoon salt*

*2 to 3 tablespoons chilled water*

**1.** In a large bowl with a pastry blender or two knives, cut shortening into flour and salt until particles are the size of small peas. Sprinkle in water, 1 tablespoon at a time, tossing with fork until all flour is moistened and pastry dough almost cleans side of bowl (1 to 2 teaspoons additional water may be added if necessary).

**2.** On a lightly floured surface, form pastry into a ball; shape into a flattened round. Using a floured rolling pin, roll pastry 2 inches larger than an inverted pie plate. Fold pastry into quarter folds and ease into plate, pressing firmly against bottom and side. Trim overhanging edge of pastry 1 inch from rim of pie plate. Fold and roll pastry under, even with pie plate; flute. Fill and bake as directed in recipe.

# Akutaq/Eskimo Ice Cream

The Inuit people of Alaska have a distinct version of ice cream. It's not creamy ice cream as we know it, but a concoction made from reindeer fat or tallow, seal oil, freshly fallen snow or water, fresh berries, and sometimes ground fish. Air is whipped in by hand so that it slowly cools into foam. They call this Arctic treat akutaq, aqutuk, ackutuk, or Eskimo ice cream. This is a delicacy that Alaska Natives have thrived on for thousands of years, and another one of those foods that you shouldn't bad mouth if you haven't tried it. It is eaten as a dessert, a meal, a snack, or a spread. Traditionally it was made for funerals, potlatches, celebrations of a boy's first hunt, or almost any other celebration. Akutaq is also used as a special traveling food.

Today, Eskimo ice cream is usually made with Crisco shortening instead of tallow and with raisins and sugar sometimes added. The region lived in usually determines what berry is used, and each family usually has their favorite recipe for Eskimo ice cream. It is said that your choice of berries used in making Eskimo ice cream is a lifetime decision. It is okay to eat any flavor made by others, but if you are caught making more than one kind, you will lose all social standing.

The people of the Arctic love to serve their favorite dish to *cheechakos* (newcomers in Alaska). When guests are willing to try their favorite foods, the Inuits feel pride at sharing their culture. At first, the host might be shy to offer any of their food for fear of rejection. If you are a guest and are offered some (you will probably be served first as a guest), at least try a small amount. Please do not express any "yucks" or other words of ridicule. If you really cannot bring yourself to eat this unusual food, accept the serving and find the oldest person in the room and offer the food to him or her. This will show that you have good manners, if not good taste, and that you respect your elders. Then quickly grab a plate and fill it with things that you can eat. Most people who try Eskimo ice cream say it is delicious.

Food is the connector to everything that surrounds the Inuit culture. Each celebration includes a huge feast, as they believe that food tastes better when it is shared with family, relatives, and many other people. Feasts are very special because they believe sharing food is an important part of their culture and an important link to their heritage. In community feasts, where everyone gathers in a public place, all food is donated by those who have food to give. In bigger communities, designated hunters provide much of the food.

## Did You Know?

Alaska has the highest percentage of men and the lowest percentage of women of any state. Alaska claims that there are ten good men for every woman. The women state, "The odds are good, but the goods are odd!"

# Akutaq

This was a very hard recipe to record, as each family usually has its own version and has never written down in an actual recipe. They generally just make it from memory and feel. After reading several descriptions on how to make akutaq, I came up with the following recipe.

The type of fat used determines how the akutaq will taste and feel, as each animal has a different type of fat. Well-aged yellow fat is usually preferred because it has more flavor and whips up fluffier than does fresh fat. Some people think that seal oil ruins the flavor, while others would not eat akutaq without it. The ice cream can also be sweetened with sweetener or with fruits. Meat and fish akutaq are not usually sweetened.

*1 cup reindeer, caribou, or moose fat (back fat)*

*1 cup seal oil*

*½ cup water or 2 cups loose snow*

*4½ cups fresh berries (blueberries, cloudberries, cranberries, salmonberries, or blackberries)*

Grate or grind fat into small pieces. In a large pot over low heat, add fat and stir until it becomes a liquid (the fat should never get hotter than it is comfortable to your hand). Add ⅓ cup seal oil, mixing until it is all liquid. Remove from heat and continue stirring the fat in big circles. While continuing to stir at a steady rate, add ¼ cup water or 1 cup snow and another ⅓ cup seal oil. As fat slowly cools and starts to get fluffy and white, add remaining ¼ cup water or 1 cup snow and remaining ⅓ cup seal oil, continuing to stir. When the akutaq is as white and fluffy as you can make it, fold in berries. Form into desired shape. Cover, and freeze to firm up.

# Modern Eskimo Ice Cream

*1 cup solid vegetable shortening\**

*1 cup sugar*

*½ cup water, berry juice, or 2 cups loose snow (optional)*

*4 cups fresh berries (blueberries, cloudberries, cranberries, salmonberries, or blackberries)*

*\*   Crisco solid vegetable shortening is preferred.*

In a large bowl, cream vegetable shortening and sugar until fluffy. Add water, berry juice, or snow and beat until well combined. Fold in berries, 1 cup at a time, until blended. Place in freezer to firm up before serving.

# Hasty Pudding/Indian Pudding

**Fath'r and I went down to camp.**
**Along with Captain Goodin;**
**And there we saw the men and boys,**
**As thick as hasty puddin'.**

—*Verse from eighteenth-century American folk song*
*"Yankee Doodle"*

Hasty pudding is also known as Indian pudding, because the colonists had a habit of calling anything made with corn "Indian." The love of pudding came with the first colonists in Virginia and was a favorite of the New England settlers. In colonial New England, the earliest Indian pudding recipe included cracked hominy and dried whortleberries. The first printed pudding recipe did not show up until the sixteenth century and the recipe called for bread. In later years, the pudding was dressed up with everything from sugar and eggs to raisins and spices.

In 1662, John Winthrop, Jr., son of John Winthrop (1588–1649), first governor of the Massachusetts Bay Colony, wrote the following about the pudding in his letter to the Royal Society in London:

> This is to be boyled or Stued with a gentle fire, till it be tender, of a fitt consistence, as of Rice so boyled, into which Milke, or butter be put either with Sugar or without it, it is a food very pleasant . . . but it must be observed that it be very well boyled, the longer the better, some will let it be stuing the whole day: after it is Cold it groweth thicker, and is commonly Eaten by mixing a good Quantity of Milke amongst it. . . .

In 1796, Joel Barlow (1754–1812), American poet and diplomat, wrote his famous poem called "The Hasty-Pudding." The poem was inspired by his homesickness for New England and his favorite cornmeal mush.

> And all my bones were made of Indian corn.
> Delicious grain! Whatever form it take,
> To roast or boil, to smother or to bake,
> In every dish 'tis welcome still to me,
> but most, my Hasty Pudding, most in thee.

In 1795, a society called the Hasty Pudding Club was organized by twenty-one Harvard College students. The club's purpose was to encourage "friendship and patriotism." Its constitution stipulated that every Saturday, two "providers" were to carry a pot of hasty pudding to the meeting. For the majority of the nineteenth century, prospective members were forced to ingest large quantities of hasty pudding. According to Harvard University historians, the club was founded by students who sought relief from the food the college provided by cooking their own hasty puddings in fireplace pots. With this ritual, the Hasty Pudding Club found its namesake. Today it is the nations oldest theater company, which annually puts on a spectacular spring production starring men in drag.

# Maple Indian Pudding

4 cups milk

½ cup yellow cornmeal

½ cup genuine maple syrup

¼ cup light molasses

2 eggs, slightly beaten

2 tablespoons butter, melted

⅓ cup firmly packed brown sugar

1 teaspoon salt

¼ teaspoon ground cinnamon

¼ teaspoon ground nutmeg

¾ teaspoon ground ginger

½ cup cold whole milk

Vanilla ice cream or light cream (optional)

1. Preheat oven to 300°. Lightly grease a 2-quart baking dish.

2. In top of double boiler over boiling water, heat milk; slowly stir in cornmeal. Cook over boiling water, stirring occasionally for 20 minutes. Remove from heat and set aside.

3. In a small bowl, combine maple syrup, molasses, eggs, butter, brown sugar, salt, cinnamon, nutmeg, and ginger; stir into cornmeal mixture. Pour into prepared dish; pour cold milk on top, without stirring. Bake, uncovered, 2 hours or just until set but quivery on top (do not overbake). Remove from oven and let stand 30 minutes before serving. Serve warm with vanilla ice cream or light cream.

Makes 8 servings.

# New Orleans Bread Pudding

**The most direct line to a Cajun's heart is through his stomach.**

—*Cajun proverb*

The classic New Orleans dessert is bread pudding, as every restaurant in New Orleans offers its own version of this favorite. Bread puddings can be found throughout the country, but the finest manifestations of this dessert are today found in New Orleans, Louisiana. The Cajun tradition of adding a whiskey sauce marries the drink's strong taste with a sweetness that will instantly make you a bread pudding fan. Bread pudding aficionados claim no distance is too great to travel for this wonderful dessert.

This dessert has its foundation in pioneer history up and down the Atlantic coast. Bread pudding is one of many kinds of food preparations that began as a result of early settlers trying to find some other way to use leftovers. Since food was hard to get and prepare, little could be wasted. Bread, being the most important staple of life during the seventeenth, eighteenth, and nineteenth century diets, was recycled into a number of different dishes. Bread pudding was the most popular way to use stale bread, especially since bread holds moisture well. Early cooks considered the main ingredients in bread pudding (bread, milk, and eggs) to be "easy on delicate digestions."

## New Orleans Bread Pudding

This recipe is from *What's Cooking America*, by Linda Stradley and Andra Cook.

3 tablespoons butter, melted

1 loaf French bread

4 cups milk

3 eggs, beaten

2 cups sugar

2 tablespoons vanilla extract

1 cup raisins

Bourbon Whiskey Sauce (recipe follows)

Preheat oven to 350°. Pour butter into a 13 x 9-inch baking pan, turning pan to coat the sides and bottom. Tear French bread into pieces; place in a large bowl. Add milk and let bread pieces soak; crush with your hands until well mixed. Stir in eggs, sugar, vanilla extract, and raisins. Pour mixture into prepared pan. Bake, uncovered, 1 to 1½ hours or until very firm. Remove from oven and cool on a wire rack. To serve, cut into squares and put into individual serving dishes. Serve warm with Bourbon Whiskey Sauce.

Makes 6 servings.

### BOURBON WHISKEY SAUCE

1 cup sugar

1 egg

½ cup butter, melted

2 tablespoons Bourbon Whiskey or to your taste

In a medium saucepan over medium heat, combine sugar and egg; stir until well blended. Add butter; stir until sugar is dissolved. Stir in whiskey.

# Persimmon Pudding

**If it not be ripe, it will drawe a man's mouth awrie with much torment; but when it is ripe, it is delicious as an Apricock.**

*—Captain John Smith (1579–1631), English explorer and colonist, describing the persimmon*

Persimmon pudding is probably the least known regional dish outside of Indiana, Illinois, and Ohio. To the families where native persimmons grow, their traditional and favorite holiday persimmon pudding recipe is an absolute must.

Unripe persimmons have a bitter, puckery flavor. A favorite prank of children is to trick an unsuspecting city boy into eating a not quite ripe or "green" persimmon. Lips, gums, and tongue will pucker up until he cannot spit or talk (it tends to dry out the mouth and cause the mouth parts to cling together). This astringent quality, due to tannin, disappears in the fully ripened fruit. To eat a persimmon, let it get so soft you almost cannot believe it is not rotten. When the fruit falls from the tree, it is ready to eat. A fully ripe persimmon is deliciously rich and sweet and is worth waiting for.

The American persimmon grows wild across Indiana, Illinois, and Ohio. Native persimmons are now cultivated, but not widely. Since they are highly perishable, they are rarely sold in supermarkets. The trees tend to be grown on small farms and are considered a specialty or heritage crop. (These native persimmons must not be confused with the Japanese variety that is cultivated in California and marketed widely.) According to local folklore, the seeds of the native persimmons play a role in forecasting the upcoming winter. First you must split one of the mahogany seeds in half with a sharp paring knife. The opaque interior will have distinctively shaped marking resembling either a knife, a fork, or a spoon. The knife shape indicates a winter of bitter cold, the fork a mild winter, and a spoon means plenty of snow.

French fur traders traveling in the Midwest in the late 1600s wrote of trees laden with "apples" that tasted so bad that they could not be eaten unless they had first been left to freeze. Native Americans ate this fruit both raw and cooked, and they also made bread, using the dried seeds of the persimmon pounded into flour.

Mitchell, Indiana, is the self-proclaimed heart of persimmon territory. Since 1946, the town has held an annual Persimmon Festival every year. During the festival you can sample persimmon puddings, cakes, cookies, ice cream, waffles and much more.

## Persimmon Pudding

*2 eggs*

*2¼ cups all-purpose flour*

*2 cups persimmon pulp\**

*1 cup buttermilk*

*1 cup sugar*

*1 cup firmly packed brown sugar*

*1 tablespoon baking powder*

*1 teaspoon baking soda*

*1 teaspoon ground cinnamon*

*1 teaspoon ground allspice*

*½ teaspoon salt*

*Whipped cream*

\*  2 large or 3 to 4 small persimmons will yield 1 cup pulp. To get persimmon pulp, cut persimmons in half. With a spoon, scoop out the pulp and puree in a food processor.

**1.** Preheat oven to 350°. Grease two 9 x 9-inch baking pans or one 13 x 9-inch pan.

**2.** In a large bowl, add eggs, flour, persimmon pulp, and buttermilk; stir until combined. Add sugar, brown sugar, baking powder, baking soda, cinnamon, allspice, and salt, stirring until well mixed and smooth.

**3.** Pour batter into prepared pans. Bake 50 minutes or until a wooden toothpick comes out clean when inserted in the center. Remove from oven and cool 15 minutes. Cut into squares and serve with whipped cream.

Makes 18 servings.

# Beverages

# Coffee Drinks

**Coffee is real good when you drink it. It gives you time to think. It's a lot more than just a drink; it's something happening.**

*—Gertrude Stein (1874–1946), American writer*

Seattle, Washington, loves and craves its coffee, and an entire coffee culture has sprung up to answer the craving of this phenomenon. Espresso stands and carts have sprung up all over town and the surrounding region, including neighbor state Oregon. You can find espresso or coffee places on street corners, in grocery stores, gas stations, hardware stores, department stores, dry cleaners, stadiums, and even in the fast food outlets. There are even drive-through espresso stands for coffee drinkers who don't have time to get out of their cars. Coffee shops continue to spring up in cities across America and also around the world. Seattle has definitely affected the way Americans drink coffee. It is more than just a trend; it is a new institution of the busy lifestyle.

As to why coffee is so popular in the Northwest, some people laughingly argue it is because people can't function in the cold, gray, and drizzly climate without it. Whatever the reason, this craving has spread throughout the United States and owes this present-day phenomenon to the Starbucks Coffee chain, which opened its first location in Seattle's legendary Pike Place Market in 1971. Starbucks was named for the first mate in the novel *Moby Dick* by Herman Melville.

The boom of coffee houses in the 1990s is nothing new, as the roots of coffee houses go back to the fifteenth century Arabia, sixteenth century Europe, and seventeenth century North America. Coffee drinking began in the American colonies as early as 1689 in Boston, New York, and Philadelphia. In fact, the Green Dragon Coffee House of Boston was where the idea for the famous Boston Tea Party was conceived in 1773. Americans revolted against England's tea tax, and the Continental Congress declared coffee the "Official National Beverage" (what better way to protest the unfair tea taxes imposed than to enjoy an alternate beverage?).

Hawaii boasts a thriving coffee industry that is mostly geared toward Island visitors and gourmets. Coffee is grown commercially on four out of the six major Hawaiian Islands and each island produces a distinctive coffee. The Kona region is considered the backbone of Hawaii's coffee industry with more than five hundred coffee farms yielding 1,800 acres of coffee. Hawaii remains the sole U.S. producer of commercially grown coffee. Coffee was introduced to the Hawaiian Islands in 1813 by Don Francisco de Paula Marin. He recorded in his journal that he had planted coffee on Oahu. This first planting failed, but in 1825, Chief Boki, governor of Oahu, brought Brazilian coffee plants to Hawaii aboard a British warship. In 1828, Reverend Samuel Ruggles, an American missionary, brought cuttings from the coffee plants in Oahu to Kona.

# Caffe Latte or Café au Lait

⅔ cup brewed hot espresso coffee

⅓ cup milk

Ground cinnamon, nutmeg, or sweetened chocolate powder (optional)

Prepare a single shot of espresso according to your coffee machine's instructions. Steam or froth the milk (150° to 170°). Simultaneously pour the espresso and the steamed milk into a large cup. If desired, top with a teaspoon of foam. Sprinkle with cinnamon, nutmeg, or chocolate if desired.

## VARIATION

**Café Mocha:** Stir 2 tablespoons chocolate syrup into the hot coffee.

Makes 1 serving.

# Hawaiian Coffee Soda

3 cups brewed cold extra-strong Kona coffee

1 tablespoon sugar

1 cup half-and-half cream

1 pint coffee-flavored ice cream

Chilled club soda

Whipped cream

4 maraschino cherries

In a large pitcher, combine the coffee and sugar; add half-and-half cream. Fill 4 large glasses halfway with the coffee-sugar mixture. Add one scoop of ice cream to each glass and then fill each glass with club soda. Garnish with a dollop of whipped cream and a maraschino cherry.

Makes 4 servings.

# Rhode Island Coffee Milk/Coffee Cabinet

**This great state was founded on the principles of rugged individualism, and we're proud of the things that make us different from people in other places. Coffee milk is one of those things.**

*—Rhode Island State Senator John W. Lyle, speaking in favor of making coffee milk the Official Drink of Rhode Island*

Coffee milk is the most popular Rhode Island comfort food, and the rest of the United States barely knows it exists. It is one of the first things that homesick Rhode Islanders write home for. The drink is served either by the glass or the half-pint (in a waxed cardboard carton).

When ice cream is added, this famous drink is called a "coffee cabinet" or "coffee cab." In Rhode Island, a milk shake is just what it says: milk to which you add flavoring, then shake. In most of the U.S., if you order a milk shake, you get ice cream blended with milk. In Rhode Island and most of New England, however, you would get chocolate powder or syrup stirred into milk without ice cream. To further clarify the milk shake question, in Rhode Island, "cabinet" is a local term for a frappe, which is a regional term for an ice cream milk shake.

Coffee milk was first introduced to Rhode Islanders in the early 1920s. Two companies, Autocrat and Eclipse, used to vie for the chocolate syrup business. Their rivalry ended in 1991, when Autocrat bought the Eclipse brand name and secret formula. Both labels are now produced by Autocrat and are available in stores and online.

Rhode Islanders' love affair with coffee milk is so intense that in 1993, after much political debate, it was made the Official State Drink of Rhode Island.

## Rhode Island Coffee Milk

*2 tablespoons coffee-flavored syrup\**

*1 cup cold milk*

\* Autocrat coffee syrup is the preferred syrup in Rhode Island.

In a large glass, add coffee syrup and milk; stir well. Taste and add more coffee syrup to taste.

Makes 1 serving.

# Hurricane

**New Orleans, the only city in the world that looks forward to the first Hurricane of the day.**

*—author unknown*

The drink known to most tourists in New Orleans is the hurricane. During celebrations (and celebrations seem to be every night in the New Orleans French Quarter), tourists carry their "to go" hurricane drinks with them. In New Orleans, you can carry your drink out of a bar and down the street, even into another bar. Hurricanes are also the cocktail of choice during Mardi Gras, when thousands come to parade and party.

The hurricane was made famous by Pat O'Brien's French Quarter bar. Other restaurants and bars now serve this drink but it has become synonymous with Pat O'Brien's. This signature cocktail is a potent fruit punch drink that is served in a special hurricane lamp glass that has become one of the most sought-after souvenirs in New Orleans. The drink was created during World War II, when liquor such as whiskey was in low supply and bar owners were forced to order large amounts of rum in order to get their quota of whiskey. Pat O'Brien's has become a tourist mecca.

## Hurricane

*1 ounce fresh lemon juice*

*4 ounces dark rum*

*4 ounces passion fruit syrup*

*Crushed ice*

*Orange slice*

*1 maraschino cherry*

In a cocktail shaker, add lemon juice, rum, passion fruit syrup, and crushed ice; shake vigorously for 1 to 2 minutes and then strain into a tall glass or hurricane glass. Garnish with orange slice and maraschino cherry.

Makes 1 serving.

# Mint Julep

**But my grandfather always insisted that a man who
would let the crushed leaves and the mangled stem-
lets steep in the finished decoction would put scor-
pions in a baby's bed. Down our way we've always
had a theory that the Civil War was not brought on
by Secession or Slavery or the State's Rights issue.
These matters contributed to the quarrel, but there
is a deeper reason. It was brought on by some
Yankee coming down south and putting nutmeg in a
julep. So our folks up and left the Union flat."**

*—Irvin S. Cobb (1876–1944), American journalist and humorist*

This wonderfully refreshing drink comes to us from
the southern states, but it is mainly credited to
the traditions of Kentucky and the famous annual
horse race the Kentucky Derby. People from
Charleston, South Carolina, also like to claim the
mint julep as their own. Mint juleps have been served
in the South since the 1700s. A visitor in 1774,
describing the southern menu and especially breakfast
as being overly luxurious, observed that the average
planter rose early and had his drink (because a julep
before breakfast was believed to give protection
against malaria).

Kentuckians maintain that when a mint julep is
made right, you can hear angels sing. Always made
with fresh mint, Kentucky bourbon, and plenty of
crushed or shaved ice, it is the official drink of the
Kentucky Derby. Traditionally, mint juleps are served in
silver or pewter cups (which frost better than glass).
Thousands of mint juleps are served each year at the
Derby, on the first Saturday in May, at Churchill Downs,
and at weekend Derby parties around the nation.

The racetrack's clubhouse began mixing mint juleps
around 1875. The drink really became popular and
became the track's signature libation in 1938 when the
management began charging 75 cents for the drink
and the small glass vessel it came in. Every year during
Derby week at Churchill Downs, more than 80,000
mint juleps are served.

# Mint Julep

Mint juleps are the perfect excuse, on a hot summer day or night, to sit back and drink what is perhaps the South's greatest contribution to civilized drinking. I've become such a mint Julep fan, that I even bought some silver mint julep cups.

*Crushed ice*

*2 tablespoons Mint Syrup (recipe follows) (prepare syrup the night before making mint julep)*

*2 tablespoons water*

*3 to 4 ounces Bourbon whiskey*

*1 mint sprig*

**1.** Fill a highball glass or mint julep cup with crushed ice; add Mint Syrup, water, and whiskey. Stir until glass is frosted. *(Note: The highball glass will not frost like the traditional silver mint julep cup. If you're a serious mint julep drinker, you absolutely must use silver or pewter cups.)*

**2.** Serve garnished with a fresh sprig of mint. *(Note: According to tradition, you must not touch the cup with your fingers, but hold it with a napkin; this is to keep the oils from your hand from leaving marks on the cup.)*

Makes 1 serving.

## MINT SYRUP

*1 cup sugar*

*1 cup water*

*1 cup fresh mint leaves*

In a medium saucepan, add (but do not stir to combine) sugar and water. Boil for 5 minutes, without stirring; remove from heat. In a large bowl or jar, pour syrup over the mint leaves and gently stir with a spoon. Refrigerate syrup mixture overnight in a covered bowl or a closed jar. Remove mint leaves and continue to refrigerate syrup. This syrup mixture will keep for several weeks.

## Kentucky Mint Julep

### from Judge Soule Smith, 1890

Take from the cold spring some water, pure as the angels are; mix with it sugar till it seems like oil. Then take a glass and crush your mint in it with a spoon—crush it around the border of the glass and leave no place untouched. Then throw the mint away—it is a sacrifice. Fill with cracked ice the glass; pour in the quantity of bourbon you want. It trickles slowly through the ice. Let it have time to cool, then pour your sugared water over it. No spoon is needed, no stirring allowed. Just let it stand a moment. Then around the brim place springs of mint so that one who drinks may find taste and odor at one draught. When it is made sip it slowly. August suns are shining, the breath of the south wine is upon you.

# Date Shake

**Dates like to grow with their feet in the water, their heads in the fires of heaven.**

*—Arabic saying*

One of the most recent and tastiest culinary creations is the date shake. Date shakes are commonly made in the date-growing region of southern California. In February every year, Indio, California, hosts the National Date Festival with its Arabian theme.

The first date palm trees in the United States were grown from seeds planted by Franciscan and Jesuit missionaries around 1769 in the San Diego, California, area. Most of the missions were established along the Pacific coast, where the damp coastal climate is not suitable for producing dates. Because of the coastal climate, only a few of these original date palms are still in existence (as landmarks only).

In 1890, the U.S. Department of Agriculture arranged for sixty-eight offshoots (the suckers that grow out around the base of the tree and produce fruit identical to that of the parent tree) to be imported from Egypt and Algeria. According to historical records, the Arab growers were very uncooperative and feared any competition. Supposedly the shoots had to be smuggled out at night.

Most of the first date trees planted in California by the missionaries were of the readily available Deglet Noor variety from Algeria. Today, this is the most common commercial variety in the United States, but there are hundreds of other varieties that have been imported. The Coachella Valley in California is the only place in the Western Hemisphere where dates are grown commercially. This desert valley is 20 feet below sea level. A canal brings water from the Colorado River, and the sun shines hot nearly all the time. Here the date palm has ideal living conditions, with "its head in the sun and its feet in the water." Date palms are planted in "harems," forty-nine females to one male presiding. Each female blossom must be pollinated by hand. Although there is some wind pollination, the natural process is too uncertain for commercial growers.

## Date Shake

½ cup pitted California dates

⅓ cup milk, divided

½ cup vanilla ice cream

In a blender, process dates and ¼ cup milk at high speed until smooth. Add remaining ¼ cup milk and ice cream, blending at low speed until well mixed. Serve immediately.

## VARIATIONS

**Chocolate Date Shake:** Add 1½ teaspoons chocolate syrup.

**Orange Date Shake:** Substitute ½ cup orange juice for ½ cup milk.

Makes 1 serving.

# Blenheim Ginger Ale

## It's good for what ails you!

*—South Carolina saying*

This ginger ale is a classic South Carolina beverage with a hot chili pepper and ginger flavor. It is definitely an acquired taste that some people do not care to acquire. Once you do, though, it's very addictive. It's hard to consider this drink in the same category as soft drinks or pops. It is brewed from a blend of spicy ground ginger root, natural mineral spring water, and other natural ingredients. The fame of Blenheim Ginger Ale is expanding, and the drink has a loyal following (sort of like Moxie lovers in New England).

The Blenheim bottling plant is the oldest and smallest independent bottling company in America. Located next to the Blenheim Artesian Mineral Springs, the bottling plant is today much as it was when it began the production of the ginger ale in 1903. Up until 1993, each bottle was taken off the production line to be shaken by hand to mix the granulated sugar into the ale. This laborious process ended when the Schafer family acquired the bottling plant and renovated the old plant to meet new standards.

James Spears, a Whig, discovered the mineral springs in 1782 while trying to escape Tory troops. According to legend, James lost a shoe in a water hole. When he returned to retrieve his shoe, he tasted the water and noticed its strong mineral content. He became convinced of the water's curative properties and spread the word. Soon people were coming to taste this cool refreshing water, and several wealthy plantation owners built their summer homes near the springs. One of these people was Dr. C. R. May. In the late 1800s, Dr. May advised his patients with stomach problems to drink the mineral water. Several of his patients complained about the strong taste of the plain mineral water, so Dr. May doctored it with Jamaican ginger to make it more palatable.

# Lemon Drop Martini

**One is all right, two is too many, and three is not enough.**

*—James Thurber, American humorist, in reference to the martini*

The martini is the premier American cocktail and has achieved a social status of its own. Served in the traditional glass with a V-shaped profile, it has become an American icon. In San Francisco, the lemon drop martini is the most popular version—a lemon drink that is truly reminiscent of childhood candy. It is sometimes known as adult lemonade. The lemon drop martini is made with fresh lemon juice, vodka, sweet vermouth or Triple Sec, and sugar, and served ice cold in a sugar-rimmed martini glass.

This sweet, lemony treat came into vogue during the 1970s. The drink was developed at a now defunct bar called Henry Africa's in San Francisco, a well-known singles bar. Henry Africa's developed and pushed "girl drinks"—drinks that are potent, yet sweet enough to cover the taste of alcohol.

San Francisco and Martinez, California, have each claimed to have originated the standard martini. According to the story accepted by everyone in San Francisco, a gold miner came into the bar of the Occidental Hotel sometime in the 1860s, threw a gold nugget on the table, and asked the hotel's legendary bartender, "Professor" Jerry Thomas, to shake up something special for him. The recipe that Jerry Thomas created was later included in Thomas's own *Bartending Book* in 1887. To further substantiate this story, a mock court, called the Court of Historical Review, was held in San Francisco. The "court" ruled that the martini was invented in San Francisco, but not before the presiding judge drank the evidence. Later, a "court" in Martinez, California, overturned this decision and the citizens of the town have erected a brass plaque in downtown Martinez proclaiming their town as the birthplace of the martini. It is confirmed by food historians that the lemon drop martini originated in San Francisco.

## Lemon Drop Martini

After making and sampling many different recipes, my husband, Don, and I declared this recipe our favorite.

*1½ ounces vodka*

*½ ounce Triple Sec*

*1 teaspoon superfine sugar*

*¾ ounce fresh lemon juice*

*Ice cubes*

*Superfine sugar for dipping*

*Twisted peel of lemon*

Mix vodka, Triple Sec, sugar, and lemon juice in a cocktail shaker half-filled with ice; shake well (supposedly the cocktail is to be shaken 40 times to make sure the sugar is well blended). Pour strained liquor into sugar-rimmed martini glass and garnish with a twisted peel of lemon.

*Note: To create a sugar-rimmed glass, take a lemon or lime wedge and rub the drinking surface of the glass so it is barely moist. Dip the edge of the glass into sugar.*

Makes 1 serving.

# Mai Tai

**Anyone who says I didn't create this drink is a dirty stinker.**

—*Victor J. "Trader Vic" Bergeron, from* Trader Vic's Bartender's Guide, *1947*

The mai tai is considered the unofficial drink of Hawaii. A potent drink, it combines light and dark rums with different fruit juices. It seems that every bartender in the Hawaiian Islands has his or her own secret recipe and that every tourist wishes to sample as many as possible.

The mai tai may be a Polynesian name, but it's American in origin. There have been heated debates regarding who first created this drink. Some say it was Donn Beach, known as Donn the Beachcomber; others give credit to Victor Bergeron, known as Trader Vic. Donn the Beachcomber, who opened Beachcomber's Bar in Hollywood in 1933, has claimed that he has documents proving that the mai tai appeared on his bar's drink menus as early as 1941.

According to Trader Vic, he created the mai tai in 1944 for a couple of Tahitian friends, Harn and Carrie Guild. On tasting the drink, Carrie reportedly exclaimed "Mai tai, roa, ae," meaning, in Tahitian, "out of this world, the best."

Syndicated columnist Jim Bishop claims that during a dinner conversation with Beach and Bergeron, Bergeron finally admitted the truth about the drink's origins. In a letter to Don Chapman of the *Honolulu Advertiser,* Bishop wrote: "In probably 1970 or 1971, Donn and I were with Vic at Vic's in San Francisco. In the 'friend-foe' relationship Donn and Vic had, Vic said in effect that night, 'Blankety blank, Donn, I wish you'd never come up with the blankety blank thing. It's caused me a lot of arguing with people.'"

## Pineapple Mai Tai

*1 ounce light rum*

*½ ounce Triple Sec*

*¼ ounce Rose's lime juice*

*1½ ounces pineapple juice*

*1½ ounces orange juice*

*1 dash Grenadine*

*Cracked ice*

*½ ounce dark rum*

*Maraschino cherry*

In a cocktail shaker, combine light rum, Triple Sec, lime juice, pineapple juice, orange juice, and Grenadine with cracked ice; shake vigorously. Strain into a cocktail glass; top with dark rum and garnish with a maraschino cherry.

Makes 1 serving.

# New York Egg Cream

This old-time New York thirst-quencher is sweet and full of fizz. Despite its name, the egg cream contains neither eggs nor cream. In the beginning, it was a soda produced almost exclusively in New York (particularly Brooklyn). The basic ingredients are milk, seltzer, and chocolate syrup. It is traditionally made in a small Coke-style glass.

True New Yorkers insist that it is not a classic egg cream without Fox's U-Bet Chocolate Syrup. It is perfectly proper to gulp down an egg cream. In fact, egg cream will lose its head and become flat if it is not enjoyed immediately. Soda fountains all over New York City have their own versions. For many years, the egg cream remained a product sold only through New York soda fountains. Today, it is being bottled by a few small companies.

There are several legends on how the egg cream was born. One version claims that it began in 1882 on the Lower East Side of New York with Boris Thomashevsky, a Yiddish actor who brought the first Yiddish play to New York from London. After tasting an egg cream–like concoction in France, he asked to have one made in New York.

A second legend says that a Jewish candy shop owner, Louis Auster, in Brooklyn, invented the egg cream in 1890. Egg creams became extremely popular, and the candy shop had lines of customers stretched down the street and around the corner. It is reported that Auster sold three thousand egg creams a day until the day he closed the shop. He died without revealing his original recipe and the origin of the name, and to this day his family has kept the secret.

*Junior's Official Egg Cream Kit includes all the essential elements for a true New York egg cream.*
*Courtesy The New York First Company at www.newyorkfirst.com.*

## New York Egg Cream

This recipe was given to me by Bonni Lee Brown, who presently lives in Bradenton, Florida. Bonni writes, "My Dad made egg creams all the time at his old-fashioned drug store and luncheonette, called Joe Fordham Pharmacy, that was at Kings Highway and East 5th Street in Brooklyn. Egg creams were traditionally made in a small Coca-Cola glass. Two-cents plain was both the cost and the name of a plain glass of seltzer. When Dad heard that my mother had given birth to me, around 11:00 A.M., he proudly offered free egg creams to everyone to celebrate!"

*Approximately ½ cup cold whole milk*

*1 cup bottled seltzer*

*2 tablespoons chocolate syrup\**

\* Fox's U-Bet Chocolate Syrup is used in New York

**1.** Pour ½ inch of cold milk into a tall soda glass. Add seltzer or club soda to within 1 inch of the top of the glass; stir vigorously with a long spoon (this will cause it to become white and bubbly with a good head of foam).

**2.** Very gently pour 2 tablespoons of chocolate syrup slowly down the inside of the glass. When the chocolate has settled in the bottom of the glass, briskly stir with a long spoon only at the bottom of the glass where the chocolate sits. The resulting drink should have a dark brown bottom and a 1-inch high pure white foam top (if you mix it too much, the foam disappears).

Makes 1 serving.

# Prickly Pear Margarita

One of the newest drink fads is the tasty prickly pear margarita, served by trendy restaurants across the Southwest. The margarita was invented to act as a coping mechanism that both tasted good and made people feel cool in the hot weather of the region. One reason for the margarita's rise in popularity is that it is a very versatile recipe that lends itself to variations in fruit flavorings. Since its original creation, many variations of the traditional margarita have been created with fresh flavors like mango and prickly pear. Whether plain, salted, straight up, on the rocks, or frozen, margaritas are made in an array of flavors and colors.

As for the creation of the drink itself, several bars and bartenders (all from Mexico) have staked a claim

The prickly pear cactus, the key ingredient in the unusual Prickly Pear Margarita, grows wild on much of the Western plains. H. Wayne Phillips photo.

to it. The strongest claim comes from Ciudad Juarez, Mexico, in 1942. Francisco "Pancho" Morales is credited with inventing the drink while working in Tommy's Bar. A woman came in and asked for a "magnolia"—a drink he had not heard of. Pretending to know what she wanted, he whipped up a cocktail of tequila, Cointreau, and lime juice. The woman loved it and asked what the drink was called. The rest is history.

Prickly pear cactus has been a staple food of Native Americans for many centuries, with many varieties of prickly pear cacti growing wild throughout the deserts of the Southwest. In the 1500s, Cabeza de Vaca, an early explorer of the American Southwest, reported that the Native Americans celebrated the prickly pear

harvest with festivities similar to today's Mardi Gras in New Orleans. Only recently has the fruit become popular in western cuisines. The fruits, or tunas, of prickly pears are commonly sold in the markets of Mexico and in the Southwest. They can be eaten fresh, dried, or used for making juices and syrups.

## Prickly Pear Margarita

My brother and his wife, Jerry and Laura Stewart, of Tucson, Arizona, did the taste testing on this recipe. They tasted and tasted until they felt the right ingredients had been achieved. They reported, "The prickly pear margaritas were fantastic! We couldn't stop drinking them. We especially like the color of the prickly pear juice, and we're margarita snobs!"

1 cup crushed ice

¼ cup (2 ounces) fresh lime juice

¼ cup (2 ounces) undiluted frozen limeade

⅔ cup (5 ounces) tequila

¼ cup (2 ounces) Triple Sec

2 tablespoons (1 ounce) prickly pear juice, concentrate, or syrup

1 tablespoon sugar or light corn syrup, or more to taste*

Lime wedges for garnish

* Depending on what type of prickly pear liquid (juice, concentrate, or syrup) is used, the sugar or corn syrup needed can vary.

In a blender, add crushed ice, lime juice, limeade, tequila, Triple Sec, prickly pear juice, concentrate, or syrup, and sugar or corn syrup; cover and mix ingredients (a pulsating action with 4 or 5 jolts of the blender works the best). At this point, a taste test will be required. Correct with additional sugar or corn syrup if it is too tart. Pour into salt-rimmed margarita glasses, garnish with a lime wedge, and serve immediately.

Note: To create a salt-rimmed glass, take one of the lime wedges and rub the rim surface of the glass so it is barely moist. Dip the edge of the glass into coarse or kosher salt.

Makes 4 servings.

# Sweet Ice Tea

**Ice tea should be like a southern lady—strong and sweet.**

*—Pamela H. Long of Mobile, Alabama*

Southerners swear by their traditional sweet ice tea and drink it by the gallons. In the South, ice tea is not just a summertime drink, it is served year round with most meals. When people order tea in a Southern restaurant, chances are they will get sweet ice tea.

Up until the late nineteenth century, most Americans drank their tea hot. At the 1904 World's Fair in St. Louis, Rich Blechynden, a merchant of Indian tea, was trying to sell hot tea to customers during the hot summer day. He poured his hot tea over ice, creating a cool tea beverage that was an instant success and changed the way Americans thought of tea. Southerners added their own twist by pouring sugar into the tea right after it was brewed.

## Perfect Pitcher of Sweet Ice Tea

The following advice and recipe comes from Pamela H. Long of Mobile, Alabama.

Listen to me, and you'll never go wrong making sweet ice tea. Other folks try to make tea by putting it in a big ole jar out in the backyard. It just ends up tasting like storm-water runoff. When I was a child, one of my favorite things to do on the weekend was to go up to my aunt Annie's house in Clanton, Alabama. Aunt Annie made, undoubtedly, the best sweet tea that has ever been made, and she always served it in anodized aluminum tumblers. Her name was really Annie Vivian Cowart Pyron, and she was my grandmother's, Gladys Ray Cowart Howell's, older sister. To this day, if someone makes a particularly tasty pitcher of tea, we always say, "This is almost as good as Aunt Annie's."

To make the best sweet tea, get out that enamel sauce pan you use for cooking noodles. Pour some cold water in it ('til it's about full). You need about 3 quarts of water. Put 4 family-size bags of Red Diamond Tea in it and bring it to a boil. Boil about 3 or 4 minutes, and then remove from heat and take the tea bags out.

Pour in about 1½ cups of granulated white sugar and stir until it's dissolved. Use a funnel and pour the tea into a gallon jug or pitcher. Finish filling up the jug or pitcher with water (I always use filtered or spring water), but stop before it gets weak.

Serve in anodized aluminum tumblers about half full of hand-chipped ice. If you don't have the anodized tumblers, Waterford glasses will do. Take it out on the porch, or under the Scuppernong grape arbor, and take along one or more of the following: the phone, a book, a magazine, a church fan, a friend!

## Juanita's Southern Ice Tea

This recipe was given to me by Juanita Daniels of Helena, Alabama. I didn't like southern ice tea when I first tried it. In Oregon, we don't usually sweeten our ice tea—but it seems to grow on you. Now I crave it.

*3 cups boiling water*

*1 family-size tea bag or 3 regular-size tea bags*

*½ to ¾ cup sugar or to taste*

*5 cups cold water*

*Ice cubes*

Pour boiling water over the tea bags; set aside 5 minutes. In a large pitcher, add sugar and pour warm tea over sugar; stirring until sugar is dissolved. Add 5 cups cold water and stir until well mixed. Cool and serve in tall glasses over ice cubes.

*Makes ½ gallon.*

# Sazerac Cocktail

The Sazerac cocktail is to New Orleans what the margarita is to the southwest. It is reported to be the first cocktail ever invented (at least in America). Antoine Amadie Peychaud, a Creole apothecary, is given the credit for first inventing the Sazerac cocktail in the 1830s. In 1795, he immigrated to New Orleans from the West Indies and opened a drugstore called Pharmacie Peychaud. Like many "chemists" of his day, he sold his own patent medicine; Peychaud's Bitters, a proprietary mix of aromatic bitters said to relieve his clients' ailments. His medical toddy soon became very popular, and friends gathered regularly to sample his late-night drinks. The drink was named after an imported Sazerac cognac, Sazerac de Forge et Fils, which was originally used in making the cocktail.

Stomach bitters were basically alcohol disguised as medicine. They became extremely popular from 1850 to 1870 due to the liquor tax laws, the popularity of temperance movements, and local restrictions on the liquor trade. Peychaud had a unique way of serving his drink. He served it in an egg cup, known to the French speakers as a *coquetier*. Most historians believe that the word *cocktail* came from a mispronunciation of this French word.

The popularity of the Sazerac cocktail led to the opening of a large bar in 1852 called the Sazerac Coffee House (*coffee house* was the term used for drinking establishments in the mid-1800s). The bar had a 125-foot-long bar manned by a dozen bartenders all mixing Sazerac cocktails for patrons. In 1870, Thomas H. Handy purchased the Sazerac Coffee House and also bought out the rights to Peychaud's Bitters. In the early days, the Sazerac cocktail was made with cognac or brandy, but as American tastes changed, rye whiskey was substituted. This unique cocktail derived its anise scent from absinthe. Beginning in 1912, absinthe was banned in the United States because of its habit-forming quality. Pernod, Herbsaint, or Ricard was substituted in place of absinthe.

The Sazerac cocktail is now associated with the Sazerac Bar at the Fairmont Hotel in New Orleans, and the hotel pays an annual fee to the Sazerac Company for the use of the name. When visiting the Sazerac Bar, if you don't want to be labeled as a tourist, be sure not to ask for Sazerac on the rocks—this drink should never be served with ice.

*A Sazerac cocktail with its essential ingredient of Peychaud's Bitters. Courtesy Sazerac Company.*

## Sazerac Cocktail

*Crushed ice*

*1 teaspoon absinthe, Pernod, or Herbsaint liqueur*

*Ice cubes*

*1 teaspoon sugar, 1 sugar cube, or 1 teaspoon simple syrup*

*1½ ounces rye whiskey*

*3 dashes Peychaud's Bitters*

*1 lemon peel twist*

**1.** Chill an Old-Fashioned glass by filling with crushed ice, or refrigerate or freeze for at least 30 minutes in the refrigerator. Add the Herbsaint, absinthe, or Pernod to the glass; swirl it around to coat the entire sides and bottom of the glass. Discard the excess.

**2.** In a cocktail shaker, add 4 or 5 small ice cubes, sugar, rye whiskey, and bitters. Shake gently for about 30 seconds; strain into the prepared old-fashioned glass. Twist lemon peel over the drink and then place in the drink.

Makes 1 serving.

# Syllabub

According to legend, the following recipe was sent to Martha Washington in the mid-1700s by Mrs. Cooper of North Carolina, after the Marquis de Lafayette was said to have praised it:

To make a fine Syllabub from the cow. Sweeten a quart of cider with double refined sugar, grate nutmeg into it, then milk your cow into your liquor. When you have thus added what quantity of milk you think proper pour half a pint or more in proportion to the quantity of syllabub you make, over beaten cream.

Syllabub is softly whipped cream that is flavored with wine, sweetened cider, and sometimes brandy. It is closely related to eggnog, but less potent because no strong spirits are used. Special syllabub churns were used to achieve the right cream texture. Some were of hand-painted china and others of glass. As you tip the glass to drink syllabub, the wine or cider comes through the frothy cream.

Originally an English recipe from the seventeenth century, the first syllabubs were made by dairy maids who would direct the warm milk straight from the cow to a pail containing sherry or cider. The froth was then skimmed off and served for breakfast. Today, syllabub is thicker and richer because it can be kept in the glass for several hours before serving. We don't have to wait until milking time to enjoy syllabub, as we have heavy cream that is ideal for whipping.

It is supposed to be served with a foamy topping that was often made "under the cow," by holding a bowl filled with wine or cider under a cow until the cow milk made a fine froth at the top of the bowl. It is rumored that King Charles II (1630–1685) of England had a special herd of cows kept in St. James Park for making his syllabubs. The English aristocracy were said to have gone to great lengths to achieve this effect. In one fashionable London drawing room, both the cow and the milkmaid were brought inside for the assembled guests to observe as the milk squirted directly into the syllabub mixture to give the desired froth. The syllabub was then passed to the guests, who ate the fluff off the top with a spoon and then drank the remaining drink.

The drink was well liked in colonial times and was a favorite drink of eighteenth-century southern ladies, especially in Maryland and Virginia. Serving syllabub to guests was a symbol of southern hospitality and was generally considered a holiday treat enjoyed while the men drank hot buttered rum. Men generally considered it a lady's drink because of its weak potation. It was often served with cookies and even children got to taste it.

## Syllabub

*1 tablespoon grated lemon peel*

*3 tablespoons fresh lemon juice*

*1 cup medium-dry sherry or white dessert wine*

*¼ cup sugar*

*2 cups heavy cream*

*Freshly grated nutmeg*

1. Chill a large bowl in the refrigerator (also chill your beaters). In a small bowl, combine lemon peel, lemon juice, sherry or wine, and sugar; stir 5 minutes or until sugar dissolves.

2. Removed chilled bowl from refrigerator and combine cream and sugar mixture. Using an electric mixer, beat continuously, skimming off foam as it rises to the top. Continue beating until all the mixture has turned to foam (it will not thicken). To serve, carefully skim off the foam and spoon into individual small glasses or mugs and sprinkle with nutmeg. To serve later, place a metal sieve in a bowl and spoon the foam mixture into the sieve. Store up to 24 hours in the refrigerator. When ready to serve, spoon the drained foam into individual serving glasses or mugs. Sprinkle with nutmeg and enjoy.

*Makes 4 to 6 servings.*

# Moxie

Moxie is such an unusual New England beverage that it could not be left out of this book even if there is no recipe to include with it. It began as a New England beverage and remains a New England beverage. It is the oldest carbonated beverage in the world. Said to resemble a bitter root beer with a strong bitter after taste, popularity of this beverage is confined largely to the New England region, as over the years Moxie has declined greatly in popularity.

Dr. Augustine Thompson of Lowell, Massachusetts, founded Moxie in 1884. Originally, Moxie was touted as a patent medicine guaranteed to cure almost any ill, including loss of manhood, paralysis, and softening of the brain. These claims were revised slightly with the passage of the Pure Food and Drug Act in 1906. Dr. Thompson then added carbonated water and called it "Beverage Moxie Nerve Food." This version was a huge success.

Moxie was also the favorite beverage of Calvin Coolidge, thirtieth president of the United States, and it is said he served it at the White House during his presidency. According to historical sources, Coolidge, upon hearing of President Warren G. Harding's death and after being sworn into office, exclaimed "Guess we better have a drink," and along with his wife, father, and a few others went across the street to where they marked the occasion with a Moxie.

In the late 1920s, Moxieland was built in Boston and was successfully promoted as a tourist attraction. Moxieland became as famous as any Boston landmark. Increased sugar prices, along with increased competition from other beverage companies, caused Moxieland to close. The company later continued operation from its Needham Heights, Massachusetts, location until the late 1960s. Today it remains as it began, a New England beverage that is still made in New England by a few bottlers.

# Bibliography

"About Racine Danish Kringles." Internet Web site. www.kringle.com/about_kringle/faqs.shtml.

Adams, Dennis. "Frogmore Stew and Other Lowcountry Recipes." Beaufort County Public Library. Internet Web site. www.co.beaufort.sc.us/bftlib/frogmore.htm.

Agte, Barbara, and Carla DeMarco. "Posole stew—A New Mexico Holiday Tradition." Southern New Mexico Online. Internet Web site. www.zianet.com/snm/posole.htm.

Alexander, George. "Deep-Fried Greenhorn: Only a Dupe Believes in Such a Thing as the Best Chicken-Fried Steak in Texas." *Houston Press*. 30 November 2000. Internet Web site. www.houstonpress.com/issues/2000-11-30/skewer.html.

Algren, Nelson. *America Eats*. Ames: University of Iowa Press, 1992.

Aliverti, Brent. "Blenheim Ginger Ale." Blenheim Bottlers. 15 August 1999. Internet Web site. theacf.com/blenheim/.

Allen, Terese. *Hometown Flavor: A Cook's Tour of Wisconsin's Butcher Shops, Bakeries, Cheese Factories, and Other Specialty Markets*. Wisconsin: Trails Media/Prairie Oak Press, 1998.

Allman, Ruth. *Alaska Sourdough*. Seattle: Alaska Northwest Books, 1976.

American Heritage, eds: *The American Heritage Cookbook: and Illustrated History of American Eating and Drinking*. New York: American Heritage Publishing Co., 1964.

"Anchor Bar: Our History." Internet Web site. www.anchorbar.com/history.htm.

Anderson, Carol. "Bean Soup: A Treat to Be Rediscovered." *The Free Lance-Star* (Fredericksburg, Va.) 2 February 2000. Internet Web site. content.fredericksburg.com/opinion/Local_Columnists/Carol_Anderson/anderson.html.

Anderson, Janet Alm. *A Taste of Kentucky*. Lexington: University Press of Kentucky, 1986.

Arnold, Jack. *The Chili Lover's Handbook*. San Diego: Jack Arnold Associates, 1977.

Auchmutey, Jim. "Central Grocery Company: Loaves of Plenty." *Atlanta Journal-Constitution*, 1 February 1998.

"Avocados: How They Got Their Name." Soilmoisture Equipment Corp. Internet Web site. www.soilmoisture.com/avocado.htm.

Bailie, Thomas B. *The Great Big Book of Chili*. Baltimore: AmErica House, 2000.

Banks, Phyllis Eileen. "Bosque Redondo—Destination of the Long Walk." Southern New Mexico Online. Internet Web site. www.zianet.com/snm/redondo.htm.

"Barbecue: Kansas City Style." Experience Kansas City. Internet Web site. www.experiencekc.com/barbeque.html.

"The Barbecue That Made Kansas City Famous." 2001 Energy. Internet Web site. www.energy2001.ee.doe.gov/BarBQ.htm.

Baumann, Richard J. *Foods That Made Wisconsin Famous: 150 Great Recipes*. Madison: Wisconsin Tales and Trails, 1999.

Beard, James. *James Beard's American Cookery*. Boston: Little, Brown and Company, 1972.

Beard, James and José Wilson, ed. *Beard on Food*. New York: Alfred A. Knopf, 1974.

Bennett, Bev. "Saluting Country Captain Chicken." *Los Angeles Times*.

Berger, Frances de Talavera, and John Parke Custis. *Sumptuous Dining in Gaslight San Francisco: 1875–1915*. Garden City, N.Y.: Doubleday, 1985.

Bergerson, Victor J. "Let's Get the Record Straight on the Mai Tai!" San Francisco 1970. Internet Web site. www.tradervics.com/maitai1.htm.

*Better Homes and Gardens Heritage American Cookbook*. Des Moines: H & G Books, 1993.

Bincoletto, William. "Early Times Mint Julep." *Purple Fee*. Internet Web site. www.wineiscool.com/purple/library/grape/grape_mint_julep.htm.

Boizot, Peter. *The Pizza Express Cookbook*. London: Elm Tree Books/Hamish Hamilton, 1976.

Boreth, Craig. *The Hemingway Cookbook*. Chicago: Chicago Review Press, 1998.

Bowen, 'Asta. *The Huckleberry Book*. Helena, Mont.: American Geographic Publishing, Helena, 1988.

Boyle, Christopher C. "Rise of the Georgetown Rice Culture." EGO's Travel Guides. Internet Web site. www.ego.net/us/sc/myr/history/rise.htm.

"Brooklyn Egg Cream: So . . . What's an Egg Cream?" The Soda Fountain. Internet Web site. www.lowcarbluxury.com/eggcream.html.

Brown, Cora, Rose Brown, and Bob Brown. *America Cooks: Favorite Recipes from 48 States*. Garden City, N.Y.: Halcyon House, 1940.

Brown, Dale, and Time-Life Books, eds. *American Cooking: The Northwest*. Alexandria, Va: Time-Life Books, 1970.

Brown, Helen Evans. *West Coast Cook Book*. The Cookbook Collectors Library, 1952.

"The Buckner Mint Julep Ceremony: History." Internet Web site. www.thebucknerhome.com/julep/history.html.

Burger, Ann. "Getting to the bottoms of things." Charleston, S.C.: *Post and Courier*, 8 October 2000.

Burger, Ann. "Shrimp and Grits." Charleston, S.C.: *Post and Courier*, 18 October 2000

Butel, Jane. *Chili Madness: A Passionate Cookbook*. New York: Workman, 1980.

———. "Sacred Stew." Jane Butel Cooking Schools. Internet Web site. janebutel.com/resource/art.html.

Buyers, Rebecca. *The Marvelous Macadamia Nut*. New York: Irena Chalmers Cookbooks, 1982.

"Cafe du Monde History." Internet Web site. www.cafe dumonde.com/history.htm.

Calloway, Karin. "Fajita Fun: Flavorful Finger Food Can Be a Versatile Addition to Any At-Home Meal." *Augusta Chronicle*, 25 May 1999. Internet Web site. www.augusta chronicle.com/stories/052699/fea_095-5516.000.shtml.

Cannon, Poppy, and Patricia Brooks. *The Presidents' Cookbook: Practical Recipes from George Washington to the Present*. Funk and Wagnalls, 1968.

Carroll, Rick. "The Mai Tai hits the Big Five-0: Celebrating the (Nearly) Perfect Mai Tai." Internet Web site. www.kevdo.com/maitai/maitaihistory.html.

Cassidy, Frederic G. *Dictionary of American Regional English*. vol 1. Cambridge, Ma.: Belnap/Harvard University Press, 1985.

Chang, Elizabeth. "Hawaii's Plate Lunches: What a Dish!" *Washington Post*, 7 March 1999. Internet Web site. www.washingtonpost.com/wpsrv/travel/index/stories/chang03071999.htm.

Chapman, Art. "Frito Fracas: San Antonio and Santa Fe Vying for Bragging Rights to Oldest and Best Frito Pie." Virtual Texas. Internet Web site. www.virtualtexan.com/writers/chapman/fritopie.htm.

"The Cheese Stands Alone." *Guide to Madison Wisconsin*, 2nd ed. Internet Web site. www.insiders.com/madison/sb-brewpubs.htm.

"Chef Ron in the News: The Amazing Spam." Internet Web site. www.chefron.com/NewsDetail.cfm?ArticleID=147.

"Chicken Bouyon (or Booyah)." The Wisconsin Gardener. Wisconsin Public Television. Internet Web site. www.wpt.org/garden/food_and_photos/recipe2.cfm.

"Chowder Has Lively History in America." *Cuisine*, 10 October 2000. GMToday. Internet Web site. www.gmtoday.com/cuisine.asp.

Clarke, Joan. "Haute Doughnut: Malassadas Goes Upscale." *Honolulu Advertiser*. 26 July 2000. Internet Web site. the.honoluluadvertiser.com/2000/Jul/26/islandlife1.html.

"Collard Greens." WholeHealth.com. Internet Web site. www.wholehealthmd.com/print/view/1,1560,FO_152,00.html.

Collin, Rima, and Richard Collin. *The New Orleans Cookbook: Creole, Cajun, and Louisiana French Recipes Past and Present*. New York: Alfred A. Knopf, 1975.

———. *The Pleasures of Seafood*. New York: Galahad Books, 1976.

"Columbia River Sturgeon." Internet Web site. www.worldstar.com/~dlarson/SturgeonoftheColumbia.htm.

The Congressional Club, eds. *The Congressional Club Cookbook*. Washington, D.C.: The Congressional Club, 1976.

Conrad, Barnaby III. *The Martini*. San Francisco: Chronicle Books, 1995.

"Crawfish." Delaware Sea Grant, University of Delaware. Internet Web site. www.ocean.udel.edu/mas/seafood/crawfish.html.

"The Crawfish Pond." Internet Web site. home.att.net/~cajunplace2be/crawfish.html.

Crooks, Mark W. "What's a Spiedie?" B&M Adventures. Internet Web site. www.bmventures.com/spiedie.htm.

Dabney, Joseph E. *Smokehouse Ham, Spoon Bread, and Scuppernong Wine: The Folklore and Art of Southern Appalachian Cooking*. Nashville: Cumberland House, 1998.

Danforth, Randi, Peter Feierabend, and Gary Chassman. *Culinaria—The United States: A Culinary Discovery*. New York: Konemann.

Delany, Jerry. "Minorcan Datil Peppers." Internet Web site. www.minorcanfamily.com/Jerry'sFile/DATILPEPPERS.htm.

DeVoto, Bernard. *The Journals of Lewis and Clark*. Boston: Houghton Mifflin Company, 1953.

Dickson, Ron. *The Great American Moon Pie Handbook*. Atlanta: Peachtree Publishers, 1985.

Dojny, Brooke. *The New England Cookbook*. Boston: Harvard Common Press, 1999.

Dunne, Mike. "Boring Diet Gave Miners Appetite for Dining Out." *Sacramento Bee*. 18 January 1998. Internet Web site. www.calgoldrush.com/part2/02food.html.

DuSablon, Mary Anna. *Cincinnati Recipe Treasury*. Athens: Ohio University Press, 1983.

Duson, Betty T. A Cooking Legacy. New York: Walker, 1975.

"The Early Days of Liberty Orchards." Liberty Orchards Co., Inc. Internet Web site. www.libertyorchards.com/newabout.asp.

Eddy, Kristin. "One Peculiar Pudding: Southern Indiana Is Home to a Rare Dessert that Owes its Heart to the Strange Native Persimmon." *Chicago Tribune*, 22 November 1998. Internet Web site. cgi.chicago.tribune.com/leisure/goodeating/ws/item/0,1308,8832-19128-19129,00.html.

"Edible Bean Ceremonies of the New Year (and First Footing)." Internet Web site. www.luckymojo.com/newyearbean.html.

Edmunds, Lowell. *Martini, Straight Up: The Classic American Cocktail*. Baltimore: Johns Hopkins University Press, 1999.

Egerton, John. *Southern Food: At Home, on the Road, in History*. Chapel Hill and London: University of North Carolina Press, 1993.

Elkort, Martin. *The Secret Life of Food: A Feast of Food and Drink History, Folklore and Fact*. New York: Tarcher, 1991.

Elverson, Virginia T., and Mary Ann McLanahan. *A Cooking Legacy*. New York: Walker, 1975.

Enna, Renee. "Toast of St. Louis: Accidental Dunking in the Deep-Fryer Has Led Humble Ravioli to Snack Stardom." *Chicago Tribune*, 17 March 1999. Internet Web site. cgi.chicago.tribune.com/leisure/goodeating/ws/item/0,1308,8832-24803-25092,00.html.

Fabrique, Polly Esther. "The Spam Story." Internet Web site. www.personal.umich.edu/~ryantm/spam-story.html.

"The Famous Senate Restaurant Bean Soup." The Honorable and Mrs. John D. Rockefeller IV. First Traveler's Choice Internet Cookbook. Internet Web site. www.virtualcities.com/ons/wv/gov/wvgvjr12.htm.

Faries, Dave. "Hog Wild: What Are Chitlins, and Why Would Anyone Eat Them?" Burning Question. *Dallas Observer*, 23 November 2000.

Farm Journal, eds. *Great Home Cooking in America*. New York: Doubleday, 1976.

Farrington, Doris E. *Fireside Cooks and Black Kettle Recipes*. Indianapolis and New York: Bobbs-Merrill, 1976.

Ferguson, Sheila. *Soul Food: Classic Cuisine from the Deep South*. New York: Grove Press, 1989.

Fertig, Judith M. *Prairie Home Cooking*. Boston: Harvard Common Press, 1999.

Flemmons, Jerry. "The Good, the Bad and the Deep-Fried." *Fort Worth Star-Telegram*, 6 July 1997. Internet Web site. www.hometownstar.net/comm/virtual/flsteak.htm.

Flores, Carlotta Dunn. *El Charro Café: The Tastes and Traditions of Tucson*. Tucson, Az.: Fisher Books, 1998.

Folse, John D., *The Evolution of Cajun and Creole Cuisine*. Gonzales, La.: Chef John Folse and Co., 1989.

Foster, Nelson, and Linda S. Cordell, eds. *Chilies to Chocolate: Food the Americas Gave the World*. Tucson and London: University of Arizona Press, 1992.

Fritschner, Sarah. "Humble or Hurried, Hoppin' John Is the Dish for New Year's." Sarah's Kitchen, 30 December 1998. Internet Web site. www.courierjournal.com/sarah/1998/1230hoppin.html.

FritzGerald, Don, ed. *The Pacifica House Hawaii Cook Book*. Studio City, Ca.: Pacifica House, 1973.

Fussell, Betty. *I Hear America Cooking: The Cooks and Recipes of American Regional Cuisine*. New York: Viking Penguin, 1986

——. *The Story of Corn*. New York: Alfred A. Knopf, 1992.

Garner, Bob. *North Carolina Barbecue Flavored by Time*. Winston–Salem, N.C.: John F. Blair, 1996.

Garrido, David, and Robb Walsh. *Nuevo Tex-Mex: Festive New Recipes from Just North of the Border*. San Francisco: Chronicle Books, 1998.

Gerlach, R. D., Nancy. "New Mexico Cuisine." Fiery Foods. Internet Web site. www.fiery-foods.com/dave/nmcuis.html.

"Goo Goo Cluster: Company History." Standard Candy Company. Internet Web site. www.googoo.com/history.cfm.

Green, Aliza. "What's in a Chowder? Just about Anything You Want." Knight Ridder News Service. *The Oregonian* (Portland) 27 February 2001.

Green, Joey. "Weird Facts: Spam." Internet Web site. www.wackyuses.com/spam.html.

Grigas, Catherine Enns. "Chow Down on Chowder." *Water's Edge*. Internet Web site. www.waters-edge.com/index.shtml.

"Gullah Heritage Excursion/Sea Island Coalition Press Release." 6 August 1997. Internet Web site. www.hartford-hwp.com/archives/45a/346.html.

Guste, Roy F., Jr. *Antoine's Restaurant Since 1840 Cookbook.* New Orleans: Carbery-Guste, 1978.

Hall, Suzanne. "New Texas Barbecue." *TravelLady Magazine.* Internet Web site. www.travellady.com/articles/article-newtexas.htm.

Hamlim, Kathy. "Cocktails/Beer." Internet Web site. cocktail.about.com.

Harmon, John E. "The Spiedie—A Tasty Morsel." Atlas of Popular Culture in the Northeastern United States. Internet Web site. www.geography.ccsu.edu/harmonj/atlas/spiedie.htm.

Harrell, Monette R., and Robert W. Harrell Jr. *The Ham Book: A Comprehensive Guide to Ham Cookery.* Norfolk, Va.: Donning, 1977.

Harris, Jessica B. *The Welcome Table: African-American Heritage Cooking.* New York: Simon and Schuster, 1995.

Heller, Lori. "Pierogi Spells Pittsburgh." *Tribune-Review,* 7 March 1999.

Herbst, Sharon Tyler. *The New Food Lover's Companion: Comprehensive Definitions of over 4,000 Food, Wine and Culinary Terms,* 2nd ed. Hauppauge, NY: Barron's, 1995.

Herter, George Leonard, and Berthe E. Herter. *Bull Cook and Authentic Historical Recipes and Practices,* vols. 2 and 3. Herter's Inc., Waseca, Minn.: 1960, 1967.

Hess, Karen. *The Carolina Rice Kitchen: The African Connection,* Columbia: University of South Carolina Press, 1992.

Hevrdejs, Judy. "Beyond Lincoln Take Time to Explore the Other Side of Springfield." *Chicago Tribune,* 3 July 1994. Internet Web site. cgi.chicago.tribune.com/travel/mid/archive/ill/4070sil.htm.

"The History of Barbecue in the South." Internet Web site. xroads.virginia.edu/~MA95/dove/history.html.

"History of Coffee in Hawaii." Kalaheo Coffee Company and Cafe. Internet Web site. www.kalaheo.com/history.html.

"The History of Coffee in Hawaii." Maui Coffee Co. Internet Web site. www.mauicoffeeco.com/history.html.

"History of Hawaii—the Pokiki: Portuguese Traditions." *Mahalo Islander.* Internet Web site. www.islander-magazine.com/port.html.

"The History of Pat's King of Steaks." Pat's King of Steaks. Internet Web site. www.patskingofsteaks.com/history.htm.

"History of Pecans." National Pecan Shellers Association. Internet Web site. www.ilovepecans.org/history.html.

"The History of Sazerac." Sazerac Company History. Sazerac Co., Inc. Internet Web site. www.sazerac.com/history.html.

"The History of Sushi." Internet Web site. sushi-master.com/usa/whatis/history.html.

"The History of Sushi." The Little Japanese Chef's Sushi Page. Internet Web site. www.geocities.com/NapaValley/5789/history.htm.

Hoover, Barbara. "Guts and Glory: 'Tis the Time for Chitlins—Whether You Love 'em or Hate 'em." *Detroit News,* 24 December 1996.

Hopkins, Jerry. *Strange Foods: Bush Meat, Bats, and Butterflies—An Epicurean Adventure around the World.* Boston: Periplus Editions, 1999.

"The Hot Brown." (pamphlet) The Camberley Brown Hotel. Louisville, Kentucky.

"If It's Mardi Gras, It's Time for Gumbo!" Tabasco Mardi Gras. Internet Web site. www.tabasco.com/html/mg_gumbo.html.

"In Praise of Spam Musubi." Internet Web site. www.pineapplehead.org/spam.htm.

"Indian Food and Cooking in Eastern North Carolina." Heritage Education Program. Fort Raleigh National Historic Site. National Park Service (pamphlet).

"The Involvement of the Métis Nation in the Pemmican Trade Was an Historic Era in Canada and the United States." Internet Web site. www.geocities.com/SoHo/Atrium/4832/buffalo3.html.

"Is It True the Senate Restaurants Serve Bean Soup Everyday?" U.S. Senate History Briefings: Frequently Asked Questions. Internet Web site. www.senate.gov/learning/brief_faq.html.

"It's Time for Gumbo." The Literary Club, Chicago. Internet Web site. www.theliteraryclub.org/cspage16tlc.html.

Jameson, W. C. "Natural History of Bread Pudding." *Log Cabin Democrat,* 9 December 1997. Internet Web site. thecabin.net/stories/120997/fea_bread.html.

——. *The Ultimate Chili Cookbook: History, Geography, Fact, and Folklore of Chili.* Plano: Republic of Texas Press, 1999.

Jamison, Cheryl Alters. *The Border Cookbook: Authentic Home Cooking of the American Southwest and Northern Mexico.* Cambridge, Mass.: Harvard Common Press, 1995.

Jones, Evan. *American Food: The Gastronomic Story.* New York: E. P. Dutton, 1975.

Julian, Debbie. "Oysters Everywhere." Asia with Pride, Teacher's Guide. Internet Web site. www.intandem.com/ NewPrideSite/Asia/Lesson14/Lesson14_Tchr.html.

Kavasch, E. Barrie. *Enduring Harvests: Native American Foods and Festivals for Every Season.* Guilford, Conn.: The Globe Pequot Press, 1995.

Keating, Kevin. "Glory on the Half-Shell." *Hemispheres* (January 1997).

Kellner, Esther. *Moonshine: Its History and Folklore.* New York: Weathervane Books, 1971.

Kimball, Yeffe, and Jean Anderson. *The Art of American Indian Cooking.* New York: The Lyons Press, 1965.

"King Cake—a Rich Tradition." Randazzo's Camellia City Bakery, Slidell, Louisiana. Internet Web site. www.king cakes.com/kinghis.html.

"The King's Cake—Kickoff to the Carnival Season." Internet Web site. www.yatcom.com/neworl/mardi/kingcake.html.

Kirkland, Chasiti. "Town Goes Hog Wild over Chitlins." South Carolina Bureau. *Augusta Chronicle,* 29 November 1997. Internet Web site. www.augustachronicle.com/stories/ 112997/met_chitlin.html.

Knickerbocker, Peggy. "Serious Crab." *Saveur* no. 25 (March 1998).

"Kolache Festival: 'Czech' Out." Burleson County Chamber of Commerce, Caldwell, Texas. Internet Web site. www.rtis. com/reg/caldwell/ent/.

Langford, David L. "Amish Attracting Tourists." *Naples (Florida) Daily News,* 22 January 1998.

Lanier, Doris. *Absinthe: The Cocaine of the Nineteenth Century.* Jefferson, N. C.: McFarland Books, 1995.

Laudan, Rachel. *The Food of Paradise: Exploring Hawaii's Culinary Heritage.* Honolulu: University of Hawai'i Press, 1996.

Lawrence, James M., and Rux Martin. *Sweet Maple: Life, Lore and Recipes from the Sugarbush.* Montpelier: Vermont Life Magazine and Chapters Publishing, 1993.

Leahy, Linda Romanelli, with Jack Maguire. *The World's Greatest Peanut Butter Cookbook.* New York: Villard Books, 1994.

Lee, Gary. "In the Land of the Gullahs." *Washington Post,* 20 September 1998. Internet Web site. www.washington-post.com/wp-srv/travel/destinations/gullah092098.htm.

Legwold, Gary. *The Last Word on Lefse.* Cambridge, Minn.: Adventure Publications, 1992.

——. *The Last Word on Lutefisk: True Tales of Cod and Tradition.* Minneapolis: Conrad Henry Press, 1996.

Lehman, J. W. "Persimmon." North American Fruit Explorers, Inc. Internet Web site. www.nafex.org/persimmon2000. htm.

Liboiron, Henri, and Bob St-Cyr. "Experiments in Pemmican Preparation." Saskatchewan Archaeology. *Journal of the Saskatchewan Archaeological Society,* 9 (1988). Internet Web site. collections.ic.gc.ca/notukeu/pemmican_e1.htm.

Linck, Ernestine Sewell, and Joyce Gibson Roach. *Eats: A Folk History of Texas Foods.* Fort Worth: Texas Christian University Press, 1989.

Lipman, John. "Cincinnati Chili." Internet Web site. w3.one. net/~jeffelle/recipes/04_chilicinc.htm.

"Local Food." InfoMaui, vol 1. Internet Web site. www.info maui.com/editorials/localfoo.html.

Lockhart, Betty Ann C., and Donald G. Lockhart, eds. *The Maple Sugaring Story: A Guide for Teaching and Learning about the Maple Industry.* Charlotte: Vermont Maple Promotion Board, 1990.

Longone, Jan. "From the Kitchen." *American Magazine and Historical Chronicle* 2, no. 1 (Spring–Summer 1986).

Loughran, Siobhan. "Experts Wild for Oregon Mushrooms." *The Oregonian.* FOODday, 23 February 1999. Internet Web site. www.trufflezone.com/recipes/oregonian.htm.

Love, Louise. *The Complete Book of Pizza.* Evanston, Ill.: Sassafras Press, 1980.

Lovegren, Sylvia. *Fashionable Food: Seven Decades of Food Fads.* New York: Simon and Schuster/Macmillan, 1995.

"A 'Lussious' Fish: Discovering Lewis and Clark." Internet Web site. www.lewis-clark.org/ftclvirtual/eulachon/fi_eula2. htm.

Mariani, John F. *The Dictionary of American Food and Drink.* New Haven, Conn., and New York: Ticknor and Fields, 1983.

Martin, Cy. *The Saga of the Buffalo.* New York: Promontory Press, 1973.

McDonald, Charlie. "Celebrate Chiles at the Hatch Chile Festival." Southern New Mexico Online. Internet Web site. www.zianet.com/snm/chilfest.htm.

Meldrum, Douglas G. *The Night 2000 Men Came to Dinner and Other Appetizing Anecdotes.* New York: Scribner's, 1994.

Mello, Tim. "Ceviche Bars: Latin America's Hot Export Adds Passion to Menu Profits." Internet Web site. www.fspronet.com/food/ceviche1.html>.

Miller, Richard L., and T. L. Bush, eds. *The Official Fajita Cookbook*. 2nd ed. Houston: Gulf Publishing Company, 1988.

"Mint Julep." Cocktail—Drink of the Week. Internet Web site. hotwired.lycos.com/cocktail/97/17/nc_drink.o.week.html.

Montoya-Welsh, Sharon, and Marjorie Speare-Yerxa. *Oyster Cookery*. Oysterville, Wash.: Shoalwater Kitchen, 1984.

"Moon Pie History." Chattanooga Bakery, USA. Internet Web site. www.moonpie.com/history.asp.

Morantz, Dave. "Blenheim to Extend Roots North." Associated Press. *Augusta Chronicle*, 9 May 1999.

Morgan, Sarah. *The Saga of Texas Cookery*. Austin, Tex.: Encino Press, 1973.

"The Moxie Collector's Page." Cyber edition of the New England Moxie Congress. Internet Web site. www.xensei.com/users/iraseski/.

"Muffuletta Sandwich: What It Is, History and Background." Internet Web site. colorpro.com/great-sandwiches/muffuletta/history.htm.

Neff, Jack, and Skip Tate. *The Insiders Guide to Greater Cincinnati*. Lexington, Ky.: Lexington Herald-Leader, 1995.

Nelson, Gordon R. *Lowbush Moose: And Other Alaskan Recipes*. Anchorage: Alaska Northwest Publishing Company, 1978.

"New Orleans Beignets." Internet Web site. www.yatcom.com/neworl/dining/cdm.html.

"New Orleans Muffuletta." *Cuisine Magazine*. August Home Publishing Co. Internet Web site. www.cuisinemagazine.com/recipes/mufleta.html.

"New York Food Museum: Communities/Tradition." New York Food Museum. Internet Web site. www.nyfoodmuseum.org/com-trad.htm.

"Nick Tahou Hots: Home of the Garbage Plate." Internet Web site. www.geocities.com/Colosseum/Loge/5981/Tahou.htm.

"Nick Tahou's Tribute and Dietary Information." Internet Web site. www.people.cornell.edu/pages/sjs16/nicks.html.

Niethammer, Carolyn. *American Indian Cooking: Recipes from the Southwest*. Lincoln and London: University of Nebraska Press, 1999.

Noble, Doug. "The Origin of the Hangtown Fry." *Mountain Democrat Online*, 31 July 2000. Internet Web site. www.mtdemocrat.com/display/inn_1999_columnists/Doug%20Noble/zcolumn29.txt.

Nolan, Cecile Alyce. *Oregon: A Feast of Delights*. Portland, Ore.: Rain Dance Publishing Co., 1991.

Oberrecht, Kenn. "How Sturgeon Depend on Estuaries." South Slough National Estuarine Research Reserve Estuaries Feature Series. Internet Web site. www.southsloughestuary.com/sturgn2.htm.

"The Official Spam Home Page." Hormel Foods Corp. Internet Web site. www.spam.com/.

Oliver, Sandra L. *Saltwater Foodways: New Englanders and Their Food at Sea and Shore, in the Nineteenth Century*. Mystic, Conn.: Mystic Seaport Museum, 1995.

Olsen, Dave. *Starbucks Passion for Coffee*. Menlo Park, Ca.: Sunset Books, 1994.

"101 Testicle Recipes and Fun Facts." Internet Web site. www.funlinked.com/testicle/recipe.html.

O'Neill, Molly. *New York Cookbook*. New York: Workman, 1992.

"Ono Grinds: Saimin—Hawaii's Fast Food, Local Style." Aloha from Hawaii. Internet Web site. www.aloha-hawaii.com/c_saimin.shtml.

"Oregon White Truffles." Internet Web site. www.oregonwhitetruffles.com/.

"The Original Hass Mother Tree." The California Avocado Commission. Internet Web site. www.avocado.org/about/2000_26.php?sd=about.

"The Original Pat O'Brien's Hurricane." Pat O'Brien's Bar, Inc., New Orleans. Internet Web site. www.patobriens.com/hurricane.html.

"Origins: A Brief History of North Carolina Pulled-Pork Barbecue." The Lexington Collection, ibiblio. Internet Web site. www.ibiblio.org/lineback/bbq/origins.htm.

Orton, Vrest. *The American Cider Book: The Story of America's Natural Beverage*. New York: North Point Press, 1973.

"Our Tradition: San Francisco Tradition." The Boudin Bakery. Internet Web site. www.boudinbakery.com.

"Owensboro, Kentucky: The Burgoo Page" Internet Web site. www.angelfire.com/ky/burgoo/.

"Paczki Day." *Polish American Journal,* February 1995. Internet Web site. www.polamjournal.com/Library/Holidays/paczki/body_paczki.html.

Pallesen, Tim. "Kringle's New Fame Brings Sweet Memories." *Palm Beach Post,* 4 September 2000.

Panati, Charles. *Panati's Extraordinary Origins of Everyday Things.* New York: Harper & Row, 1987.

"Peanut Butter." Supermarket Product History Lesson. Internet Web site. www.pe.net/~checker/peanut.htm.

"Peanut Folklore." The Nut Factory. Internet Web site. www.thenutfactory.com/kitchen/facts/facts-peanut.html.

"Pecan History." Bragg Pecan Farms, Hondo, Texas. Internet Web site. www.texaspecans.com/htdocs/main/history.htm.

Pedersen, Cathy A. "Boiled peanuts: Delicacy for Many in the South." *The Log Online.* Internet Web site. www.destin.com/news/archives/aug98/peas.shtml.

Perl, Lila. *Red-Flannel Hash and Shoo-Fly Pie: America Regional Foods and Festivals.* Cleveland and New York: World Publishing Co., 1965.

Rabb, William. "Birth of the Moon Pie: Has Mystery Been Solved?" *Mobile (Alabama) Register,* 6 March 2000.

Randolph, Mary. *The Virginia Housewife.* Birmingham, Ala.: Antique American Cookbooks, 1984.

Rattray, Diana. *Southern U.S. Cuisine.* Internet Web site. southernfood.miningco.com/mbody.htm.

Raven, John. "Traditional Texas Fare: Barbecue 101." Texas Cooking Online. Internet Web site. www.texascooking.com/features/nov97ravenbbq1.htm.

Reardon, Joan. *Oysters: A Culinary Celebration with 185 Recipes.* New York: The Lyons Press, 2000.

Rector, Sylvia. "Ethnic Breads Symbolize Easter for Generations of Detroiters." *Detroit Free Press,* 31 March 1999. Internet Web site. www.freep.com/fun/food/qbread31.htm.

Reynolds, Edward B., and Michael Kennedy. *Whistleberries, Stirabout, & Depression Cake: Food Customs and Concoctions of the Frontier West.* Federal Writers' Project (1935–1942). Helena, Mont.: The Globe Pequot Press, 2000.

Rice, William. "Po' Boys Rich in Taste and History." *Chicago Tribune.* Reprinted in *The Detroit Free Press,* 14 April 1999. Internet Web site. www.freep.com/fun/food/qpoor14.htm.

———. "Yankee Know-how." *Chicago Tribune,* 24 February 1999.

Richman, Vicki, and Chuck Taggart, eds. "About Absinthe in New Orleans." Gumbo Pages. Internet Web site. www.gumbopages.com/food/misc/beverages/absinthe.html.

Roberson, John, and Marie Roberson. *The Complete Barbecue Book.* New York: Prentice-Hall, 1951.

Roberts-Dominguez, Jan. "Tex-Mex Ranchmen Rolled the First Fajitas in the '40s." *The Oregonian,* 13 June 2000.

Rochowansky, Sandra. "Barbecue—K.C. Style." Kansas City Dining. Guest Informant CitySpin. Internet Web site. www.cityspin.com/kansascity/dining/dining.htm.

Rogov, Daniel. "Crab Louis—The Absolutely Perfect Combination." Rogov's Ramblings. Internet Web site. www.stratsplace.com/rogov/crab_louis.html.

Root, Waverley. *Food: An Authoritative and Visual History and Dictionary of the Foods of the World.* New York: Simon & Schuster, 1980.

Root, Waverley, and Richard de Rochemont. *Eating in America: A History.* New York: The Echo Press, 1981.

Rosenberg, Judith Pierce. "Hawaii's 'Local Food': A Fusion of Ethnic Flavors." *Christian Science Publishing Society,* 3 June 1998. Internet Web site. www.csmonitor.com/durable/1998/06/03/p14s1.htm.

Rubin, Cynthia, and Jerome Rubin. *Old Boston Fare: In Food and Pictures.* Charlestown, Mass.: Emporium Publications, 1976.

Saveur Magazine, eds. *Saveur Cooks Authentic American.* San Francisco: Chronicle Books, 1998.

Schnebel, J. J. "Who Cooked That Up? Deep Dish Pizza." Internet Web site. members.home.net/jjschnebel/Cookup16.html.

Schodolski, Vincent J. "Lights! Camera! Salad!" *Chicago Tribune,* 26 August 1998.

Schulz, Phillip Stephen. *As American As Apple Pie.* New York: Simon & Schuster, 1990.

Schweid, Richard. *Hot Peppers: Cajuns and Capsicum in New Iberia, Louisiana.* New Orleans: New Orleans School of Cooking, 1987.

"Scuppernongs." Still Pond Vineyard, Arlington, Georgia. Internet Web site. www.stillpond.com/about.htm.

Sheldon, W. Lynn, Jr. "Presidential Places to Arrive (and Stay) for the Night: Taft's Role in a Charleston Delicacy." Internet Web site. www.lynnseldon.com/article26.html.

Sheraton, Mimi. *The Bialy Eaters: The Story of a Bread and a Lost World.* New York: Broadway Books, 2000.

Sherley, Connie. *Texas Style: Cooking, Gardening, and Entertaining in the Lone Star State.* New York/Avenel, N.J.: Crescent Books, 1992.

Shimabukuro, Betty. "Airy Cake a Triple Guava Delight." By Request, *Honolulu Star-Bulletin,* 12 January 2000. Internet Web site. starbulletin.com/2000/01/12/features/request.html.

Shribman, David. "On a Roll." *Fortune,* August 2001. Internet Web site. www.business2.com/articles/mag/print/0,1643,16548,FF.html.

Sietsema, Robert. "Cajun Country: Stalking Boudin and Crawfish." Chowhound's Articles and Special Reports, April 2000. Internet Web site. www.chowhound.com/writing/sietsema/sietsemacajun.html.

Skrabanek, Robert L. *We're Czechs.* College Station: Texas A&M University Press.

Smith, Andrew F. *Pure Ketchup: A History of America's National Condiment with Recipes.* Columbia: University of South Carolina Press, 1996.

Smith, Kathie. "Favorite foods from around the region." *Toledo Blade,* October 1999. Internet Web site. www.toledoblade.com/apps/pbcs.dll/forside.

Smith, Rick. "Call Goes Out for Best Frito Pie in West Texas." *San Angelo Standard-Time,* 29 October 1999. Internet Web site. www.texaswest.com/archive/99/october/29/4.htm.

Smoler, Roberta Wolfe. *The Useful Pig: 150 Succulent Pork Recipes.* New York: HarperCollins, 1990.

Solley, Patricia G. "Food Tale: Oysters." Soup of the Evening: Beautiful Soup. Internet Web site. www.soupsong.com/foyster.html.

Solomon, Alan. "Chicken-Fried Steak: A Wonderful Artery-Clogging Dish Holds a Special Place Deep in the Heart of Texas." *Chicago Tribune,* 7 October 1998.

Sparks, Elizabeth Hedgecock. *North Carolina and Old Salem Cookery.* Kernsville, N.C.: Dowd Press, 1964.

"Springfield—A Great Place to Write Home About." Springfield, Illinois Convention and Visitors Bureau. Internet Web site. www.visitspringfieldillinois.com/pressroom/ideas.htm.

Stanforth, Deirdre. *The New Orleans Restaurant Cookbook.* Garden City, N.Y.: Doubleday 1967.

Stern, Jane, and Michael Stern. "Beef on Weck." *Splendid Table,* 4 September 1999. Internet Web site. table.mpr.org/whereweeat/stern_beef.html.

——. *Roadfood.* New York: Harper Perennial, 1992.

Stevens, Patricia Bunning. *Rare Bits: Unusual Origins of Popular Recipes.* Athens: Ohio Univerity Press, 1998.

Stradley, Linda, and Andra Cook. *What's Cooking America.* Helena, Mont.: The Globe Pequot Press, 2000.

"Sturgeon: The Northwest's Hottest New Fishery?" Great Outdoor Recreation Pages. Foghorn Press. Internet Web site. www.gorp.com/gorp/publishers/foghorn/fis_stur.htm.

"Sturgis Pretzel: The History of Sturgis Pretzels." Internet Web site. www.sturgispretzel.com.

Taggart, Chuck. "Gumbo Pages." Internet Web site. www.gumbopages.com/.

Tannahill, Ray. *Food in History.* New York: Crown, 1988.

Taylor, John Martin. *Hoppin' John's Lowcountry Cooking: Recipes and Ruminations from Charleston and the Carolina Coastal Plain.* Boston and N.Y.: Houghton Mifflin, 1992.

"Things Japanese: Mochi, a Good Steeped in Tradition." Internet Web site. mothra.rerf.or.jp/ENG/Hiroshima/Things/61.html.

Thompson, Sharon. "Are You Up to This? Picture-Perfect Chiffon Cake Can Be Tall Order." *Kentucky Connect and the Lexington Herald,* 31 August 2000. Internet Web site. www.kentuckyconnect.com/heraldleader/news/083100/youdocs/chiffon31.htm.

Thorne, John, with Matt Lewis Thorne. *Serious Pig: An American Cook in Search of His Roots.* New York: North Point Press, 1996.

Thrasher, Alice. "Hold the Frogs: Frogmore Stew Gets Its Name from the Community." *Fayetteville Observer,* 17 November 1999.

Tolbert, Frank X. *A Bowl of Red.* College Station: Texas A&M University Press, 1994.

Toupin, Elizabeth Ahn. *The Hawaii Cookbook and Backyard Luau.* Norwalk, Conn.: Silvermine Publishers, 1967.

Trager, James. *The Foodbook.* New York: Grossman, 1970.

——. *The Food Chronology: A Food Lover's Compendium of Events and Anecdotes, from Prehistory to the Present.* New York: Henry Holt, 1995.

Treutlin, Theodore F., trans. *Sonora: A Description of the Province.* Tucson: University of Arizona Press, 1989.

Tyndall, Ruth R. *Eat Yourself Full: Pennsylvania Dutch Cookery for Feinschmeckers.* New York: David McKay, 1967.

Tysh, George. "Fat Tuesday Fanatics." Best of Detroit '99: Stuffing Your Face. *Detroit Metro Times,* 17 March 1999. Internet Web site. metrotimes.com/19/24/Features/bodRestaurantFat.html.

"The Ultimate Local Grind: Loco Moco." University of Hawaii at Manoa. Internet Web site. www.botany.hawaii.edu/faculty/bridges/eschool/projects/proj4/locomoco.htm.

Vennum, Thomas, Jr. *Wild Rice and the Ojibway People.* St. Paul: Minnesota Historical Society Press, 1988.

Volk, Thomas J. "Tom Volk's Fungus of the Month for January 1997." Internet Web site. www.wisc.edu/botany/fungi/jan97.html.

Voltz, Jeanne, and Elaine J. Harvell. *The Country Ham Book.* Chapel Hill and London: University of North Carolina Press, 1999.

Voltz, Jeanne, and Caroline Stuart. *Florida Cookbook.* New York: Alfred A. Knopf, 1993.

Wall, Alie Patricia, and Ron L. Layne. *Hog Heaven: A Guide to South Carolina Barbecue.* Lexington, S.C.: Sandlapper Store, 1979.

"Wall Street Journal Story Chips Away at Legend of Where Frito Pie Was Invented." Associated Press. *Corpus Christi Caller Times,* 27 October 1999. Internet Web site. www.caller2.com/1999/october/27/today/texas_me/85.html.

Walsh, Robb. "Pralines and Pushcarts: A Six-Part History of Tex-Mex." *Houston Press.* Internet Web site. www.houston-press.com/issues/2000-07-27/cafe.html.

Walters, Lon. *The Old West Baking Book.* Flagstaff, Ariz.: Northland Publishing, 1996.

Ward, Susie, Claire Clifton, and Jenny Stacey. *The Gourmet Atlas: The History, Origin, and Migration of Food of the World.* New York: Simon & Schuster/Macmillan, 1997.

Watts, Edith Ballard, and John Watts. *Jesse's Book of Creole and Deep South Recipes.* New York: Weathervane Books, 1985.

Watts, Kelly. "Put the Kettle on for Popular Frogmore Stew." *Milwaukee Journal Sentinel,* 15 October 1999. Internet Web site. www.jsonline.com/food/kiss/oct99/wattcol17101499.asp.

"What in the Heck Is Burgoo?" Village of Arenzville, Illinois. Internet Web site. www.burgoo.org/burgoo.htm.

"What's a Calabash?" Hurricane Fleet, Calabash, North Carolina. Internet Web site. www.hurricanefleet.com/calabash.html.

"What's Jambalaya?" Jambalaya Festival, Gonzales, Louisiana. Internet Web site. www.ascensionparish.com/festival/whatis.html.

"Where the Knish Is Delish." The New York First Company. Internet Web site. www.newyorkfirst.com/gifts/9022.html.

White, Jasper. *50 Chowders: One-Pot Meals—Clam, Corn and Beyond.* New York: Simon & Schuster, 2000.

"Why Do YOU Eat Black-Eyed Peas on New Years?" Free Public, Fresco, California. Internet Web site. www.freerepublic.com/forum/a3a50a64c0f1a.htm.

Williams, Barbara. *Cornzapoppin'!* New York: Holt, Rinehard and Winston, 1976.

Wilson, Jose, and Time-Life Books, eds. *American Cooking: The Eastern Heartland.* Alexandria, Va.: Time-Life Books, 1971.

Wong, Cynthia. "Japanese Mochi Making." UCLA Folklore 15 Multimedia Project. Internet Web site. www.humnet.ucla.edu/humnet/folklore/folk15/Cindy%20Wong/home.html.

"World's Largest Catsup Bottle Web Site and Fan Club!" Internet Web site. www.catsupbottle.com.

Wyman, Carolyn. *Spam: A Biography.* Orlando, Fla.: Harcourt Brace, 1999.

Yankee Magazine, eds. *The Yankee Magazine Cookbook.* New York: Harper & Row, 1981.

# Recipes by Region

*I'll Have What They're Having*

# Index

New Orleans Bread Pudding, 200

Ozark Pudding, 171

Persimmon Pudding, 201

Pueblo Indians, 38

Purvis, William Herbert, 190

## Q

Query, Archibald, 180

## R

rainbow trout, 83

raisins

in Country Captain Chicken, 92

in Lady Baltimore Cake, 176–77

in New Orleans Bread Pudding, 200

Raleigh, Sir Walter, 120, 192

Randolph, Mary, 104

Rauch, Ambrose, 61

Ravioli, St. Louis Toasted, 20

Red Eye Gravy, 93

Rego, Leonard, 59

reindeer fat in Akutaq/Eskimo Ice Cream, 196–97

Rhett, R. Goodwyn, 43

Rhode Island Coffee Milk/Coffee Cabinet, 206

Ribs, Kansas City Barbecued, 98–99

rice

in California Roll, 6–7

in Cashew Chicken Chop Suey, 89

in Country Captain Chicken, 92

in Hawaiian Spam Musubi, 18–19

in Hoppin' John, 118

in Loco Moco, 97

in Old Clothes/Ropa Vieja, 103

Popped Wild or Maple Rice, 16

Rice Pilaf with Peas, 126

in Shrimp Gumbo, 34–35

in Shrimp Jambalaya, 36–37

Robert E. Lee Cake, 178–79

Rock Creek Lodge, 17

Rockefeller, John D, Sr., 148

rocket sandwiches, 143

Rocky Mountain Oysters, 17

Rogers, Will, 44

Romberault, Abel Rene, 10

Roosevelt, Franklin D. (President), 92

Ropa Vieja/Old Clothes, 102–3

roux, 34

Rubio, Ralph, 141

Rubio's—Home of the Fish Taco (San Diego), 141

Ruggles, Reverend Samuel, 204

Runza Drive-Inn (Lincoln), 135

Runzas/Bierocks, 135

rutabagas in Cornish Pasties, 138–39

rye bread in Limburger Sandwich, 145

## S

Saimin, 41

Saki (Hector Hugh Munro), 13

salads

Crab Louis Salad, 116–17

Florida Lobster Salad, 113

Olive Salad for Muffuletta, 150–51

Swamp Cabbage/Hearts of Palm Salad, 128–29

salami

in Italian Hoagie, 143

in Muffuletta, 150–51

Sally, Aunt, 184

Salmon, Smoked, 80–81

salsa in Breakfast Tacos, 136

salt pork in Boston Baked Beans, 110

salvation fish (smelt), 78–79

Sam Choy Poke Festival (Hawaii), 124, 125

sandwiches, 133–59

Beef on Weck, 134

Bierocks/Runzas, 135

Boiled Lobster/Lobster Roll, 148–49

Breakfast Tacos, 136

Buffalo Burgers, 137

Cornish Pasties, 138–39

Cuban Sandwich, 140

French Dip Sandwich, 142

Grilled Fish Tacos, 141

Horseshoe Sandwich, 144

Indian Tacos, 152–53

Italian Hoagie, 143

Limburger Sandwich, 145

Muffuletta, 150–51

Navajo Fry Bread & Indian Tacos, 152–53

Original Hot Brown, 146–47

Oyster Po' Boy Sandwich, 156

Philadelphia Cheese Steak, 154

Slugburgers, 157

Soft-Shelled Crab Sandwich, 155

Spiedie, 158

Walleye Sandwich, 159

San Francisco

San Francisco Cioppino, 28

San Francisco–Style Sourdough French Bread, 62–63

# About the Author

Linda Stradley, a native northwesterner, was raised in Longview, Washington, and now lives in Newberg, Oregon. Linda says, "My mom was a great cook, but she cooked the typical foods of the '50s—overcooked meat and vegetables. It wasn't until I really got interested in cooking for my family that I discovered the wonders of great food using simple, fresh ingredients! I also discovered the love of eating and the problems of weight gain!"

A member of the Portland Culinary Alliance and the International Association of Culinary Professionals, Linda originated and maintains an online cooking site (since 1997) called What's Cooking America. The Web site is a continuation of her first cookbook, also called What's Cooking America (coauthored with her friend Andra Cook of Raleigh, North Carolina).

Linda has appeared on numerous local and national television programs during her book tours of the United States.